AUSTRALIANS at HOME
WORLD WAR I

AUSTRALIANS at HOME
WORLD WAR I

MICHAEL McKERNAN

The Five Mile Press

The Five Mile Press Pty Ltd
1 Centre Road, Scoresby
Victoria 3179 Australia
www.fivemile.com.au

Part of the Bonnier Publishing Group
www.bonnierpublishing.com

Copyright © Michael McKernan, 2014
All rights reserved.

First published as *The Australian People and the Great War* by Thomas Nelson in 1980. This redesigned edition published by The Five Mile Press in 2014

Printed in China

Page design and typesetting by Shaun Jury
Front cover © Getty Images

National Library of Australia Cataloguing-in-Publication entry
   McKernan, Michael, 1945– author.
   Australians at home: World War 1 / Michael McKernan.
   ISBN: 9781760063689 (hardback)
   Includes index.
   World War, 1914–1918–Social aspects–Australia.
   Civilians in war–Australia.
   Australia–History–1914-1918.
   Australia–Social life and customs.
   994.041

PREFACE TO THE NEW EDITION

I began dreaming of and planning for this book when I should have been doing something else. I was working as a doctoral researcher at the Australian War Memorial – one of two long-term researchers there – supposedly reading chaplains' diaries, sermons and theology for a thesis on Australian churches in the Great War.

But the attractions of browsing the Memorial's extraordinary collection were too strong. Instead of a morning tea break I would start looking at school magazines from the war years and beyond, reading of boys who walked straight out of school and into the recruiting office. Or, after a quick sandwich for lunch, I'd sit down with a bound issue of the *Sydney Mail* to see how sportsmen responded to the war; what fundraising efforts women were making; how children were devotedly engaging with the war. Improbably, as a trusted reader, I was allowed to browse the private records (manuscript) collection opening boxes of records at random to see what the Australians were up to away from the battlefields.

I wasn't long before I realised that there was a book on the homefront at war in that wonderful collection alone. With the thesis out of the way and an academic job that gave me paid access to research, I started to work on what I had long been dreaming of. Now a resident in Sydney I also used the wonderful Mitchell Library collections, but on regular trips to Canberra, partly funded by a modest War Memorial research grant, I continued to mine the library's holdings there.

Thomas Nelson, publishers, came to the party contracting me for a homefront book on the strength of their great success with Patsy Adam-Smith's *The Anzacs* (1978). At least one Australian publisher had found that there was an interest for the story of Australia in the Great War. Few others were at all interested and I was thought, by academic colleagues, to be a bit strange for working on a war topic. How times have changed!

The Australian People and the Great War first appeared in 1980 and was reissued in paperback in 1984. Others have described it as a pioneering book and I suppose it was, although it seemed to me, at the time, just the next logical step in my writing life. It is offered again to readers exactly as it appeared in 1980, without amendment, correction or amplification.

Many things are missing from this book, but such was the state of my historical understanding then. And the state of the profession, I might add. Today, most obviously, I would seek to include the story of Indigenous Australians on the homefront, as I have done for more recent books. I should also have written about Australian nurses in my chapter on Australian soldiers. I might also have looked more closely at unemployment and the downturn in the economy that the war caused. I apologise to those who look to find these important themes, but such were my limitations then.

Since it was first published there have been many books devoted to what I confined to a chapter in this book. So the study of women in war has exploded; where I gave schools a chapter, others have devoted entire books to an individual school or to a segment of the Australian school system. Where I wrote on Australian soldiers on leave, another historian has given an entire book to the problems of ill-discipline in the Australian Imperial Force.

Yet this summary volume still has its place. *Australians at Home: World War I*, as it is now called, gives a broad picture of the astonishing Australian response to the war. It puts in an Australian context a war that dominated almost the entire world for four years. It shows a unique Australian approach to that war.

This is not a specialised book. It was not designed to speak only to professional historians. Rather it was always a book for the broad Australian community, showing now an extraordinary patriotism and community involvement then. It still speaks to Australians because as we know from bushfires, floods and other natural disasters, when an Australian community is challenged we, as a nation, will rise to that challenge. Just as did the men, women and children of Australia in the years of the Great War.

CONTENTS

Preface to the new edition		v
Chapter One	THE WAR IN AUSTRALIA	1
Chapter Two	A HOLY WAR?	14
Chapter Three	SEEDPLOTS OF EMPIRE LOYALTY: THE SCHOOLS AT WAR	43
Chapter Four	'TO WAIT AND TO WEEP': AUSTRALIAN WOMEN AT WAR	65
Chapter Five	'MUDDIED OAFS' AND 'FLANNELLED FOOLS': SPORT AND WAR IN AUSTRALIA	94
Chapter Six	FROM HERO TO CRIMINAL: THE AIF IN BRITAIN 1915–19	116
Chapter Seven	MANUFACTURING THE WAR: 'ENEMY SUBJECTS' IN AUSTRALIA	150
Chapter Eight	THE OTHER AUSTRALIA?: WAR IN THE COUNTRY	178
Chapter Nine	THE GREY YEARS	201
Notes		225
Index		237

CHAPTER ONE
THE WAR IN AUSTRALIA

Wars have shaped the history of nations. They have stimulated or resolved political change, they have hastened technological change and they have contributed to profound social change in the lives of the people who have endured them. Students of history have traditionally devoted much of their time to the study of war, the reasons for its appearance, the course of the war and the complexities of the peace discussions. Although no war or long-term revolt has been fought on Australian soil since the dispossession of the Aboriginals, Australian thinking has concentrated on war and the threat of invasion and Australians have always been ready for war: ready to repel imagined invaders be they French, Russian or German in the nineteenth century, or Japanese, Chinese or Russian, in the twentieth. Australians depended on the strength of the British Empire, and especially upon the British navy, for the defence of their country and so they encouraged an exaggerated loyalty to the monarch and to the Empire. The smaller imperial wars towards the end of the nineteenth century gave Australians the opportunity to demonstrate their loyalty and love for the Empire in the hope that such demonstrations would compel Britain to recognise her obligations when Australia's own time of trial arrived. So war formed a constant backdrop against which Australians acted; the expectation of it gave point and purpose to many Australian aspirations.

By the time the long expected clash with Germany eventuated Australians were well used to the idea of war. Yet despite this tradition of preparedness and expectation, they greeted the news of the declaration of war on 4 August 1914 with the naïveté and innocence of a people with no experience of suffering and large-scale disruption. Australians lacked that sense of pessimism and fatalism found in the French, the Russians, or the Irish, people who knew how devastating were the consequences of war. While the peoples of other nations may have been sorrowful at heart at the departure of their troops but outwardly cheerful to keep up morale, the Australians were genuinely cheerful, excited and hopelessly optimistic. War to them was not a scourge but the greatest of all games, a sport, at which the home team, the Empire, invariably excelled. Experience of the bloodiest war in history

Outside the *Argus* office, Melbourne, at the outbreak of war

shattered that innocence, forcing Australians to reassess their ideas about war, the world, and themselves.

Reassessment proved difficult. We know with what enthusiasm Australians embraced the Empire's cause, unquestioningly, unhesitatingly, as soon as the news flashed across the cables. Or so it appeared on the surface. The political parties vied with one another to express and demonstrate their loyalty. In a climate which indicated that the voters preferred Labor, a senior opposition spokesman, W. M. Hughes, shortly afterwards attorney-general in the Fisher government, suggested that the federal elections under way be suspended, to allow Mr Cook's Liberals to be returned to government. Hughes's suggestion was legally impossible and in the event Mr Fisher's Labor Party won a handsome victory, but Hughes's readiness to forego the chance of winning the elections shows to what extent Empire loyalty transcended domestic political battles. It also indicates that Hughes did not conceive of the possibility of a lengthy war and that he believed that Labor would benefit in the long term by parading its loyalty.

Whether such self-sacrificial devotion to the cause of Empire was quite as developed amongst the people as amongst the politicians remains a question for us to ponder. People showed their feelings in the mad rush to do something to help. Men of all ages and at all levels of physical fitness crowded to the recruiting offices, and, while many were rejected, the government's initial offer of 20,000 men was quickly filled and further recruits found place in a force, the size of which now had no upper limit. By December 1914, 52,561 men had enlisted and the rush showed no sign of abating. Women, too, showed how intense their Empire loyalty was. Denied the opportunity of direct involvement, they organised themselves into charitable voluntary groups, to raise money for the victims of war and to provide 'comforts' for Australia's best sons. Superficially, at least, the nation seemed united in a common concern to expend itself in serving the Empire.[1]

Rarely is an issue ever so simple. There was excitement in Australia and intense interest, but there was caution and scepticism, too. There were small groups who, for ideological reasons, opposed war or the Empire. There were others, particularly in the working classes, who suspected war. A letter from 'D.R.', published in the *Australian Worker* on 6 August 1914, but written, presumably, before the outbreak, alleged '"war mongers" in the form of capitalists' stood to profit from war, while the suffering fell heavily on the working classes: 'It is we, the workers who when mortally wounded are left to rot on the battlefield'. But the worker suffered not only

Volunteers enlisting, Melbourne Town Hall

at the front. Employers panicked when war was announced, fearing the economic consequences. Prices rose rapidly in the expectation of shortages. Wholesale grocers in New South Wales, for example, raised prices of imported commodities by between 7 and 20 per cent during August alone. As early as 13 August the *Australian Worker* reported that the Eight Hours Committee had called on the government to stop increases on the prices of necessary items; the public were asked to remember the firms that had offended and to refuse to do business with them. The Victorian government was forced to act; it prepared a bill to check price increases in the face of a revised grocery price list, which showed 'a considerable increase'. Unemployment increased dramatically, too. Between 10 and 31 August unemployment in New South Wales rose from 13,500 to 29,313, and although these are official figures, it is likely that they underestimated the true picture. Other workers were placed on half-time instead of being dismissed. Such a sudden increase in unemployment, particularly severe in places like Broken Hill or on the west coast of Tasmania, whose copper and zinc mines relied on export markets, caused great unease amongst unionists and other workers.[2]

Faced with these severe economic conditions, working-class Australians were sceptical about the sacrifices others claimed to be making in the name of patriotism. The *Australian Worker* scoffed at 'the large-heartedness' of two Melbourne companies, each of which gave £5,000 to a patriotic fund; such generosity was not 'conspicuously displayed in their dealings with their employees'. Monetary sacrifice from such 'capitalists' seemed too easy: 'Having thus vicariously displayed their patriotism they return to the business of profit sharing while the other fellow goes fighting'. Appeals on behalf of distressed Belgians left some workers cold. 'Commercial magnates' were accused of flag-waving patriotism and public generosity, while at the same time amassing huge wartime profits: '"Patriotic" employers, who have donated large amounts to the Belgium, Patriotic and other war funds, have sacked thousands of bread-winners'. There were calls for a realisation that charity begins at home. Indeed, several local funds were started to aid Australians in need, unemployed owing to the war. The Glebe Political Labor League, for example, organised a procession and a carnival at Wentworth Park to raise money for the unemployed.[3]

The reaction to the news of war varied, then, between those who felt economic distress almost immediately and those who were better placed, with secure jobs, to meet the effects of rising prices. At the outbreak of war, while there was discontent about the disproportionate nature of the sacrifice, there was little opportunity for these varied reactions to find an airing, so completely had patriotism gripped the preachers, politicians and pressmen. Opposition to war was based almost solely on its immediate economic impact on Australia; there were few indeed who questioned the Empire's motives or who even discussed the causes of the war. Some people mocked the recruits who flooded the army depots, labelling them 'six-bob-a-day' tourists who

Gallipoli

would never see any fighting. But most agreed that the Empire's cause was a worthy one and that German expansion must be checked. At that level the nation was united, but at another level of debate about equality of sacrifice and disproportionate burden, there was conflict. The seeds of that division lay germinating from the first months of the war.

Perceptive observers who saw these divisions believed that they would be overcome when Australian troops went into action. Those who had laughed at the recruits realised, by December 1914, that victory would not be swift and that the Australians would play a part in the fighting. A mood of anticipation grew in 1915 as Australians waited for the first reports that their troops were in action: loyalists who wanted to stir all the people to the heights of patriotism and nationalists who wanted the Australians to show their worth. It was pure chance that their first encounter with the enemy at Gallipoli should have been so dramatic: indeed it is hard to imagine how the Australian troops could have begun with more impact. The Canadians, by comparison, slipped quietly into the trenches in France alongside the British and French, creating no separate identity for themselves. Sent on a fool's errand, the Australians faced the impossible task of scaling cliffs from the sea against a well-entrenched enemy, fortified and alert. They failed to remove the enemy but, at great cost, they forced the Turks to yield them enough ground to enable them to dig in and then to endure a Western-front type of stalemate.

At home, this remarkable feat of devotion and determination fired the imagination of all Australians, instantly created the legend of the Anzac, and united the people behind their troops. Or so the evidence of memorial services, recruiting, speeches and editorials would have us believe. Preachers boasted that 'the troops exceeded the most sanguine expectations in steadiness, dash and military efficiency' that the landing was an event 'which nothing in the history of human bravery has surpassed'. The minister of defence, Senator George Pearce, a Western Australian, explained that the Australians had been 'pitted against the flower of the Turkish army' although they were 'untried men ... [indeed] the greater part of them had had no military training at all'. 'It could have been said', he continued, 'that the test was too great to ask any soldiers to face. But the Australians not only landed and scaled the Gallipolean heights in the face of machine-guns and trenches, but they took trenches and held them with the determination of the British bull-dog'. Possibly for the first time, Empire loyalty fused with Australian patriotism, to create a peculiar type of dual loyalty to which all classes in Australia could give their allegiance, in varying proportions, Australian or imperial.[4]

The Australians failed at Gallipoli and were eventually mercifully evacuated. The casualties had been enormous but the rush of recruits continued: in July and August 1915 a further 62,289 men joined the AIF. Few issues disturbed the outward calm of unity in Australia: competition meant showing who could do most for the Empire and the AIF. The Australians reached France early in 1916 and suffered stunning losses, greater than anything experienced at Gallipoli. The rush of recruits slowed, probably, not because of the effects of the losses, but because the pool of available, eligible men had been drained. The loyalists, whose interpretation of the war passed almost

Men of the 3rd Australian Division in Armentieres, November 1916. This was their first taste of a French winter, as they had only recently arrived. The mud indicates how welcome frequent changes of socks would have been

beyond the limits of rationality, despaired at the slowdown in recruiting which showed, they argued, that the spirit of the nation was unsound. Some of these patriots, churchmen particularly, had developed a semi-mystical interpretation of the meaning of the war, arguing that only through sacrifice would the nation be saved; others concentrated on the supposed iniquities of the Germans, or 'Huns' and 'baby killers' as they called them; others, again, emphasised the threat to Australia. Much of this rhetoric passed beyond the limits of the plausible, straining the credulity of Australians always cautious in forming opinions. The apparent indifference, apathy even, distressed the patriots almost beyond endurance and they began to demand the conscription of those apparently unable to see their duty for themselves.[5]

While the federal government possessed the power to impose conscription by a simple act of parliament, W. M. Hughes, who had succeeded Fisher as prime minister, anxious to avoid a confrontation with the Labor majority in the Senate and a public party brawl, submitted the question to the people in a referendum. This decision to allow the people to choose might well have earned Hughes the reputation of a great democrat but instead he was derided as a coward by the loyalists and as a class traitor by many Labor supporters.

To ask the people to vote on such a contentious issue while the war raged and the Australians suffered dreadful casualties was foolhardy. The conscription campaign opened up the divisions and played on frustrations hitherto masked by the superabundance of the rhetoric of patriotism. Those who opposed the proposal or the war now found the need to speak out and in doing so they demonstrated the nation's disunity and confusion. After a bitter campaign the result showed the voters almost neatly divided into two equal camps, with a slight 'No' majority. In general, traditional Labor voters followed most of their politicians and officials into the 'No' camp. Electorates that had always returned Labor members gave strong majorities against conscription. Middle-class voters, on the whole, voted 'Yes', or at least those electorates that had invariably returned conservative candidates were in the 'Yes' camp. But there were significant swings in some of these conservative electorates which make generalisation difficult. Country voters in New South Wales particularly, diverged from the pattern and voted 'No'; only one rural electorate voted 'Yes' in New South Wales. Farmers were concerned about the availability of labour, especially as they were just breaking clear from the effects of a severe drought. But in the aftermath of the referendum, these subtleties escaped most observers. Superficially it seemed that the vote had been determined along class lines and the patriots, particularly in the newspapers, were quick to brand the workers and their political party as disloyal, even traitorous.

During 1917 and 1918 these accusations increased in ferocity and divided the classes dangerously. Middle-class patriots seemed to forget the solid enlistment in the AIF that had come from workers. Working-class Australians, from the outset suspicious that the burdens of war fell unequally, and resentful of the attacks upon them, drew together and began to give closer attention to the problems of living in Australia than to the war overseas. Despite the frenzied efforts of recruiters, enlistment dwindled. Hughes had said during the conscription campaign that Australia needed to provide 16,500 recruits each month. In the early months of 1917 never more than 5,000 volunteers offered themselves for service, and this dropped to 2,500 in the second half of the year and to 1,500 in some months in 1918. The AIF continued to suffer heavy casualties in France and in 1918 was forced, much against the wishes of the men, to amalgamate battalions that could not be lifted to full strength in any other way.[6]

While patriots bemoaned the drop in recruiting, they were driven to despair by workers who went on strike with increasing frequency as the war progressed. The largest of these was the 'great strike' in New South Wales which began in August 1917. Workers at the Randwick tramway workshops objected to the 'speeding-up' efficiency methods which their employer, the state government, had introduced. Initially only a few thousand workers were involved in the strike but so tense was the industrial-social situation in Australia that it spread rapidly. Eventually, 76,000 workers (about 14 per cent of the workforce) went out in New South Wales, throwing the fuel, food and transport industries into chaos. That such a huge disruption could arise out of an apparently trivial dispute showed how deep were the antagonisms that had developed in Australia.[7]

The middle-class housewife, with a son at the front, was energetically working for the Red Cross and could not understand any less intense commitment to the Empire's cause. Roused by the stories of German atrocities and Australian heroism, she and thousands like her also believed newspapers, which had branded workers as disloyal. The defeat of conscription confirmed her views, strikes magnified them. She met few wives of workers at Red Cross working groups or on the committees of fund-raising ventures; the spokesmen of patriotism were invariably middle-class, professional men. The working-class woman, on the contrary, viewed the middle-class patriot with suspicion and distrust. The patriot's food bills were paid, she could still afford to clothe her family, her husband stood in no fear of losing his job. Such a woman could afford to be patriotic as before the war she had afforded an afternoon of card-playing or idle socialising. The working-class woman knew no such luxuries, particularly as prices were rising and strikes reduced her husband's income. Her son, a valued weekly contributor to the family's budget, was now overseas with the AIF, and provided only minimal support.

In such a climate of antagonism and resentment, Hughes tried again to introduce conscription through a referendum in December 1917. All the passions aroused during the first campaign re-emerged, even more strongly this time. The campaign destroyed any remaining illusions of unity and, not surprisingly, Hughes's proposal was defeated by a slightly larger majority than in 1916. So distracted were people by events at home that the war began

HE: *"And how are you getting on with your collecting for the soldiers?"*
SHE: *"Perfectly! I've had my name in the papers four times already."*

One view of middle-class patriotism. *Bulletin*, 6 December 1917

to recede from view. By the end of 1917 Australians seemed emotionally exhausted. There was constant anxiety about the outcome of the war and the fate of Australia's 'best sons'. There were tensions and anxieties caused by class and religious divisions; there was the overwhelming fear that Australia would never be the same again. Australians had embraced war lightheartedly, in a spirit of adventure and excitement. In so doing they had shown themselves to be a naïve and innocent people, complacently sheltering beneath the Empire's might. By the time the war ended they had experienced bitterness and sorrow to the full. Australian casualties had been very high and many men who did return would never be able to settle down to normal civilian life. Most importantly, however, the war had disrupted the outward calm of Australian life and forced awareness of sectional interests and class conflict. Such was the price of Empire loyalty.

Because it brought such elemental emotions into play World War I has attracted the attention of many Australian historians. The official historians, led by C. E. W. Bean, recounted, in amazing detail, the story of the AIF in action. Bean's admiration for the Australians whom he saw as a newer, finer race of Englishmen nurtured in the bush helped him to fulfil his ambition of describing every significant action in which the Australians took part. Recent writers have returned to the World War I period to probe more deeply areas that the official historians covered in summary. They have combed the soldiers' letters and diaries searching for new insights on their ideals, motives and how they described the fighting. They have resorted to oral history, too, probing the memories of old men for whom the war remained an ever-present reality. Other writers have turned their attention to the home front, excited by the confrontation and division that the conscription referenda, in particular, inspired. These studies of the home front grew out of the earlier political histories which dominated Australian historical writing until recently. In concentrating on political and industrial turmoil these studies tend to minimise the impact of the war as a unique event and seek an explanation in existing political and industrial conditions. In the broad sweep, of course, they are right but their accounts neglect to show what an enormous effect the war had on the lives of ordinary Australian men and women.

This book seeks to concentrate on the war as it impinged on the Australian people. It leaves to others discussion of tactics and battles, of political intrigue and high diplomacy. It seeks to show how the war stimulated patriotism and loyalty; dull, vague concepts until fleshed out by living people forcing themselves to knit, to raise money, to spend themselves, however trivially, in the service of their country. War increased tension and anxiety. For four years the people heard only bad news, or bad news dressed up as good – ultimately more devastating. These worries brought the other side of patriotism to prominence, the mean, hating, divisive spirit which forced people to judge others on slim evidence, to lose their natural tolerance and to turn savagely on those they perceived as the enemy.

My aim, then, was to concentrate on the ordinary people; the difficulty, of course, was to find them. By definition 'ordinary people' do not leave their papers to libraries and archives where historians traditionally congregate. Nor do 'ordinary people' write newspaper editorials, or read speeches into Hansard and, if they preach in pulpits, it is at small undistinguished churches which reporters never visit to summarise the sermon. The historian's traditional sources were of very general use at best, so I determined to look elsewhere. I searched school magazines, written by the pupils, to find how the war affected them and found ardent patriotism and acceptance of the duty of enlisting when the time came. I found great pride in the sacrifice of those who had enlisted and I experienced an overwhelming sense of astonishment and despair at the extent of the sacrifice and its failure to shake the headmasters and teachers out of their platitudes. I combed parish records to find the story of the pacifist Methodist preacher at Hay, New South Wales, and found, too, an easy-going tolerance on the part of his congregation. Patriotism did not always command intolerance of divergent viewpoints. I looked at Red Cross reports for the response of women to the war and found devotion and generosity on a huge scale, indicating what an important place the AIF occupied in the hearts of the people, the mothers, wives, fathers and brothers.

I looked too for evidence of the extent of women's suffering and anxiety and found in rare letters to politicians stories which hinted at the unhappiness the war caused.

Then I turned to the AIF itself, impressed by the use other historians had made of soldiers' letters and diaries. I tried not to see that source only as a document but as an exchange between real people immediately affected by the contents of letters. Australian attitudes were shaped by the experiences of the AIF as reported home, seen through the eyes of the writers. Soldiers wrote at length of their impressions of British society and in these unguarded comments showed how different British attitudes and ideals were where they had expected similarity. These comments throw new light on perceptions of Australia and explain why many members of the AIF determined to preserve unchanged conditions they had known in Australia before they departed. I consulted many newspapers, too, in my search for the ordinary Australian, looking more at the sports' pages than at the editorial, more at letters to the editor than at statements by politicians. In particular, I made extensive use of newspapers published in rural Australia to see if country people differed from those in the cities.

The individual war experience of each Australian differed and often a generalisation on the basis of one or two instances may seem unwarranted. Of course we cannot be sure now of the majority response and the method here has often been to hint and suggest. Impressions can be confirmed by discussion with those who lived through it all but I am haunted by an interview with an aunt, part-German, wholly Catholic, and a student at ultra-loyalist Melbourne University from 1915 onwards. She found no antagonism or intolerance, or none that she could recall. The records of Council and student bodies suggest that her memory was faulty and further discussion showed that as a Catholic she felt very much out of place and ignored. And so we generalise.

While it is useful to try to paint a general picture, groups within society will, of course, react differently to events. Society is not one, whole undifferentiated mass of people with common aims and ideals, but a series of groups and classes undergoing similar experiences but reacting in many diverse ways. Family tradition and religious upbringing will shape some perceptions, region or locality others, and class loyalties and interests will also affect reactions to an event of the magnitude of war. Many of these influences are interlocking, although they link the individual with several different groups. My German-Catholic-working-class aunt was not unique, and all those influences helped shape her responses to the war. Class loyalties were probably most important in Australia despite the complacent view that Australia was an egalitarian society where 'Jack was as good as his master'. Only in the sense that class position depended largely on income rather than birth, that movement between the classes was possible, did egalitarianism seem a relevant description of Australian society.

Perhaps there were fewer manifestations of class in Australia in 1914 than in other countries. While the clothing worn to work and the area and type of housing might have indicated one's social status, at leisure, there were fewer observable differences of accent or demeanour such as would identify class background as surely as in Britain. Income was the principal determinant of class. Australian workers lived comfortably in the good times but, never able to save much, suffered whenever the economy deteriorated. The memory of the 1890s depression cut deep and as many workers feared that war would cause inflation and unemployment, they viewed it with concern. There were, of course, gradations in all this. The worker who owned his home, who had acquired a saleable skill, was clearly more secure than a shop assistant or an office worker struggling to maintain appearances with a heavy mortgage in a 'middle-class' suburb.

Income, then, was not the sole determinant of class, although an important one; culture mattered too. The man who worked with his hands, wore working clothes and possibly belonged to a union, saw himself and his family as different from men who worked in offices and who ate 'dinner' rather than 'tea'. These differences provoked mild antagonism between the classes but it was often encased in humour, as much contemporary literature shows. C. J. Dennis, the poet of the 'Sentimental Bloke', delighted in poking fun at both middle-class pretensions and working-class imitations of them. His book, *Digger Smith*, published in 1918, opens with a typically humorous account of a socially aspiring working-class wife and mother:

> My wife 'as took the social 'abit bad.
> I ain't averse – one more new word I've learned –
> Averse to tea, when tea is to be 'ad;
> An' when it comes I reckon that its earned.
> It's jist a drink, as fur as I'm concerned.
> Good for a bloke that's toilin' on the land;
> But when a caller comes, 'ere I am turned
> Into a social butterfly, off-'and.
>
> Then drinkin' tea becomes an 'oly rite.
> So's I won't bring the family to disgrace
> I gits a bit uv coaching overnight
> On ridin' winners in this bun-fed race.
> I 'ave to change me shirt and wash me face,
> An look reel neat, from me waist up at least,
> An sling remarks in at the proper place,
> An not make noises drinkin', like a beast.[8]

At other times, when working conditions were threatened, or the power of the state seemed to be unfairly thrown on the side of the employers, there was more than mild, good-humoured antagonism. Then a man was expected to show loyalty to his class and his mates; his woman was expected to stand beside him. At such times the rhetoric of union officials and the labour press made more sense; men could then see the influence of 'capitalists', 'trusts' and 'combines' and how distinct were these interests from those of the workers. In this sense, class conflict might often seem to have been absent in prewar Australia, but it emerged whenever there was economic dislocation or hardship: predictions of the unity of all Australians under the pressure of war were more a middle-class ideal than a description of reality.

Despite these differences, middle-class ideals predominated in Australia, possibly because many Australians invariably expected to move up in social status, rather than down. Working girls would have preferred not to work; Australians on the whole regretted the necessity for a woman to work after marriage. Schools inculcated middle-class virtues such as hard work, thrift and home ownership; teachers also ensured that patriotism and loyalty gained widespread acceptance, before the war. All Australians aspired to own their homes, to tend their gardens carefully and to manifest 'good taste', but by no means all could afford to do so. Economic position and fears often dominated reaction to episodes in the war experience. Quite obviously patriotism was a less expensive virtue for some than for others. A contribution to a fund, a donation of time to serve on a committee or to work, was easier for people not totally concerned to feed and clothe a family. It was regrettable that an appreciation of these differences and difficulties escaped many Australians, leading them to reflect on the motives of others.

Australians were ill-prepared for war. School texts and popular writers had fed them with stories of war's romance for too long. The 'thin red line' of British troops, 'the deeds that had won the Empire' were constituent parts of Australia's perception of war. The reality proved totally different. The war was not over quickly, the navy was not dominant, there were few decisive battles and little point in plotting the movement of troops on the war maps the newspapers published so enthusiastically. Instead there was stalemate, enormous loss of life, a frightening display of the might of modern weapons, actions against civilians that had seemed unthinkable, and internal political dispute almost everywhere.

Within Australia the war provoked class conflict and religious and racial hatred; it confirmed the male dominance of society and produced massive displays of confrontation. At its conclusion the acting prime minister spoke of an enormous sigh of relief going up all over Australia: such a comment indicates what war-weariness and exhaustion was all about. Because the initial response was so optimistic, the ultimate revulsion went deeper. Never again would there be such certainty in Australia or such a ready identification with the cause of Empire. Australians would go to war again, but more realistically, with no high hopes.

CHAPTER TWO
A HOLY WAR?

In 1914 the Australian Christian churches played an important part in the life of the individual and the nation. The 1911 census showed that the vast majority of Australians allied themselves with one of the major denominations; only 0.24 per cent of the population claimed to have no religion. A certain degree of scepticism about the depth of religious commitment is justified, however; it may be that many Australians were Christians in name only as an energetic Melbourne Anglican, L. V. Biggs, lamented. He spoke of the 'average parish' of between 12–13,000 nominal church members at which attendance at the various services 'rarely exceed[ed] a few hundreds'. Nevertheless, the clergy invariably officiated at the important moments in a family's history, to celebrate a birth, to solemnise a marriage and to comfort the bereaved at a funeral. Performance of these 'rites of passage' won clergymen an accepted place in society, gave them a legitimate role to perform, and from this secure base they gave a Christian interpretation of most of the events that concerned Australians and argued the case for a Christian morality in season and out.[1]

The clergy's involvement in the family's affairs was paralleled by their role in the nation's history: they had a speaking part but were certainly not leading actors. At moments of national crisis or celebration, however, clergymen came to the fore. Australia's short history meant that no home-grown ceremonies had evolved to express national identity or unity, such as a coronation or the inauguration of a president. Existing rituals – the ceremonies to open parliament, for example – were borrowed and ill-fitting, designed to emphasise the links with Britain rather than to reflect an Australian character. The churches, while not developing indigenous ceremonies, came to the rescue by adding colour and theatre to formal occasions and by expressing in the grandeur of the language of the liturgy the often tired platitudes of parish-pump politicians.

This identification between church and state was informal and, given the claims of the competing denominations, nervy: one archbishop would never suffice, all the leaders of all the denominations must officiate at state occasions. This was illustrated most graphically in the squabbles about precedence at the inauguration of the Commonwealth in January 1901. The Anglican archbishop of Sydney, as primate, and the Catholic archbishop, a cardinal, were given much higher ranking in the official procession than the leaders of the other denominations, who accordingly protested. Then a dispute arose as to the precedence of the two central clerical characters. Cardinal Moran insisted that ordination date should determine the issue and that he be allowed to read a prayer for the Commonwealth before his Anglican rival. When the government refused, Moran withdrew from the proceedings but, pointedly, sat in state, watching the procession pass his cathedral, flanked by 3,500 Catholic schoolchildren.[2]

Even so, these twin roles as family and national masters of ceremonies had been accepted by 1914; it was natural for the nation to turn to the church at the outbreak of war and, for the time being at least, clergymen occupied the centre of the stage.

In Australia, unlike Britain, there was in 1914 no obvious anti-war lobby, no group that would appeal for the calm dispassionate debate that a decision to go to war should evoke. The politicians, too dependent on party and too anxious to please their electors, rallied to the Empire's cause, making extravagant rhetorical flourishes. The federal opposition leader, Andrew Fisher, in the midst of an election campaign when war broke out, immediately pledged Australia's 'last man and last shilling' to the Empire's cause. His conservative opponent, the Liberal prime minister, Joseph Cook, matched this extravagance. The press was as unrestrained. Lacking an eloquent, authoritative radical newspaper such as the *Manchester Guardian*, Australians read in the *Argus*, the *Sydney Morning Herald*, or the *Age*, how wise was the Empire's course of action and how prompt must be Australia's response.

Nor were Australian university staff prepared to subject the Empire's war aims or Australia's actions to independent, intellectual scrutiny. Perhaps the fate of George Arnold Wood, professor of history at Sydney University, served as a warning. Wood had determined that the Empire was in the wrong in her war in South Africa against the Boers. He wrote and spoke eloquently against that war and suffered vilification and professional ostracism as a result. There were even suggestions that Wood would be dismissed because of his anti-war position. In 1914 Australian academics gave the Empire's cause early and enthusiastic support. The University of Melbourne organised a series of 'War Lectures' examining the war from every conceivable academic aspect, including 'Chemistry and the War' by Professor Orme Mason. The professor of history at the University of Adelaide lectured on the war, in Adelaide and in thirty country centres, drawing a total crowd of over 10,000. Even George Arnold Wood at Sydney embraced the war enthusiastically.[3]

The only other group of educated persons adept in public speaking and debate was Australia's clergy. Many of them, certainly, were of the second rank, who chose advancement to high office in Australia rather than relative obscurity in Britain. Thus a senior clergyman wrote of John Charles Wright,

Anglican archbishop of Sydney and primate of Australia, that 'He held the Church in peace and amity, but he has not led it forward on any great spiritual or moral enterprise'. A perceptive Catholic doctor wrote of his archbishop of Sydney, Michael Kelly, that at church functions invariably he gave 'long addresses which touched on all subjects without illuminating them'. Nor were the Australian-born clergy, though rarely in the highest positions, of better quality, it seemed. An Anglican bishop, in 1916, asked his fellow bishops in conference to think about the type of man who offered himself for the ministry: 'How seldom can we say that there is a set of men of the highest type, physically and mentally. Is it not rather true that the finest type of man is conspicuously rare?' To this catalogue of woes must be added the fact that clergymen were as ignorant as all other Australians of the causes of the war, and as innocent in their assessment of its impact.[4]

Nevertheless, their response deserves our attention because the nation expected them to have something to say and listened attentively to what they did say. In their pronouncements, clergymen set the tone for the nation. They might have urged caution, at least until all the facts were known, they might have reminded Australians of the need for tolerance and charity, or they might have set a realistic limit to the extent of the nation's involvement, weighing the Empire's claims against Australia's needs. In doing so, given the enthusiasm, even hysteria, that gripped Australia from the announcement of war onwards, clergymen would have been unpopular; they would have stood out as cautious conservatives. But unpopularity might have been no bad thing. Instead, clergymen embraced the war as enthusiastically as any other Australians, and indeed, immediately surrounded it with religious and divine significance. In this way they locked themselves into positions that eventually sounded odd even to patriots. Rather than stemming the tide of war hysteria, clergymen contributed to it and indeed shaped it. Their contribution exceeded their influence in other areas of national life because the nation looked to them for guidance at the outbreak of war and then found them willing allies during all its phases.

Lowther Clarke, the English-born Anglican leader in Melbourne since 1902, became the nation's spokesman at a service of intercession on the first Sunday of the war. He was, perhaps, not the most qualified person for the task; his own dean described his cathedral sermons as 'Sunday School talks delivered in a somewhat portentious and pompous style'. Nevertheless, Melbourne was the federal capital city and the Anglican service commanded the presence of the governor-general, Sir Ronald Munro-Ferguson, the Victorian governor, the lord mayor and leading federal and state politicians, as well as a distinguished congregation of leading business and professional men. All had come to ask God's blessing for the nation: the archbishop must have been aware of the pressure to avoid contentious ideas, if, indeed, he had any. Through the newspapers he spoke to a much wider audience. Clarke gave a rather dull performance; he preached from the text 'Be still and know

Archbishop Wright preaching in Sydney Domain, 1916.

that I am God' which emphasised that God was in control, that the believer would not despair or be concerned unduly. He was optimistic: 'these days will bring their own blessing ... they will teach very many better than they know it now the value of religion'. Such sentiments were commonplace in all the churches on that national day of prayer.[5]

As with the press and politicians who had given an early, unrestrained assurance to the people that the cause was just, the clergy accepted the war, showing how noble Britain was to rush to the help of a weaker neighbour and to honour a long-standing pledge. At a service in the Domain, which attracted 20,000 people, the dean of Sydney, A. E. Talbot, suggested that Britain had obeyed God's command in seeking to repel the German invader. Clergymen throughout Australia reassured the people that God was on the Empire's side.[6]

From this it followed that Australians must strain every resource to bring the war to a swift, satisfactory conclusion. Churchmen sounded the call to arms and the call to prayer. Those who were able were exhorted to enrol in the expeditionary force that the government had offered to the Empire. So complacent were most Australians, including clergymen, that few expected the troops to be trained and despatched in time to participate in significant action. Most expected Australian sacrifices to fall within the economic sphere: the disruption to trade would increase unemployment and the price of goods; clergymen asked the people to accept the hardship graciously. Prayer was mobilised quickly. In Perth, the Anglicans set aside Monday, 10 August, as a special day of humiliation and prayer. There were five separate services at the cathedral throughout the day with large crowds gathering for each. In Brisbane, clergymen decreed that the following Sunday should be observed as a special day of prayer to ask for peace 'and for the Divine blessing to rest upon the cause on behalf of which [we] are now engaged in war'. So large were attendances at Adelaide services that clergymen petitioned the Lord Mayor for the use of the Town Hall for daily lunchtime intercessory services; he readily agreed. Clergymen rejoiced to find their services so popular and envisaged a reformed Australia in which the churches might come to dominate national life.[7]

More than a simple love of Empire lay behind clergymen's eager acceptance of the war. They presumed to see God's hand directing this momentous event in human history. They argued that as God had permitted an event as disastrous as war, he must have ordained that good would come from it; so sure was their faith in God's providential care for the world that they were confident that God could not permit destruction and waste without producing a positive effect. Henry Howard, a fiery Methodist preacher in Adelaide, announced that 'any discipline, whether of war or pestilence, of famine or fire, of drought or flood, that can break down our trust in the material and strengthen our faith in the spiritual ... is a discipline which should be welcomed and acquiesced in rather than deplored'. He regretted aspects of Australian life 'its intemperance, uncleanness, mutual distrust, commercial dishonesty, political chicanery' which war would help reform.[8]

This became a standard and early theme with Australian clergymen. It must be, they reasoned, that God was using the war to call the nations, and Australia in particular, back to the paths of righteousness. They saw the war as a worldwide revival crusade, causing reform and renewal in the lives of nations and individuals. Clergymen everywhere spoke of the cleansing effect of sacrifice, indeed, they postulated that as nations only achieved greatness through sacrifice, the war was Australia's opportunity to become a nation. John Walker, a senior Presbyterian minister at Ballarat, dreamed of Australia after the war as a 'fire-purged civilisation, [in] which the King of Kings and Lord of Lords shall rule'. Thus Australians were counselled not to be dismayed by the news of war, but rather to accept it from the hands of a loving Father, who would turn evil into good. It was standard Christian doctrine that through suffering would come glory; however, it is remarkable that clergymen applied it literally to Australia's situation. It allowed Christians to accept more easily the reality of carnage and destruction while committed to an ethic that included a condemnation of violence and whose highest law was the law of love.[9]

It is understandable that clergymen, with a very imperfect understanding of the European situation and faced with the necessity of preaching about it, should have relied on basic Christian principles. But having outlined this Christian view so forthrightly at this early stage, clergymen found themselves committed to hold it ever more fiercely as the war progressed, if they wished to be consistent. Clergymen might have hesitated before making such unequivocal pronouncements. However, they shaped the course of the people's reaction to the war; they reduced substantially the opportunities for caution and reasoned discussion and laid the churches open to increasing turmoil.

These views about sacrifice and duty which clergymen gave out so consistently and so frequently during the early months of the war became a central part of Australia's wartime rhetoric. The cause was just, duty universal, the outcome would be a fundamental renewal and reform of Australian society. Although Catholic spokesmen agreed with their Protestant counterparts on the basic issues and gave the illusion that all Christians were united, nevertheless Catholics had a far less exalted view of the consequences of the war. They looked less for moral and religious renewal than for practical and pragmatic benefits. They hoped that just as Ireland, by proving her loyalty to England, would win Home Rule from grateful politicians, so Australian Catholics, by proving their loyalty, would win concessions from the dominant Protestant majority. In advising Catholics to join heartily in the war effort, Melbourne's Archbishop Carr stated that 'religious principles, loyalty and interests' suggested it. Archbishop Kelly, in Sydney, believed that as a result of the war 'there would be no more disabilities put upon their schools, and the question would not be asked with regard to ... public work whether a person was a Catholic or not'. While Catholics hoped to advance their integration with the wider community through loyal participation in the war, Archbishop Carr still spoke of securing 'education justice' as 'the main anxiety'.[10]

The pressure to conform influenced Catholic preachers less because they saw themselves as an alienated minority within the larger community. The church drew its leaders and most of its priests from Ireland; slightly less than 200 of the 808 diocesan clergy in Australia in 1914 were Australian-born and almost all of the 224 priests in religious orders came to Australia from overseas, mostly from Ireland. This ensured that, while the majority of church members were Australian-born, the church had a strong Irish orientation. The battle over Home Rule for Ireland had reached its peak in 1914 and many observers believed Britain to be on the brink of civil war: Australian Catholics had followed the arguments and were involved in the antagonisms, their loyalty was not directed unswervingly towards the Crown. Secondly, the composition of the Australian Catholic church differed from that of the Protestant churches in that a majority of Catholics were low on the social scale; they were workers rather than employers, or members of the professional classes or clerks. Herbert Moran, in *Viewless Winds,* recalled that in the 1890s 'the great majority of [Catholics] were to be found in the lower strata of society (at least, economically), – their political sympathies were given to the radical-liberal element in politics which later became the Labour Party'. This situation continued in 1914; the 1911 census showed that Catholics had the highest illiteracy rate amongst the denominations, with 4.29 per cent of Catholics over five unable to read, compared with 2.5 per cent of Presbyterians.[11]

This predominantly working-class ethos in the Catholic church increased feelings of alienation: their employers were more likely to worship elsewhere than to rub shoulders with them in the pews at mass. Rarely did a governor or civic dignitary grace a Catholic cathedral to celebrate the moment of national crisis, because Catholicism was a minority faith. This allowed Catholic preachers greater freedom to scrutinise their government's response and to suggest, cautiously, that the war was not a moment of supreme importance in the divine plan but rather merely an event in human history. This freedom from the restraints of conformity, this more pragmatic view of the war, was barely perceptible in August 1914 but was to become more marked later. At first, superficially, it seemed that all church spokesmen agreed: their views were a vital section of the unanimous chorus celebrating Australia's acceptance of the obligations of Empire.

Church enthusiasm for the war went beyond rhetoric: churchmen constructed ceremonies and celebrations designed to give vent to the patriotic instincts of the people. Flags appeared at church services, guards of honour were pressed into service, medals were worn in the pulpit and departing troops were elaborately farewelled with ritual and liturgy. A new type of church ceremony appeared: the patriotic service, a variant, no doubt, on divine service. Typical of such services was that held at the tiny Methodist church at Uralla, twelve kilometres south of Armidale in New South Wales:

> The church was crowded and extra seating accommodation had to be provided. Members of the Gestwych Shire Council and the Uralla Municipal Council were present officially. A church parade of the Commonwealth forces and the rifle club was held, and led by the local Salvation Army band, the troops marched to the church. The Rev. J. W. Dains preached from the text 'the ambassadors of peace shall weep bitterly'. The church was decorated with flags of our Nation, and a reverent and attentive congregation followed the discourse. The service closed with the hymn 'God bless our native land'.[12]

The rhetoric of the preachers and the activities at parish level were reinforced by the editors of the many church newspapers and by the governing bodies of the churches when they assembled. Editors, usually clergymen, concentrated on the plight of 'poor, weak Belgium', applauded the noble motives prompting Britain to take up her cause, and damned Germany as the source of militarism and absolutism. The governing bodies, synods and assemblies, completed

Melbourne street scene on a recent Saturday afternoon

A comment on the lack of 'seriousness'. *Bulletin*, 18 March 1915

the picture of churches united in support for the nation at war. Resolutions called on all Australians to co-operate in the nation's crusade and to embrace reform in their own lives thus bringing the possibility of victory nearer. From pulpit, platform, editor's desk and chapter house a single message came forth: God called on Australians to accept suffering and sacrifice to defeat the evil ambitions of Germany and to bring forth a higher civilisation in Australia.

It is difficult to know how the message was received by the people to whom it was directed. It is likely that most churchgoers accepted it happily enough but that as the initial burst of patriotic fervour died away amongst the population at large, the rhetoric of the church leaders was seen as but one stream in the torrent.

Almost coincidental with the outbreak of war was the call in Adelaide that hotel trading hours be reduced. While opponents regarded this move as an example of clerical opportunism it was, in fact, quite consistent with clergymen's thinking on the nature and purpose of the war. The forces of social reform, located largely in the Protestant churches, had campaigned for many years to regulate the drinking, gambling and other pleasures of the common man. The war made these reforms more urgent. In line with their argument that God was using the war to call the nations back to the paths of righteousness, churchmen stressed that moral reform was a precondition of victory. Only an upright moral nation could expect to win. From the outset clergymen had scrutinised the community for signs of reform and a new seriousness but, after an encouraging beginning when large numbers of people had attended church services, by Christmas 1914 the mood seemed as careless and frivolous as ever. The special daily lunchtime prayer services were cancelled in Sydney, Adelaide and elsewhere; high attendances at regular church services dwindled, crowds at sporting events returned to normal after a temporary tremble, and the summer sun beckoned holiday-makers who appeared indifferent to the serious issues at stake.

In criticising these normal, innocent recreations, clergymen showed what a total commitment they expected from the nation. The apparent indifference of the people mocked the clerical analysis of the meaning of the war, disheartening many of the clergy. Seeking to recapture the enthusiasm of the early days, Anglican leaders called their people to a national day of repentance and prayer on 3 January 1915. Again they explained how the war would show people 'the vanity of human affairs' and draw them to Christ, but again the call seemed to fall on deaf ears. The people remained unmoved.

Clergy returning from the British Isles fed this enthusiasm for reform by reporting what wonders the war had wrought on the British population. John Ferguson, a senior Presbyterian minister, had been holidaying in London in June 1914 where he saw much that distressed him. People lived for pleasure: 'there were ... balls, theatres, picture-shows galore. People were talking cricket and all kinds of sport'. Selfishness motivated political actions: Ireland and the suffragettes were in revolt, Ferguson reported. When war came, Britain changed instantly. The devotees of pleasure dedicated themselves to the cause of their country, the suffragettes retired, Ireland forgot her troubles and striking workers returned to their jobs. Young men rushed to enlist and hostesses abandoned their dances and parties; the King pledged to abstain from alcohol, a sacrifice he honoured, at least in public.[13]

Ferguson's undoubtedly was a superficial view, tinged with more than a little romanticism. But the comparison stung his Australian fellow clergymen. They read eagerly the reports of the splendid behaviour of the British troops in France contrasting them with the news from Cairo, where the Australians were unexpectedly quartered. C. E. W. Bean, the official Australian correspondent, cabled that numbers of Australian troops had damaged Australia's reputation by riotous, drunken behaviour, giving credence to the early jibe that the AIF would never be anything more than 'six-bob-a-day tourists'.[14]

These two aspects of the clergy's disappointment, the renewed level of British life compared with Australian and the misbehaviour of the Australian troops, came together in the minds of many of the clergy. The difference between the two societies, clergymen perceived, was that the British troops were in the thick of the fighting. And so, these clergymen came to share the dream of many of the Australian troops in Egypt: that they would soon be called on to show their mettle on the field of battle. Only then, the argument ran, would the Australian people open themselves to the reform that the war could work amongst them.

Australian artillery in action at Anzac Cove. This scene demonstrates an early British assessment that the Anzacs wore 'no superfluous clothing'

It is not hard to understand the eagerness of the troops to engage the enemy: they were bored with drill, hated the unpleasant conditions of their camp at the foot of the pyramids, the heat and the sand, and wanted to 'get a shot at the real thing', as they put it. But a similar anticipation amongst clergymen in Australia seems callous, even indecent. Bishop Stone-Wigg, who edited the Anglican *Church Standard* in Sydney, wrote that not until the war had dealt Australians 'a shattering, sledgehammer blow' would the people awaken to war's 'cleansing ... spiritual revelation'. Ironically, the bishop published this call for sacrifice and suffering on 30 April 1915, just as the news of the bloody landing at Gallipoli was being cabled home. W. H. Cooper, the leader of the Victorian Presbyterian church, was even more emphatic:

> if in this awful sacrifice of the nations we emerge unchastened, having made only pecuniary sacrifice, there is danger of over-weening pride and boastfulness, but if with the brave fighters from the British Isles and Canada and India our soldiers mingle their blood ... then sacrifice will hallow all our Australian life.

Crowds awaiting news from Gallipoli outside the *Argus* office, Melbourne. Note the prominent war map

Such calls are explicable only at the level of the greater good beyond mere victory that clergymen expected from the war; it was not only an episode in the human drama but had taken on a religious aspect. Otherwise how could a clergyman ask his congregation to look forward to the loss of Australian lives when some of the people sitting beneath him might have had sons or husbands in the AIF?[15]

The calls for sacrifice were answered with bewildering speed. First came the brief announcement that the Australians were in action; then Ellis Ashmead-Bartlett's romantic account of the landing was reproduced in almost every Australian newspaper. He glorified the deeds of the Anzacs, as they came to be called, writing of them as practical men, calm in action, 'this race of athletes' who handled a difficult job with ease. The attitude of the wounded amazed him: 'Though many were shot to bits, without the hope of recovery, their cheers resounded throughout the night'. Ashmead-Bartlett thrilled all his Australian readers when he concluded that 'There has been no finer feat in this war' and that 'These raw colonial troops in these desperate hours proved worthy to fight side by side with the heroes of Mons, the Aisne, Ypres …'.[16]

Then came the casualty lists. So novel an experience was this that at first many Australian newspapers attempted to print the names of all who had died or had been injured at Anzac Cove. Column after column of names, edged in black, many set in heavy type indicating death, pushed a realisation of the tragedy of war before Australians. The horror of these lists entered the nation's consciousness; newspapers began to publish short pen portraits and photographs of the young men who had died on those first days. Each morning the lists were renewed, setting a pattern for the next three-and-a-half years. Lest anyone miss them, the lists were also displayed at public places, such as suburban railway stations, as a constant reminder of the cost of Empire loyalty. Clergymen, so prominent at ceremonies of birth, marriage and death, celebrated Australia's sacrifice at special memorial services to overflowing congregations; they found the words to give utterance to the confused emotions of their fellows.

Many preachers at these services rejoiced that Australians were, at last, under fire, and they took great pride in the achievements of the AIF. They regarded this first experience of war as a test of national character and a refutation of those who believed that British virtues had been eroded by colonial conditions. Lowther Clarke, of whom it was said that he 'scarcely ever concealed his contempt for Australians', expressed frank relief that the AIF had lived up to the finest traditions of the British army: 'no-one doubted the spirit and courage of our men, but we waited with trembling hope in the confidence that they would not turn back on the day of battle'. John Ferguson rejoiced that the Australians had proved themselves 'worthy of their race, worthy of their forefathers, worthy of their country and worthy of their God'. Other preachers concentrated on the landing itself. A Melbourne Presbyterian, W. Borland, spoke of it as an event 'which nothing in the history of human bravery has surpassed', while J. C. Wright advised his congregation to glory in the deeds of the AIF, the fame of which was ringing throughout the Empire. Some preachers, too, spoke words of comfort to the bereaved. Archbishop Carr believed that a soldier who unselfishly laid down his life for his country had 'no bad chance of salvation', while Borland said that God accepted the supreme act of consecration of those who had died: 'they brought their strength to God and He glorified it'.[17]

A more onerous task awaited the clergy. When, in the early months of the war, the government had asked the churches to accept responsibility for the delivery of telegrams informing next of kin of death at the front, church leaders had readily agreed. It showed, they said, the relevance of the church and the close ties between a minister and his people; who was 'so fit to carry the sad news', one clergyman asked. By mid-1915, however, after Gallipoli, many clergymen began to regret a contract so lightly entered into. In many cases they entered the home as a stranger, with no knowledge at all of the bereaved family, who might rarely have been to church and who may have seen the clergyman as an opportunistic intruder or an embarrassing

> **WHY SHOULD I BE ASKED TO ENLIST?**
> **IS MY COUNTRY IN PERIL?**
> **YES!**
> **THEN WHY AM I HANGING BACK?**
> **AM I A COWARD?**

Recruiting poster

presence at a moment of private sorrow. What could the clergyman say of the deceased, perhaps unknown to him entirely? What words of comfort could he convey to these shocked strangers? Furthermore, clergymen found that this new task seriously jeopardised the more mundane aspects of their work. At a time when very few clergymen owned motor cars, most walked around their parish, engaged on routine matters. As the war progressed and men enlisted from virtually every street, the arrival of a clergyman in an area caused terror in the hearts of anxious parents and wives. To see a clergyman at the door was a horrible shock. An Anglican minister from Mackay wrote that normal parish visitation became well-nigh impossible: 'when the door was opened and it was seen who was there, faces became pale and voices trembled'. Some ministers sought to allay anxieties by wearing 'peculiarly shaped hats' or 'coloured badges' when delivering the telegrams, so that they would be welcome in the streets when not so dressed. Before long, clergymen referred to the government's commission as 'this dread duty' or 'this terrible ordeal'. A clergyman's son wrote nearly sixty years later that the work 'was extremely distressing' to his father, who 'never forgot how it hurt'.[18]

Although by June 1915 clergymen were in a better position to count the cost, their involvement in the sufferings of the bereaved caused no substantial revision to their understanding of the war, which they still saw in religious and moral terms. They led the way in calling for recruits to replace the men who had fallen at Gallipoli; indeed, well before the government found it necessary to sponsor any sort of recruiting campaign, clergymen were calling on eligible young men to enlist. The Rev. T. E. Ruth, for example, preached on the topic 'Wanted Men, Wanted More Men' as his contribution to the national day of prayer on 3 January 1915. In reality, this was absurd, as the Defence department was only just able to cope with the recruits who were still flooding the various depots. The motives of these clerical recruiters were more complex than a simple desire to sustain or increase the size of the AIF. If the war was a noble crusade with the potential to raise Australian life to a higher moral plane, then it was necessary that all Australians show how important it was, by providing as large a body of troops as possible. As St Clair Donaldson, the Eton Anglican archbishop of Brisbane, put it, 'the main indication of the national spirit is the eagerness of the nation's manhood to get to the fighting line'. Clergymen, therefore, constantly scanned the recruiting tallies as eagerly as they counted numbers in their churches, to see if the Australian people had at last grasped the importance of reform.[19]

When, in July and August 1915, various state governments inaugurated recruiting campaigns to make up for the losses at Gallipoli and perhaps to resolve that stalemate by increasing the numbers of Australians there, clergymen joined in enthusiastically. They showed their usefulness, if not necessarily their persuasiveness. In the first place, they gave tone and respectability to the words of the politicians, more used to appealing for votes than for lives. Thus, when the New South Wales premier, W. A. Holman, opened his state's recruiting campaign in August 1915, he was supported by both Sydney's archbishops, united in a rare display of common purpose. The South Australian campaign was opened at a large rally with speeches from the premier, leader of the opposition, and three Adelaide clergymen, one of whom, Father Edward Le Maitre, spoke of the Kaiser's 'ruthless, relentless butchery of defenceless old men, women and children'. Other clergymen helped the campaigns in more traditional ways: at Brighton, Victoria, the local Anglican minister insisted on beginning the recruiting rally with prayers and hymns. Clergymen were useful, too, because they were schooled in the art of public speaking and were also able to provide facilities to support the campaigners. While rallies were held at street corners, at sporting events, or at the cinema, others too were conducted in church halls, freely available, with reassuringly large audiences often comprising the minister's loyal, if largely ineligible, congregation.[20]

The presence of clergymen on recruiting platforms raised questions about the role of individual clergymen in wartime. Some showed how sensitive they were to these questions by appearing ill-at-ease as recruiters. They tried to justify themselves, some pointing out that they were too old, others that they had been rejected for such non-combative work as the chaplaincy to the troops, others that a son, or more, had enlisted, as if they themselves were serving vicariously. Younger clergymen, in particular, were often deeply troubled about determining how best they might serve the nation, at home in the parishes, or in some capacity with the troops. The conflict of interests at a personal level must, at times, have been acute.

The Anglican bishops counselled their young clergymen to remain at their posts, arguing that their war work at home, comforting, consoling and inspiring the people, was of greater value than the limited good they might do at the front. The bishop of Wangaratta likened the enlistment of a minister to the use of a razor to cut wood: 'any strong, healthy man of ordinary intelligence can do the duties of the rank and file [soldier]. But every such man is not called, trained and consecrated to be a priest in the Church'. When the Methodists in Victoria debated the propriety of ministers enlisting, as early as February 1915, some said that the public would listen more closely to the church's message about the war if the church showed that it was serious by releasing eligible ministers to the army. Others demanded that the church set its face against such public pressure and thus show its commitment to the spiritual message of the war. The debate aroused tensions similar to those generated by the recruiting campaign in more secular places. One clergyman, the Rev. Henry Worrall, who supported the enlistment of eligible ministers, accused his opponents of cowardice, asking whether 'if a few German shells came through the window of the church just then, [would not] the brethren opposing the resolution be amongst the first to run?'. In the end, younger clergymen made up their own minds: fifty-one Anglicans, eighty Methodists and six Presbyterians joined the forces as rank and file soldiers. Again, the

An inducement to clerical enlistment?
Bulletin, 10 May 1917

SHE: *"I can't understand why more of you young parsons don't go to the war."*
HE: *"Yes, my deah! But who is to stay behind to guard our flock from the black sheep?"*

Catholics stood out. Only one Catholic priest in Australia seems to have departed for the front as a combatant; he was a French missionary, subject to French conscription laws, although he enlisted voluntarily. All others apparently remained at their posts.[21]

The accusation that the opponents of the enlistment of ministers were cowards showed how, despite the emphasis on the spiritual and moral lessons that the war would teach, clergymen had succumbed to the war hysteria and bad temper which, certainly by mid-1916, had disrupted the traditional calm of Australian life. The solemn rhetoric of the early days gave place to strident appeals, name calling and abuse, which were certainly not unique amongst clergymen but were evidence, nevertheless, of the increasing polarisation of Australia at war. Many clergymen assumed that there was only one response possible for the patriotic citizen: to enlist if he were eligible, otherwise to devote himself wholeheartedly to the war effort at home. Those who watched sport, gambled, drank, or pursued other forms of pleasure, were presumed indifferent to the supposed message of the war and aroused the antagonism of clergy. Words as offensive as shirker, coward, slacker, traitor, parasite and even murderer, were on their lips freely, while at recruiting rallies some clergymen behaved with an amazing lack of restraint. While the Rev. Edward Schweiger assisted Sir John Forrest at Casterton 'by singing numerous patriotic songs', the Rev. Frank Lynch of Williamstown aided the cause by rushing to an interjector and dealing him 'a violent blow on the nose'.[22]

Such excesses in clerical behaviour matched some of the more frenzied actions of other Australians. Frank Lynch's outburst was not his only attempt at violence. In August 1916, he observed three men who remained seated while the national anthem was sung; referring to them as 'damned disloyal men', Lynch announced that only the restraining presence of the police prevented him from 'kick[ing] them out of the hall with the toe of my boot'. He called them 'donkeys' and invited them on to the platform to fight him. A Presbyterian minister, Rev. R. G. Hoisler, changed his name to Reynolds early in 1915 because of the shame he felt 'at the German atrocities and injustice'. The Methodist minister at Rochester, Victoria, sent, in October 1915, a white feather and an insulting letter to the shire president who had not enlisted. The minister, George Tregear, felt no shame for his action, but defended himself publicly saying that a minister had the right to recruit. Less fervent, but perhaps more widespread, was the lament of another minister: 'I can't keep the war out of my sermons'.[23]

This unusual clerical behaviour, of which these are only a few examples, is evidence of deep emotion, anxiety and confusion. Instead of exercising restraint and appealing for charity and tolerance, some clergymen, at least, encouraged war hysteria seemingly betraying their own calling. Clergymen professed to loathe violence and to abhor war; some surely found difficulty in reconciling the insensitive, belligerent statements of men such as W. M. Hughes with the Gospel teaching of Christ. For this reason they had to give the war a nobler purpose, to remove it from the realm of sordid human endeavour. Simple, good men like Canon John Hart, a theological teacher in Melbourne, whose parish ministry had earned the respect of his people, found the war a constant emotional strain, heightened, no doubt, by the frenzied behaviour of some of his brother ministers. War revolted him and the constant casualty lists depressed him. He was not a pacifist, but his concern and that of like-minded people ensured that the very few pacifists who did emerge in the Australian churches received a sympathetic hearing from some, at least, of their brethren.[24]

Perhaps the most consistent pacifist in wartime Australia was the Methodist minister at Hay, New South Wales, B. Linden Webb. Webb, born in Bathurst in 1883, had managed to avoid all reference to war in his preaching, until, on the occasion of the first national day of intercession on 3 January 1915, he was forced to say something. Preaching from the text 'My kingdom is not of this world', Webb made a clear distinction between church and state, explaining that as the state's aims were materialistic and therefore in conflict with Christian ideals, it was absurd to suggest that the state might be an agent in promoting spiritual regeneration. He dismissed out of hand the central clerical justification for the nation's involvement in the war. War, he asserted, made devils, not saints. Webb developed his theme in two further sermons and then published them all under the title *The Religious Significance of the War,* which attracted considerable attention, despite the obscurity of his position.[25]

His congregation at Hay apparently accepted Webb's sermons in good spirit and he continued to preach pacifism until, in November 1915, the first signs of friction emerged. A junior church official resigned his position, explaining that he felt bound to do so because he disagreed with Webb's views on the war. At a church meeting called to discuss the matter, three speakers supported Webb's views: one was non-committal, and three opposed him, describing his preaching as 'idealistic and unpracticable'. There was no hint of a censure for Webb and no one suggested that he be replaced: no bad result for pacifism or for tolerance in a small country town. Such a result warns us against assuming a widespread acceptance for the pro-war sentiments of the official church spokesmen. When Webb did resign from his ministry in October 1916, he explained that it was not from any sense of local difficulties but that, as the leadership of the Methodist church had so wholeheartedly endorsed conscription, he felt he could not remain a paid agent of the church. Even so, his congregation regretted his departure, presenting his wife with a silver teapot and a handbag, and giving Webb himself a cheque to help him establish a new form of life. Webb saw out the war running a chicken farm and hawking fruit and clothing from door to door. Pacifism had lost an eloquent exponent.[26]

Not so tolerant were Queensland's Presbyterians, who reacted vigorously to pacifist argument at their 1917 Assembly. The most prominent pacifist in

Dr Merrington preaching to Australians at Gallipoli

Queensland was the Rev. James Gibson, who had explained his case, gently, in the church newspaper which he edited. He provoked no opposition but, even so, found the strain of war too great and accepted a quiet country parish in 1916. He was absent from the 1917 Queensland Presbyterian Assembly when a brother minister moved an extremely bellicose war motion calling on Presbyterians 'to support the National Government in every possible way ... [to obtain] a decisive victory' but a disciple countered with the pacifist argument which relied heavily on Gibson's earlier exposition. These views aroused several members of the Assembly. The Rev. Dr E. N. Merrington, a returned chaplain, soon to re-enlist, confessed that he was ashamed to belong to an Assembly which contained pacifists. He suggested that their speeches were 'distinctly savouring of disloyalty'. In the context of wartime patriotism, this was as serious a charge as could be made. Certainly the Queensland debate unleashed emotions that were not evident in the discussion of Webb's position at Hay, but then a year had elapsed during which Australians had endured the turmoil of the conscription referendum campaign and a federal election, and were shortly to go to the polls to vote again on conscription. In such a climate, pacifism received short shrift.[27]

The bad temper that had surfaced during this debate and had been evident during the recruiting campaigns, gathered its own momentum as churchmen divided people into categories, branding some classes as loyalists and others as disloyalists. They continued to apply tests to determine the patriotism of groups and individuals and damned whole sections of the community whose understanding of the war was not as intense as their own. To watch a boxing match at the stadium or to spend a few hours in a hotel bar was enough to earn the contempt of these patriots who saw the war as a divine crusade in which every citizen must play a part. Men and women who ignored their duty were slackers to whom compulsion might rightly be applied. Catholic spokesmen, who had never accepted the war as an instrument by which Australia would be reformed, were not nearly as fanatical, playing a part in recruiting, to be sure, but always in a restrained, cautious way.

Events in Ireland accelerated the realisation of these Catholic-Protestant divisions. Australian and Irish Catholic leaders had counselled their people to assist the Empire and, in thus showing their loyalty and usefulness, they hoped Catholics would win major concessions such as Home Rule in Ireland and state aid in Australia. And yet, traditionally, Britons doubted if a Catholic could maintain both his spiritual allegiance to the Pope and his temporal allegiance to the monarch. These fears survived in Australia and are typified in the example of Herbert Brookes, 'school captain, able student, mining engineer, workshop executive, elected spokesman of the nation's infant secondary industries'. Brookes organised the Citizens' Loyalist Committee, later the Loyalist League, in Victoria, to counteract what he regarded as the disloyalty of Catholics. His biographer, Rohan Rivett, suggested that he dedicated himself to the anti-Catholic cause because of 'the lessons learned at the knee of his mother, that seamstress from Portadown, who brought from her Ulster home suspicion of the Irish priesthood'. Brookes had also idealised the British Empire and could not tolerate any criticism of it. He brought together many of Melbourne's leading Protestant ministers, among them T. E. Ruth, Waiter Albiston and Dr Alexander Leeper, who co-operated with him in speaking at rallies and in forming processions and deputations to alert people to the dangers of Catholicism.[28]

The rebellion against English rule in Ireland at Easter 1916, which the Sinn Fein engineered, confirmed these Protestant suspicions. The loyalty of Catholics apparently could not be relied upon. Catholic leaders in Australia condemned the Sinn Fein revolt immediately they learned of it, in such uncompromising terms that showed how much they feared it would resurrect these traditional suspicions. Archbishop Carr of Melbourne described the uprising as 'an outburst of madness, an anachronism and a crime', while Archbishop Kelly in Sydney and Archbishop Duhig in Brisbane explained it as a plot hatched in Germany, paid for with German gold. Such denunciations cut no ice with those Protestants brought up to suspect Catholic loyalty. An eminent Sydney Methodist, J. C. Carruthers, dismissed Kelly's striking condemnation of the Irish rebels, saying he could 'read between lines so expressed and get at the real sentiments of this clamorous Popish prelate'.[29]

It was impossible for Catholics to overcome such deep-seated, traditional antagonisms overnight. And so, throughout 1916, doubts spread about the loyalty and patriotism of Australian Catholics, a dangerous situation as they comprised nearly a quarter of the community. Extremist Protestants alleged that Catholics refused to enlist or that their priests discouraged them from enlisting. How bitterly such charges must have been resented by the Catholic mother whose son had been killed or maimed at the front, or by the Catholic priest delivering casualty telegrams and ministering to the bereaved. Charges of disloyalty and of alien interests drew the Catholic community closer together and became, in a sense, self-fulfilling, as Catholics despaired of winning acceptance by their sacrifices. The divisions increased anxieties and endangered the war effort, for it was no small thing to lose confidence in Catholics, a substantial proportion of the community.

While the religious element accounted for part of this growing division in the community, class questions reinforced the conflict, From the outbreak of war it had been apparent that Australian workers were not nearly so single-minded in their devotion to the Empire's cause as the 'professional patriots' would have desired. Unionists passed motions affirming their loyalty and support for the Empire and thousands of their members rushed to enlist in the ranks. But they worried too about prices which rose alarmingly immediately war broke out and about jobs which disappeared with equally bewildering speed. On 13 August 1914 the *Australian Worker* reported a union resolution calling on the government to prevent the increase in the price of necessities that was taking place and advising unionists to remember the firms that were pushing up the prices and to refuse to do business with them. This illustrated that the widespread anticipation that war would bring economic dislocation was fulfilled almost immediately as employers panicked, increasing prices and putting off workers. In this sense, from the beginning, the war demanded sacrifices from Australian workers. They suspected, with some justification, that patriotism was a cheaper virtue for affluent, middle-class Australians.[30]

So intense was the preoccupation of many patriots, particularly clergymen, that they puzzled over the apparent indifference or apathy of the workers, and could not understand the preoccupation with prices and jobs. When they observed that working men and women also continued to attend sports competitions, to drink and to gamble, they grew suspicious and concluded that the war had not become real to them. These patriots awaited events that would dramatise the war for the workers. And yet, as the war progressed, despite high enlistment, resolutions of loyalty and an intense anti-German sentiment, the patriots continued to bemoan the indifference, the disloyalty even, of men and women who would not abandon all interests other than those of the Empire.

These suspicions fell doubly on Catholics. There were few Catholics in the professional classes able to contribute prominently to the various patriotic causes. Indeed, as many Catholics belonged to the working class they felt a double alienation. They shared the resentment of their fellow workers that the high enlistment from unionists was apparently overlooked in the haste to condemn those workers who went to the races or the stadium. They also

Compulsion shown as overcoming the temptation of football, movies, racing, cricket and tennis. *Bulletin*, 15 November 1917

resented attacks from the patriots about the alleged disloyalty of their priests and co-religionists. They gloried, too, in the enlistment of lads from the parish and boys from the Catholic colleges but this sacrifice was also largely overlooked by the Leepers and the Worralls, who charged that Catholic enlistment lagged. Catholic workers had very good reason to repudiate the loyalists and to feel bitter about the accusations they made.

As persuasion failed, the middle-class patriots turned to compulsion to bring the apathetic or disloyal section of the community to a sense of its obligations; if they would not enlist they must be compelled to do so, if they would drink they must be prevented. Clergymen, who for decades had advocated compulsion as the method of making Australians respectable, now led such cries. Their longstanding dissatisfaction with Australian moral standards, which had caused them to initiate 'social reform crusades' from the 1880s onwards, received new impetus. Now, of course, the imposition of higher standards of conduct was not merely an end in itself but would contribute substantially to the Empire's cause. Large battalions alone would not win the war, victory would go to the Empire only when it had shown it had learned God's lesson. The campaigns to limit drinking, to outlaw gambling, to impose Sunday observance, took on an ever greater urgency as the war progressed. Churchmen redoubled their efforts to make Australians conform, at least outwardly, to respectable Christian standards of conduct.

Catholic leaders rarely sympathised with such campaigns to 'make men good by act of parliament', as they put it. In part, this derived from a theological objection and in part from an appreciation of a strong sense of class loyalty on the part of some of their people. Catholics believed that man achieved salvation through the mediation of the church, by the reception of sacraments dispensed by the church's priests. They were less inclined than Protestants to emphasise outward conformity to moral standards as a precondition for salvation. They were also reluctant to condemn the pleasures of the working man – drinking and gambling – when they perceived that such prohibitions as parliament might enact would barely impinge on the wealthier classes. They objected to 'class legislation' in the proposals to restrict drinking hours or to limit the opportunity of the worker to 'have a flutter on the horses'. Furthermore, with an expensive education system to finance, Catholic priests relied heavily on wheels of fortune and raffles to raise money and, no doubt, feared that legislation would outlaw such money spinners. Thus, while a climate of compulsion developed within the Protestant churches, Catholics regarded such measures with distaste.[31]

Nevertheless, Catholic leaders did not reject out of hand the conscription of Australians for service overseas, when the Universal Service League first advocated this in September 1915. Indeed, Archbishop Kelly in Sydney offered to speak at the League's inaugural rally, signed its manifesto and eventually became one of its vice-presidents. Editors of Catholic newspapers supported the call for conscription in 1915, basing their arguments on the need for efficiency and economy and the best use of the available manpower. Such support preceded working-class opposition to conscription, for at this stage the question was theoretical. But when it became a matter of practical political debate after Hughes returned from Britain in August 1916, spokesmen for the working class quickly expressed their opposition, mobilising the labour movement against any form of compulsory service overseas. On the whole, the Catholic newspapers followed their lead, the editor of Adelaide's *Southern Cross* showing how deftly the change of opinion might be effected. He wrote that while he still supported the principle of compulsory service, he objected on practical grounds to its implementation: 'in Australia we have not arrived at [the necessity] yet. It is not likely that we ever will'.[32]

The Sydney Mail Referendum Number

ALTHOUGH I have no authority to speak for the Congregational Union, which will make its own pronouncement on the question of the referendum this week, I do not hesitate to say that personally I can do no other than vote "Yes" next Saturday. My position is somewhat this: I have accepted all the privileges of citizenship. Everything I possess, all that makes life worth living I owe to association with my fellow-citizens. I have received from the State more than I have contributed to it or can ever repay. It is simply unthinkable that I should be so craven as to accept these privileges and ignore the responsibilities which they necessarily entail. But to me there is something higher still. "The reign of law, the control of right, the enforcement of freedom," as Principal Forsyth reminds us, "are supernatural," and he pertinently asks, "Is it a Christian thing to repudiate our trusteeship of those things in the world, refuse to be fellow-workers with God, and consent to be walked over with all our responsibilities? What are we to do when it is clear that our non-resistance will tend to our death? becomes the procreation of evil, offers it ungodly, fosters its increase, and gives up the world to scoundrels?" Personally, I am under no delusion as to what would happen if Germany were triumphant. It would lead to more than the world's vassalage. It would mean a return to barbarism, and the surrender of ourselves and our loved ones to the control of men with instincts which should govern only the beasts of the field. I simply cannot understand that anyone could accept life, under such conditions as Germany would impose, rather than death. But to me true freedom is so indissolubly associated with the Christian gospel that I regard this war, which has been thrust upon us, more as a crusade in the best sense than a war as ordinarily understood. The issues are so much more deeply spiritual than material that I should like our soldiers to feel that they can be as truly soldiers of Jesus Christ as in any work to which they could ever be called. I have not hesitated so to place the matter before my only son, in whose moral insensibility as his parents share, an only parent can feel not without loss, made deeper by the pain. For the sake of some who may have conscientious scruples about taking life—even though it be the lives of men who have lost all claim to consideration and pity—I should like to quote again the

MOST REV. JOHN CHARLES WRIGHT, D.D.
Archbishop of Sydney and Primate of Australia.

MOST REV. MICHAEL KELLY, D.D.
Roman Catholic Archbishop of Sydney.

In this great conflict all is at stake, and no man who takes the privileges of Australian citizenship has a right to refuse Australia's call. I repeat here the words of our Australian Prime Minister in his manifesto to the people: "No patriot can deny the necessity of reinforcements; no democrat can impugn the right of the nation to demand this duty from its citizens." We tell the leaders of our nation that the sacrifice has already been too great to stop short of anything less than decisive victory, and a premature peace would be a betrayal of our nation.—R. G. Macintyre, Moderator of the Presbyterian General Assembly of Australia.

author I have mentioned. "It should be remembered," he says, "that the object of war is not to kill, but to bind the superman. And, if he is so strong, infatuate, and criminal that nothing will stop him in his unrighteousness but honest, judicial killing, such killing is not murder, nor is it hate. It is a form of judgment. If it violate the right to live and be free, it does so as capital punishment does, or indeed all punishment. If killing is murder here, no Christian can be a judge, and certainly not a sheriff charged with execution."

BUT the objection will be raised by some that, while all this may be granted in so far as our own attitude is concerned, I have no right to impose this view upon others, especially when it may lead to the sacrifice of their lives. Just here I am on the horns of a dilemma, and so are we all. Several hundred thousand men have enlisted voluntarily. It is a glorious result, and if anyone had predicted such a thing five years ago he would have been held in derision. Five millions have so enlisted in the old land! This will be considered in all history as one of its marvels, and yet this is not enough. The German Moloch has been dangerously but not mortally wounded, and the leaders, who would not deceive us, tell us that there is now needed every available man. We have compulsory service in Australia. We were not hesitated when it became law, and it is a pity we are now being asked to decide whether Australia is being so garishly defended in Europe as it ever could be on its own soil. The Government might well have decided that, and risk'd the consequences. But this is no time to badger those who are charged with such grave issues. I accept the assurance of the Prime Minister and agree with him. I am asked if I doubt whether the men who have gone voluntarily, nobly responding to their country's call, shall be sacrificed unnecessarily because others who accept the privileges of citizenship prefer to shirk the responsibilities it entails. On the ground of common fairness, I say to such, you cannot have it both ways. It is too late now to get away to a country where they may be too proud to fight. Vote "Yes" and save your souls at any cost; then come back and help others to restore to the State as citizens of whom we all can be proud, and for whom we shall ever humbly thank God. There are grave crises when, after the State has given the utmost room for the plea "You ought" it is my duty bound to substitute the compulsion "You must," and this I believe to be one of them.—W. L. PATISON, Chairman-elect of Congregational Union.

REV. PROFESSOR MACINTYRE,
Moderator-General of the Presbyterian Church of Australia.

"AUSTRALIA stands by the cause—the cause of Christian civilisation and world freedom—to the end. It may importantly our country, but a thousand times better to be poor but free."

REV. GEORGE BROWN, D.D.
President General Conference, Methodist Church of Australasia.

"A RIGHT decision of the momentous issues at stake can only be arrived at after full recognition of the duty which we owe to God; to the Empire to which we belong; to the men we fight; and also to our own individual character and conscience."

REV. W. L. PATISON,
Chairman-elect of the Congregational Union of New South Wales.

"WE have compulsory service in Australia. We were not hesitated when it became law, and it is a pity we are now being asked to decide whether Australia is being so garishly defended in Europe as it ever could be on its own soil. The Government might well have decided that, and risk'd the consequences. But this is no time to badger those who are charged with such grave issues. I accept the assurance of the Prime Minister."

REV. DAVID STEED,
President of the Baptist Union of New South Wales.

"TO vote No is to imperil the safety of the democracy we hold as priceless. The good name of this fair country depends upon the answer we give. Our men at the front, when tired and fall an easy prey to the enemy, and we shirk their necessary necessity of the same we have if we call to provide help and save life. Nothing less than a clear-cut Yes can save Australia from the love of all."

Many Labor supporters felt Hughes had betrayed them. He had made a very favourable impression in London in the first half of 1916 and was paraded around Britain as the 'man of the hour'. His triumphs were handsomely reported in the Australian press but there were many who believed that the adulation had turned his head and that he was prepared to force conscription on Australia to prove his loyalty to his British hosts. Labor supporters began to complain that Hughes had been 'duchessed' abroad, an easy complaint for Australians, traditionally suspicious of the 'tall poppy'. Catholic Labor supporters felt doubly betrayed when they observed some of their religious leaders sharing common ground with the conscriptionists. Abandoned by Hughes, abandoned by bishops like Kelly and Clune, who was the working-class Catholic to follow?

Daniel Mannix, the assistant archbishop of Melbourne, who had arrived in Australia from Ireland in 1913, accepted this leadership by default; there was no one else of stature. Mannix was a striking figure, tall, erect, a splendid speaker, quick and witty and a supreme controversialist. He spoke only twice about conscription during the first referendum campaign, on both occasions briefly, touching lightly on the question in speeches devoted to other matters. That he has been seen as the leader of the 'No' campaign in 1916 bears eloquent witness to the leadership vacuum that the 'antis' experienced. Most of the opinion-makers, the politicians, the press and the pulpit, supported 'Yes'. The battle was simply to find someone to put the case against conscription with vigour and confidence. The official leader of the 'No' cause was Frank Tudor, the minister for customs in Hughes's government, who had resigned from cabinet to oppose Hughes. Tudor was a conscientious man but he was no match for the prime minister. In 1917, particularly, Mannix became Hughes's most prominent critic, attacking him with a ferocity rarely found in an archbishop.

Mannix intervened in the conscription debate because he had noticed that 'certain authorities of the Anglican Church have given their public support for conscription'; he believed that he was entitled to put the other side. He accepted their right to speak: 'We all have equal right to contribute to the discussion, and in the exercise of that right I have spoken tonight'. The Protestant leaders claimed not to be exercising a democratic freedom to discuss political questions in public, maintaining that the issue was not a political one, but a moral one about which churchmen must speak. Monotonously, Protestant church leaders and church assemblies repeated this point: 'the issue is a moral one and therefore comes within the sphere of Church action'. This attitude depended upon, and was the culmination of, the Protestant argument that the war had religious significance, that it was a moral crusade from which no citizen might excuse himself.[33]

Opposite: Prominent Sydney churchmen appealing for a 'Yes' vote

Catholics disagreed. The Pope's representative in Australia, Archbishop Cerretti, reminded all Catholic clergy that 'it would be altogether unreasonable to involve the Church, as a Church, in an issue which its members as citizens, in common with others, are called on to decide'. This fundamental disagreement about the nature of the conscription debate arose from the different perceptions about the war held by Catholics and Protestants. Mannix opposed conscription, speaking as a private citizen, giving his views on a political question. Protestants supported conscription as clergymen, from their pulpits, giving their people moral advice as they would about questions of sexual morality or gambling. Nevertheless, few Catholic bishops followed Mannix into the 'anti' camp in 1916, whether from conviction or because they were unwilling to offend the Protestant majority. Some of them, indeed, argued that for practical political reasons, not for moral ones, Catholics should vote 'Yes'. Mannix, almost alone amongst the bishops said 'No'.[34]

To the surprise of most observers Australian voters rejected conscription, even if only by the slender margin of 72,476 in a poll of about 2,500,000 voters. Three states, New South Wales, Queensland and South Australia, voted 'No', with the majority in New South Wales (117,739) determining the outcome. Explaining the result has intrigued political commentators, whose theories have ranged from the unwillingness of farmers to lose more rural labour, to the anxieties of middle-class voters about the rate of venereal diseases in the AIF. On the whole, class loyalties predominated, in that electorates that voted for Liberal candidates in the 1914 general election generally voted 'Yes' and Labor electorates generally voted 'No'. Within each electorate, however, there were swings severe enough to make generalisation difficult. Voting at a referendum, particularly a referendum as emotionally charged as this, is not strictly comparable with voting at a general election.[35]

Some Protestant clergymen had warned their churches that the laity would not vote solidly for conscription. Donald Cameron was the Presbyterian director of home missions in Victoria, a position which enabled him to travel extensively throughout the state; unlike other ministers he was not bound to one small parish area. His observations convinced him that Presbyterians were divided over conscription, that people believed that the church had sunk to the level of party politics and that they did not regard the issue as a moral one. He urged the church 'to resume its attitude of impartiality and toleration'. Such advice was ignored. Instead, Protestant clergymen berated the selfishness of the people, spoke of Australia's shame and laid the blame for the defeat squarely on the shoulders of the Catholics, who, with the German-Australians, were now 'proved' to be disloyal. The aftermath of the referendum showed what folly it was to ask people to vote at such a time on such an issue. All the frustrations and anxieties that had been held in check by the impetus of patriotism came spewing out. An 'anti' was a traitor, a friend of the Kaiser, an ally of the baby-killers. Hughes was a Labor 'rat' intent on the destruction of the party and its main planks, unionism and White Australia.

THE SOWER OF TARES

Low's view of Mannix. *Bulletin*, 1 November 1917

Sectarianism reached new depths. Mannix became the scapegoat for all this frustration and disappointment, as he had been such a prominent 'anti'.[36]

When the people were asked to vote on conscription for a second time in December 1917, most of the Catholic bishops changed sides, now supporting Mannix, because they had become aware of the feelings of their people and dared not offend them again. Catholics had shown their opinions clearly enough. They gave Mannix tumultuous receptions whenever he appeared. As the Vatican secretary of state wrote: 'it must not be forgotten that Monsignor Mannix, wrongly or rightly, enjoys great influence on the working classes – proofs of this are the imposing and clamorous demonstrations of Melbourne and Sydney.' Sydney Catholics abandoned their pro-conscriptionist newspaper, the *Freeman's Journal,* in favour of its 'anti' rival the *Catholic Press.* Archbishop Kelly, the most prominent Catholic conscriptionist, received condemnatory letters from his flock. Patrick Cunningham, a Catholic layman, complained to Kelly that when Catholic committees were formed 'you never condescend to ask the working man[;] you have Lord Mayors[,] M.L.C.[s,] Drs. and Judges' [sic]. He advised Kelly to 'follow Christ's example and come amongst the poor and leave the rich for a time'. An Irish-Catholic warned Kelly that 'hundreds [are] leaving the Catholic Church, they think it is of no use to the people … the priests, all like yourself are studying the politicians, and the whims of rich people'. Kelly also suffered the disgrace of an anti-conscription demonstration by his people while he entertained the apostolic delegate, Archbishop Cerretti, and the New South Wales premier, W. A. Holman, at the St Patrick's Day Sports in 1917. The demonstration even continued as Cerretti attempted to give the papal blessing to the people.[37]

Catholic antagonisms increased during the second referendum campaign; there was a tendency for Mannix and his supporters to see the issue in rather simple class terms, the rich against the poor. Mannix's Catholic opponents were certainly all wealthy, professional men. This did not overawe him. In November 1917 Mr Justice Heydon wrote to the *Sydney Morning Herald* that Mannix had shown himself 'to be not only disloyal as a man, but (I say it emphatically, Archbishop though he be, and simple layman though I be) untrue to the teachings of the Church'. Mannix replied that 'if [Heydon] were to address Catholics in Sydney … he would not get as many to listen to him as would fit into a lolly shop'. In March 1918, Mannix travelled to Sydney 'to thank the people of New South Wales for saving Australia' by again decisively rejecting conscription and to assist at the laying of a cornerstone at the Catholic college at Sydney University. His charisma worked in Sydney, almost as well as in Melbourne. There was a large crowd at St John's College and Mannix entertained them with an attack on his 'enemies', wealthy Catholics. He observed that 'Here in Australia we do not want higher education to produce men who are more Catholic than the Pope and more loyal than the King. We don't want that type of Catholic … [they think] that they are able to instruct their bishops'. The tension between wealthy and poor Catholics prompted the College rector, Fr Maurice O'Reilly, to abandon the building appeal; he objected, he said, to 'bleeding the workers to educate the rich'. Mannix later visited a Catholic girl's school at Balmain, a working-class suburb. The scene at his arrival 'was one of the most remarkable witnessed in Sydney. When Dr Mannix stepped from his car he was literally mobbed by folk of his own faith, and seemed in danger of losing his robes, so great was the struggle to touch or kiss some portion of his clothing'. Mannix expressed frank relief to be amongst the workers, because they always welcomed him generously. He voiced the suspicion that many working-class Catholics felt for those of their faith who had risen in society: no Catholic in New South Wales had achieved a position of pre-eminence, he said, without having 'denied the faith he had been brought up in or denied the country to which he or his father belonged'. To defend themselves, Catholics drew together in class and religious solidarity, attacking those of their faith who sided with the patriots as 'renegade' Catholics: Mannix was their eloquent spokesman and working-class Catholics recognised it, giving him devoted loyalty.[38]

The outcome of these bitter years of political confrontation was to raise sectarian animosities to new peaks, to divide the community disastrously in several directions, and thus to reduce to nonsense Protestant thinking about the war. By December 1917 it made no sense to claim that the war would produce a new Australia hallowed by sacrifice, willing to accept the moral and ethical standards of Protestantism, to abandon materialism and a superficial view of life. In the eyes of many Protestant clergymen, Australia stood revealed as a country where sacrifice counted for nothing, where selfish impulses predominated. Worse still, the conscription fiasco apparently demonstrated how small an influence the Protestant churches exercised over the people. While Protestant leaders had treated conscription as a moral issue and had spoken in unison and in clear, unequivocal terms about the path of higher duty, the people had set this guidance aside, following their own lights, voting in accordance with their material interests and their perceptions of political reality. This was a disastrous result for the churches, but only one Protestant clergyman, W. H. Fitchett, examined the implications of the failure in print. He believed that no minister could claim to have influenced his people's vote and he concluded that:

> it is surely a matter for profound regret that when the Churches of the land have agreed in judgment on a moral question affecting national affairs, and have declared their judgment in a form so public and in terms so impressive this has not arrested and influenced public opinion in a higher degree than is proved to be the case.[39]

Had church leaders thought about the reasons for their minimal influence, their conclusions would hardly have cheered them. The analysis of the war that clergymen had given the community centred on certain theological propositions. They had discussed war in terms of sin and reform, of God's overall plan, of the conditions he demanded before granting victory. Many Australians rejected these arguments as irrelevant, as exaggerated and unreal. They saw the war in more familiar terms.

Even many of the most enthusiastic patriots refused to follow clergymen into the tangles of theology, so that while they might have used similar language and have supported the war as wholeheartedly, their basic reasoning was dissimilar. These patriots, for example, argued against the continuance of spectator sport on the grounds that it distracted men from the war, encouraging them to delay their decision to enlist. Clergymen attacked the continuance of sport because it indicated an indifferent spirit amongst the people, who were unable to turn from trivia to higher issues. The important point was not the numbers of people clergymen won by their arguments, but how their passionate support for the war minimised the possibility of calm, reasoned debate emerging in Australia. The turmoil over conscription brought the emotion and division to a peak and Protestant clergymen participated in that by their wholehearted acceptance of conscription as a moral obligation. But that acceptance depended upon their earlier theories about the war. Catholic leaders, in particular Mannix, had divested the war of any major significance in the divine redemptive plan, treating it as an event in human history that need not be dressed up in confusing religious terms. Speaking more directly to the people, using concepts the people themselves employed, Mannix won a more attentive hearing.

Many clergymen, of course, contributed substantially to Australia's war effort. They raised money for war victims at home and abroad, although not on the scale of the organisations designed specifically for war purposes. They accepted the awful task of bringing the sad news of death at the front to thousands of Australian homes, and they counselled and comforted the lonely, often heart-broken women, whose men were absent for as long as four years. All these 'unremembered acts of kindness and of love' no doubt helped morale in Australia. Clergymen, too, had their victories. They helped to push through some of the social reforms that they had advocated for so long. The hours of drinking were restricted in most states and not liberalised again for many years; opportunities for gambling and sport were reduced.

Whether these achievements contributed at all to the Empire's eventual victory may well be doubted. Despite these achievements, war represented an opportunity missed for most Australian clergymen. Instead of helping to unite the nation in a common purpose, they eventually helped to divide it; instead of encouraging calm, reasoned debate, they contributed to the worst excesses of wartime hysteria. The people had reason to feel disappointed in their clergy.

CHAPTER THREE

SEEDPLOTS OF EMPIRE LOYALTY: THE SCHOOLS AT WAR

While clergymen attracted headlines with their more bellicose statements, we cannot be sure that they attracted even a large minority of the people to their churches. In terms of commitment and support, the school was a far more important institution, at the heart of the nation's life. A member of the Victorian Education department claimed that the extent of the school system enabled the department 'to get in touch quickly with nearly every home in the State'. If this was so – and we have no reason to doubt it – study of the response of the nation's schools to the war should show much about the people's spirit and their patriotism. Through the school we may come closer to the feelings and concerns of the people. In addition, because the schools were established expressly to produce good, useful citizens, the war became the chief test of their success and an important stimulus to this ideal. If the schools taught values that the community shared, then examining the schools in action as they encouraged patriotism and love of Empire should help explain the real spirit of the Australian people.[1]

By 1914 the school system throughout Australia was divided into three sections. First there were the government schools, funded and staffed from the public purse, established in the 1870s and 1880s to provide 'free, secular and compulsory' education. Owing to the size of this task, governments had concentrated on establishing a network of primary schools so that, for example, in New South Wales the state educated 272,317 children of whom only 5,220 were in secondary schools; there were 3,258 schools throughout New South Wales staffed by 6,881 teachers.[2]

Despite the forcefully expressed fears of the Catholic bishops that these schools would become 'seed-plots of future immorality', they were anything but 'value-free'. Neutral on the question of religion, they were far from neutral about the ideals and duties of citizenship. School texts emphasised the extent of the Empire on which 'the sun never sets', and stressed doctrines that taught children their duty to the Empire. Readers and, no doubt, teachers gloried in the exploits of Britain's invincible navy whose might held the

Empire together, reinforced by her army, a small band of heroic, highly trained troops, equally adept in resisting the French or Russians as in quelling a native uprising in India or Africa. School ritual supported this doctrine. Indeed, the annual celebration of Empire Day on 24 May, the anniversary of Queen Victoria's birthday, was the highlight of a year-round emphasis on Empire loyalty and patriotism. Throughout the country on Empire Day schoolchildren marched, produced patriotic displays, gave patriotic concerts, and listened, how attentively we know not, to addresses on the spirit of the Empire from dignitaries such as the mayor, the local member of parliament, or a clergyman. Ex-pupils demonstrated the success of this teaching as they scaled the cliffs at Gallipoli, determined to measure up to their teachers' image of troops of the Empire.[3]

The founders of the government schools had hoped to strengthen Australian democracy and the equality of opportunity by giving all young Australians a common start in life. Such was the nature of the secular compromise that the Catholic bishops determined to set up their own schools to provide the religious element they believed essential to the educational process. Thus Australians possessed a dual education system by which 'tribes' in the community were divided rather than united. While standards of arithmetic and spelling remained much the same in both systems, the aim of the church schools differed in that the Catholics hoped to produce useful, loyal, Catholic citizens. In practice this meant that the Catholic schools emphasised the Irish heritage for, in the eyes of the predominantly Irish bishops and priests, Catholicism and reverence for Ireland went hand-in-hand. Devotion to Ireland and Australia replaced that single-minded devotion to Empire found in the government schools, which led, as we shall see, to a slightly less enthusiastic acceptance of the war by Catholic scholars. Still, patriotism, as a Christian virtue, received due prominence in the Catholic schools, although, significantly, Catholic children anticipated present-day Australians by celebrating Australia Day rather than Empire Day although they celebrated it in June.

Because the state catered for only a small number of secondary school students, and because of the prestige and status of private schools in England, the Australian private school system made up the third strand of the education system. These schools, misleadingly referred to as public schools, existed by dint of the fees charged, and so drew pupils from amongst the moderately affluent, middle-class Australians. They imitated their English progenitors in the values they enshrined, the classical education that they adopted, their emphasis on games, and the 'old-world', ivy-covered buildings they erected. They imported many of their staff and almost invariably their heads from the British Isles and so it is not surprising that Empire loyalty assumed an important place in these schools. Their pupils, because of their affluent background and the fact that they had access to higher education, tended to dominate the professions and commercial life.

A LESSON IN GENDERS
THE SMALL BOY: *"Masculine, feminine—an' I forget the other, Miss!"*
THE AUSTRALIAN GIRL: *"Shirker!"*

Learning *the* lesson. *Bulletin*, 3 February 1916

Among the boys' schools an 'old school tie network' had evolved; certainly the products of the public schools felt that they comprised a special section of the community, sharing values others only dimly perceived. Their response to the war showed how dominant these values were. 'Sister schools' catered for the education of the daughters of the middle-class, leading some girls to higher education but training all to manage efficiently the homes of the lawyers, doctors and businessmen that they would marry.

The aims of each strand of the education system would determine how the schools would respond to the outbreak of war. Naturally war will always excite and stimulate young minds romantically attuned to notions of heroism, courage and sacrifice. Many pupils no doubt saw the war as the great adventure of their time and could not fully understand its tragedy and cost. The pages of school magazines, usually written by pupils themselves, are full of this love of adventure and enthusiasm for war, and it would be easy to exaggerate the patriotism of the schools by concentrating on these sentiments. Were these easy words matched by actions? In a sense these schoolboy sentiments captured exactly the first mood of Australia at war: after all, the young men who rushed to enlist in the first heady months were not so much older than the schoolboy editors who wrote so earnestly and so longingly about the opportunities of the war.

Pupils and teachers, nurtured on war stories and devoted to Empire ideals, welcomed the outbreak of conflict in Europe with almost indecent enthusiasm. They never doubted that Britain would triumph quickly and they delighted in the excitement of it all. At Fort Street Boys' High in Sydney the 2A class reported that 'a martial spirit' pervaded the classroom while members of the 1B class drew 'excellent maps of the war area ... in the playground', which doubtless resounded to the noise of all sorts of martial games. Across at Sydney Grammar School on 18 August 1914, 'a most important day in the history of the School', the boys with 'tremendous cheering and piercing, deep-rooted enthusiasm' hailed the troops as they marched past the school. The schoolboy editor of their magazine, the *Sydneian,* wondered what effect the war would have on examination results 'if it lasts until November'. Down at Geelong College in Victoria excitement reached fever-pitch when word arrived that the citizen forces, including seventeen Collegians, were to be mobilised to secure the Heads at Queenscliff. The football match against Wesley College set down for 7 August was cancelled, and eight of the boys remained in camp for two weeks. Many other schools abandoned sporting events and dances to allow pupils to appreciate the 'seriousness' of it all.[4]

Whether or not this lesson sank in, pupils quickly made their own the patriotic rhetoric beloved of politicians, editors and clergymen. School captains, class captains and other leaders, eagerly imitated headmasters and teachers in speaking of 'might against right' and the students' duty. In formulating such sentiments, pupils drew on the language and ideas that had figured so prominently in the stories of gallantry and heroism in their school texts and leisure reading. In this sense they were well prepared for war. Paling, captain at Fort Street Boys' High, wrote of old boys who would 'answer to the roll call' and sacrifice their lives, 'their all at the call of their country'. Kershaw, editor of the *Record* at Sydney Boys' High School, wrote an editorial that might have been borrowed from *Boys' Own Paper:*

> It is a time of self-denial – this of war – and it is fitting that we, as a school, should have our share in the general renunciation. Of what sacrifices we have made, let us say 'It was our duty', nay more, 'It was our privilege'; of what unknown, and perhaps greater sacrifices may come, let us say, not only is it our duty, not only is it our privilege, but that it is our opportunity of fulfilling those obligations to our country and Empire, to which a thousand material kindnesses have given birth.

Reading this, masters may have reflected how well they had succeeded in their aims.[5]

Literature came to the aid of editors less able with words than Kershaw. Thus, poets reprinted in the *Fortian* included Shakespeare, Southey, Thomas More, Thomas Campbell, Lord Byron, Lord Macaulay, Sir Walter Scott ('Where's the coward that would not dare/To fight for such a land'), Robert Burns, and even W. E. Henley, who asked, 'What is there I would not do/ England, my own?' More telling, perhaps, is the literature the pupils created themselves to express the thoughts that arose in them. The *Bathurstian*, magazine of All Saints College, Bathurst, offered its readers a poem that, while borrowing its language and imagery from thousands of mightier predecessors, sought to describe Australia's situation:

> Right gladly the offspring of Freedom heard
>   tell of the Mother's resolve
> And swiftly they gird them together, the
>   wheels of their war schemes revolve;
> From all the wide lands and dominions that
>   ever her justice have known
> Comes the help that has never been asked
>   for – she reaps but the crop she has sown.

Editors delighted too, to print essays on patriotism and duty, probably set by thousands of masters in these early months of war. Marjorie Spencer, for example, from Sydney Girls' High School, argued that patriotism was 'a feeling of deep love' for one's country, an emotion that 'seeks her advancement in all things'. The bulk of her essay concentrated on the ways by which soldiers showed patriotism, but also conceded a role for the patriotic woman who could knit useful things such as socks for the soldiers, but whose principal task was 'to breed a race of strong, true people'.[6]

Marjorie Spencer's essay highlighted the need the patriot felt to contribute in a personal sense at a time of crisis. School children were no exception. At first some believed that self-sacrifice was a virtue that would, in some way, help the Empire, and so they merely gave up pleasures or convenience on the Empire's behalf. Thus, a writer in the *Sydneian* argued that everyone should make sacrifices to help the Empire: 'we can walk instead of taking the tram, we can deny ourselves an evening paper, we can do without our cakes and our picture-shows ... This is the only temper that will bring our Empire triumphantly through'. It might have been argued that, on the contrary, such self-sacrifice on a national scale would merely have increased unemployment in Australia, but no doubt the sacrifice fulfilled the psychological need to become involved personally in the Empire's troubles. Elsewhere, boys gave up their sports to learn drill, and boys and girls dug into their own or their parents' pockets to assist various needy causes.[7]

At North Sydney Girls' High, when the headmistress assembled the school to make a special appeal for contributions to 'alleviate suffering' the

A Christmas gift to the boys at the front from the children of New South Wales, circa 1915

girls immediately raised £20. In September, when the Old Girls' Union held a concert to raise funds, the whole school assisted by making sweets which the senior girls sold at interval; the concert raised £60. Soon after, the girls decided that every pupil was to be levied one penny per week on behalf of the Belgian Fund, organised for the war's first victims: by November they had raised £10. The girls also began to make goods, clothes and bandages, for the Red Cross and the Belgian Fund. This is not an isolated example of the concern of one particularly patriotic school but rather is typical of the sentiments that gripped Australian girls and boys from the beginning of the war. By the time the annual ritual of speech day and break up arrived in November–December 1914, such patriotism was commonplace. At school after school headmasters proudly announced that the pupils had decided to forego their prizes, contenting themselves with a certificate, donating the money thus saved to the patriotic funds.[8]

At Geelong College this student-led sacrifice netted £158 for the funds. Children, girls particularly, came under strong pressure from their peers to demonstrate their patriotism. At Ascham School in Sydney the editor of the *Ascham Charivari* lamented that the November offering to the Red Cross showed a 'falling off' in the numbers of garments completed. 'The money and time we spend on one blouse [of our own] would perhaps clothe entirely a Belgian Baby. Can any of us really think that it is more important that we should have an extra blouse than that a Belgian Baby should have warm clothes?' Thus was patriotism stimulated.[9]

Pupils also fulfilled this need to involve themselves personally by identifying themselves more closely with their school; they believed that the loyalty they gave to the school would stimulate the loyalty they owed to the Empire. The war, then, became an argument for a greater measure of 'school spirit'. The *Sydneian* exhorted scholars at Sydney Grammar to show their patriotism by taking a greater interest in the school: pupils should attend 'its every football, cricket, rowing or shooting match, the meetings of the Debating Society and the entertainments of the Musical and Dramatic Society and, indeed, every indoor and outdoor function of the School life'. Institutions always extract commitments from schoolchildren but the war made this so much more. In the name of loyalty and patriotism, children, and their parents, were expected to reach peaks of devotion that had hitherto seemed unattainable. As the war progressed, schools became increasingly important in stimulating patriotic concerns such as enlistment and 'comforts' work, and also became increasingly political as children were taught how right-thinking citizens behaved in a crisis.[10]

There was little to separate the three strands of the education system in this initial same. Much of this, of course, relied on children's love of adventure and excitement, and their perception of war as a romantic, heroic event which coloured the pages of otherwise dull history books. So the state school children and those at the most exclusive private schools, shared common ideals and enthusiasms; their patriotism knew no class or religious boundaries. And yet subtle differences did emerge which reflected the schools' or 'the parents' influence, directing this spontaneous, childish loyalty. The private Protestant schools gave closer attention to the concept of the Empire, as in the *Bathurstian*'s poem ('Right gladly the offspring of Freedom') than did either the Catholic or the state schools.

A pupil at the Marist Brothers' St Joseph's College in Sydney, Frank Hammond, stressed Australian themes when he argued that the war would promote the 'dawn of nationhood' in Australia. Hammond suggested that the 'well-meaning fools' who had guided Australia's destinies to this point, had retarded her development by excessive reliance on the advice and the markets of the British. Their stupidity was triumphantly demonstrated by the victory of the Australian cruiser *Sydney* over the German *Emden* at Cocos Island: the 'well-meaning fools' had argued against the establishment of Australia's own navy, preferring to rely on British help. Hammond expected that in the commercial field the war would show Australians how important it was to develop their own resources and to encourage their own manufacturing industry. Hammond's article shows that optimism and love of country

Typical of thousands of young girls throughout Australia for whom knitting and other patriotic work became almost a part of the school syllabus

found in other school magazines but it is unusual in its concentration on the development of Australia without much attention to the wider sphere of Empire. While others prophesied that the war would strengthen the ties that bound the Empire together, Hammond believed it would stimulate a greater measure of Australian independence. The tone of the Catholic school magazines differed from the Protestant in the same way that the early war sermons of the Catholic leaders differed from those of their Protestant counterparts. They were loyal and enthusiastic but much less concerned with the Empire than with Australia. Hammond and other Catholic schoolboy writers simply reflected this Catholic spirit.[11]

The subtlety of such differences should not distract us from the overwhelming commitment to the cause which poured from the nation's schools once war was declared. The early efforts to raise money and to make goods and thus to share in the Empire's sacrifice became institutionalised, demonstrating how intense was that patriotism. The amount of money raised by the various branches of the school system over the entire war period is quite staggering and testifies to the enthusiasm of the teachers and the constancy of the pupils and their parents. Many New South Wales government schools raised an average of £100 per pupil during the war years, many more averaged £50 per pupil. These figures are quite astonishing in comparison to wages paid in the New South Wales public service, for example. Assistant schoolmasters received between £200-£300 per year, a junior clerk started at £60 per year and a labourer received £156. The growth of the department's patriotic fund demonstrates the extent of the school network. Established in August 1914, within two months 1,560 schools had sent £200 to the fund; a month later the fund received £500 from 2,890 schools. Clearly, weekly collections had been instituted in many of the schools in the system. In this way the departmental fund raised £24,000 during the war years. Impressive as this result is, it dwindles to insignificance when compared with the £422,470 raised by Victorian government schools.[12]

An explanation of this staggering success must be found, at least partially, in the personality of the director-general of education in Victoria, Frank Tate, who placed enormous importance on imbuing Victorian children with ideas of loyalty and patriotism and who regarded the war as the great opportunity to demonstrate what Empire obligations involved. Given the size of the sum raised, it is not unfair to suggest that patriotic efforts became an important part of the Victorian school syllabus. The department encouraged all manner of activities that would return pupils a profit, as its publication *How We Raised the First Hundred Thousand* shows. The children in country schools:

> gathered bones, fat, bottles, wool from the fences and scrub, iron, kerosene tins; they have snared and skinned rabbits, trapped foxes, caught fish, dug gardens, cleared tracks, caught horses, done odd jobs before their home duties commenced in the morning, given up holidays, handed in all their pocket money, swept schools, cleaned chimneys, caught frogs and leeches, worked by moonlight when school-work and homework filled all the daylight hours.

The children in the city schools were no less patriotic: 'they have sewn and knitted, made paper and leather flowers, fashioned things of wood and wire, grown wonderful beans on pocket-handkerchief allotments, planned concerts and bazaars . . .'.

The Victorian *School Paper* organised and directed all this activity because, as Mr Tate said, the war gave teachers 'a capital opportunity to impress upon children their civic obligations, and to promote a zeal for social service'. The department instituted the Victorian State Schools' Patriotic League, which William Gillies, author of *Stories in British History for Young Australians,* recommended to readers of the *School Paper,* saying 'you must give up something that it hurts to give up, do something that it goes against the grain to do. Only then will you feel that you are taking part in the great adventure'. The war dominated the *School Paper,* indeed it was not until October 1915 that the editors published the first article ('The Value of Bird Life') not related to the war. The March 1915 issue, for example, comprised Sir George Reid's address to the Australian troops, a story entitled 'Under Fire', a poem 'How They Brought the Good News from Ghent to Aix', and articles 'How We are Helping in War Time', 'The Australians in Egypt' and 'The Progress of the War'. Thus stimulated children joined groups such as the War Relief Gardener's League in which pupils worked together to create gardens on school land and to sell the produce, or the Young Workers' Patriotic Guild, which was to 'develop in pupils zeal for social service' and 'to promote habits of industry' as well, of course, as augmenting the war funds. Frank Tate, in recommending the Guild, wrote that 'We want all to join who really love their country and are ready to work for it. This personal service is the true test of patriotism'. In the event Victorian children showed that they were super-patriots.[13]

This extraordinary the mere raising of money; pupils contributed in kind as well. The Victorian department set up a receiving depot in South Melbourne to centralise the distribution of goods, and received, over the war years, 11,691 shirts, 59,981 pairs of socks, 18,426 pairs of gloves or cuffs, 43,604 handy bags or kit bags, 69,742 handkerchiefs and many hundreds (often thousands) of nightshirts, nightingales, cardigans, balaclava caps, scarves and pillowslips. Much of this work appears to have been done by schoolgirls. There seems to have been a clear perception of sex roles even at school: the boys prepared themselves for enlistment while the girls organised themselves into sewing circles and knitting groups. As the *Chronicle* of Sydney Girls' High put it, 'Mothers and wives are giving up their sons and husbands for service to their country – girls can at least give money, time

Boys from the Mudgee District Public School grimace as patriotism forces them to take on traditional girls' work. The *Sydney Mail* said: 'These children are actually doing more towards winning the war than hundreds – aye, thousands, unfortunately – who are living their lives entirely heedless of the clarion call of Duty'

and work'. The *Babbler* showed how dominant war work had become at North Sydney Girls' High. By 1917 each form had established its own sewing circle, which met one afternoon each week where the girls made garments for the French-Australian League, the Babies Kit Society, the 30th Battalion Comforts Fund, and the War Chest. Letters of thanks from soldiers and others which appeared regularly in the *Babbler* no doubt stimulated the girls' zeal as did the semi-regular homilies which stressed how the goods helped soldiers' morale, giving the girls the hope that their patriotic work really was significant.[14]

A similar pattern of war work emerges at school after school. Some of the church schools provided additional motivation for the girls with a religious gloss, as at the Presbyterian Ladies College, Croydon, New South Wales, where girls were encouraged to join the Australasian League of Honour, the object of which was 'to uphold the honour of our nation by furthering the cause of righteousness, purity and temperance; and, by thoughtfulness, prayer and self-denial to serve our King and Country during the most intense crisis'. Regardless of motivation, the result was much the same: girls in sewing groups, girls working back at school after hours, girls sacrificing weekends knitting and sewing for 'lonely soldiers' or homeless Belgians. As the *Ascham Charivari* had it: 'men must fight and women must knit socks'.[15]

The amount of work completed may unintentionally lead to exaggeration. These girls were not automatons, but children with a wide range of interests and activities, for whom war work must have been on many occasions boring, repetitive and uninteresting. There must have been many occasions when the enthusiasm of even the most 'patriotic' girl waned as she pored over drab khaki cotton or wool. The school magazines testify to the necessity of keeping up the girls' ideals. As we have seen, organisers made much of the importance of the work, both for the troops and for the girls themselves, as it moulded their characters and fitted them for their future roles as the wives of the returning heroes. Not everyone, of course, accepted the challenge so there were constant exhortations for new workers and better efforts. At North Sydney the *Babbler*, realising 'that the workers were but few in a School as large as ours' wished 'to apply the principles of Universal Service to our School War Work'. Given the motivational framework and the attention teachers and officials devoted to war work, it is perhaps remarkable that any girl was able to stand out; the schools, the magazines, the patriots, all developed enormous pressures to conform. How consistent with the reactions of the patriots in the wider community is the suggestion that compulsion be applied to the 'slackers' who disregarded war work. At school, as elsewhere, there was little room for dissent.[16]

Such concentration on knitting, sewing and raising money reduced pupils' devotion to more traditional school work, as many scholars themselves testified. At Sydney Girls' High, a correspondent from the second form reported that knitting was '*much* more interesting' than academic work,

Harry Roddam, aged 4, of Pyrmont, Sydney, was an enthusiastic patriot. By March 1915 he had collected nearly 4,000 pennies for the Australian Voluntary Hospital organised by Lady Dudley in England. It was quite common for mothers to dress young children in versions of soldiers', sailors' and nurses' uniforms

which, consequently, suffered. At North Sydney the *Babbler* wondered 'Why is it considered more virtuous to construe Latin than to feed the hungry' as if the girls' academic progress should take second place to their war work. However, at Fort Street Girls' High, traditionally a school with an emphasis on intellectual attainments, a correspondent noted that although sewing and knitting circles prospered, more helpers could be expected at the conclusion of the examinations.[17]

In all the many school magazines and departmental reports examined, only at Rockhampton Girls' Grammar was the contradiction between academic progress and war work openly discussed. The headmistress there, Miss W. G. Jameson, answered the accusation that the school ignored patriotic war work in her annual report for 1916. She announced that she 'utterly disapproved' of war work if it infringed at all on the time normally devoted to studies. The educational value of such work she dismissed as 'infinitesimal'. She would not encourage the girls to spend more time knitting and sewing 'while it still happens occasionally that one-fifth, or even one-fourth, of the upper school has to be detained in the afternoon for lessons unsatisfactorily done'. From other reports, Miss Jameson emerged as a headmistress firmly committed to the ideal of the higher education of women. Doubtless many teachers believed they were teaching the girls useful skills by encouraging them to spend such a disproportionate amount of time and energy on the repetitive tasks of knitting and sewing relatively simple garments and Miss Jameson's ideals conflicted with those of most of her colleagues in the teaching profession and stand quite at odds with the rather immodest boasting of the Victorian Education department, which gloried in the patriotic achievements of its pupils.[18]

The boys, lacking the serviceable skills of their sisters or the motivation to acquire them, concentrated more closely on their school work. They suffered less from an anxiety to make themselves useful because they realised that they would fulfil their obligations by enlisting, should the war still be raging when they reached the age of eligibility. No doubt the boys fell in happily with suggestions that they give to their games a new, 'manly' seriousness to prepare themselves for the 'game' of war but the normal round of school activities was rarely interrupted for the boys – except in exceptional circumstances such as in the great strike of August 1917 in New South Wales. Many of the senior students from Sydney private schools enrolled as 'loyalist workers' for the duration of the strike, with thirty boys from The King's School, for example, working for several weeks in the railway or tramway sheds to keep Sydney moving. At Newington College, Sydney, 'all the boys were eager to do their bit' and indeed they found the experience educational: 'it is now

These boys from Sydney Grammar School seem to be enjoying their stint at the Eveleigh government railway workshops. They had taken the places of some of the 'slackers' on strike in August and September 1917

easy to understand workingmen's feelings and anyone who had before railed at unions, became as good a unionist as the strikers. Only so far, of course, as it is possible for a scab to be anything good'. At Sydney Grammar, too, an average of 150 boys worked for three weeks at the Eveleigh workshops, infused no doubt with sentiments of patriotism and loyalty and unable to see how their patriotism increased the divisions between the classes. How the strikers must have resented the arrival of these schoolboy strike-breakers claiming exclusive hold on the patriotism that the workers had thought they had shown in their earlier sacrifices. But this was an interlude, a minor disruption in the life of the schoolboys. For most of the time although they raised money, conducted 'patriotic sports' or listened to earnest exhortations to patriotism, they found war work much more restricted than did their sisters. They would prepare themselves to fight while the women knitted.[19]

If war was regarded as a test of the spirit of the nation, it was also seen as a test of the patriotism of individual schools, a test to be answered by the numbers of old boys who enlisted in the AIF. Schools led the way for clubs, companies and churches in compiling lists and erecting honour boards commemorating both those who had enlisted and, no doubt, the institution itself which had in some undefined way created the climate in which such generosity could flourish. On the whole, as the state primary schools did not follow up the careers of their ex-pupils, they could not participate in this exercise, but the private schools, which through past-pupils' associations

The King's School cricket team 1909–10. As the *Mirror* said: 'Eight members of this team have given their services to the Empire'

maintained contact, provided accurate figures of enlistment which they published regularly in their journals and magazines. While it would be tedious to give a detailed account of the very high level of enlistment from these schools, the schools were successful in imparting their values and ideals.

The Catholic schools used their record of war service to refute charges of Catholic disloyalty. A Sydney priest, Father Forrest, produced figures in July 1918, which showed the extent of Catholic enlistment. St Joseph's College, Hunter's Hill, led the way with 'over 400 recruits', then came St Ignatius, Riverview, with 274, Marist Brothers', Darlinghurst, 230, Christian Brothers', Waverley, 155, including a Victoria Cross winner who enlisted straight from school. Other figures from the Sydney Catholic schools seem more like estimates: 200 from Christian Brothers', Lewisham, 100 from Holy Cross College, Ryde, and 200 from St Aloysius' College, North Sydney.[20]

The record of The King's School was outstanding, as the headmaster reported in 1918:

> We have already on active service as many Old Boys as the School turns out during a period of twenty years, so that, allowing for those who have passed through the School and for various reasons have been unable thus to serve, The King's School is represented by well nigh all its Old Boys for a quarter of a century past.

Newington College boasted not only of the total number of enlistments, 580, but more that those who had distinguished themselves at the school were most ready to enlist. Of Schofield Scholarship holders since 1905, thirteen out of seventeen had enlisted; of prefects since 1902, seventy-two out of 118; from the 1912 1st XV, thirteen joined the AIF as did ten of the 1914 1st XI. From Caulfield Grammar in Melbourne, the 1914 football team presented to the recruiting sergeant as a group: he enrolled fourteen of whom four were subsequently killed. Like King's, Scotch College, Melbourne, produced figures for the 1904–16 period that could not, surely, have been surpassed. Every captain of the school, every dux, every captain of cricket and football for the period either enlisted or had been rejected. From the ranks of the prefects 165 of the available enlisted, how many were rejected was not known. Never fewer than ten of each 1st XVIII enlisted; the peak years 1909–15 saw almost all of every team in the AIF. The top cricketers showed no less enthusiasm. All in all, 1,207 Scotch College boys served the Empire during the war. These comparative figures are more interesting than lists of total numbers from many schools because they show the size of the pool of enlistees available. It is very difficult indeed to calculate the numbers of old boys from the period 1900–14 without knowing the enrolment at each school for each year. There is no point, for example, in comparing Scotch's 1,207 with Xavier's 410, because we do not know precisely what percentage of eligibles these figures represent. Enough to say that enlistment from the schools seems to have been very high and that the comparative figures confirm this impression.[21]

Schools gloried in such sacrifice believing that it showed their worth to the community. They paraded it before the boys at the school, the parents and the wider community, by causing prayers to be said daily for those on service, by erecting boards in the school's most prominent place, and by printing letters and notes from the old boys at the front in the school magazines and journals. Headmasters spoke of the war at all major school functions, sharing the fascination that clergymen showed for strategy and national spirit, presumably they often drew upon the war to illustrate their addresses at the more private school assemblies and gatherings. At first departing old boys were farewelled elaborately by the school with speeches and presentations, but as their numbers grew this became impractical.

The emphasis on enlistment created an atmosphere that forced current boys to regard their own enlistment as the only possible option when each became eligible. The *Scotsman* reported that each senior boy saw the question as not whether he would go, but when. With most it was merely a matter of age, so that school authorities battled hard 'to force boys to work whose minds have been distracted by thoughts of the great quest'. At Geelong Grammar School three schoolboys enlisted as soon as news of war reached the school; in December 1915 the *Corian* published a picture of eleven boys

When the local member of parliament, J. S. T. McGowen, unveiled this honour board on Empire Day, 24 May 1916, at the Cleveland Street Intermediate High School, it contained the names of 540 ex-pupils who had enlisted. Such commemorations of patriotism served two purposes, to honour the heroes who had gone before and to stimulate others to follow them

leaving school to enlist. The headmaster, F. E. Brown, regretted that they had to go because 'Though strong, some are too young, and want a year or more yet before they are sufficiently set to endure a hard campaign'. Mr Brown called for 'some organized system of military service' to replace 'the haphazard methods which now obtain'. This in 1915. The *Sydneian* reported in 1915 that the enlistment of 'Tug' Mason, a member of that year's crew, had set all the senior boys thinking. Indeed, at Sydney Grammar, the authorities encouraged such thoughts: the senior boys were advised to 'weigh with themselves the great question of enlisting ... we feel confident that one and all ... will do their utmost to help the Empire in its struggle'. In the event, 1,714 old boys of Sydney Grammar enlisted but whether R. E. G. Cunningham should be included as an 'old boy' is questionable. He enlisted at the age of fifteen and saw service for two years seven months, taking part in the evacuation at Gallipoli and serving with the artillery in France. Wounded and badly gassed at Passchendaele, he returned to Australia and in 1918 resumed his life as a scholar at Sydney Grammar to 'make up some of the work he missed'. The *Sydneian* noted that Cunningham gave valuable assistance with the cadets.[22]

With such numbers of recruits from the schools, it followed inevitably that increasingly the school magazines would be filled with obituaries and casualty lists. Even today, so many years afterwards, these magazines make grim reading. Young men photographed in tennis or football outfits one year appear the next in khaki and slouch hats, and often are listed the following year as among the dead or injured. Confronted with sacrifice in this magnitude, schoolmasters tried to make sense of the slaughter in much the same way as had the clergymen. They spoke of the nobility of sacrifice, the righteousness of the Empire's cause and the good the war would produce in Australia. It is horrifying that some of these schoolmasters also appealed to the senior boys to take the places of the 'heroes' killed, as if the ritual of the school and the celebration of the 'school's contribution' to enlistment was not pressure enough.

One of the most affecting deaths reported from the schools was that of J. D. Burns, an ex-pupil of Scotch College, Melbourne. Burns had an outstanding career at Scotch from 1911 to 1914. A prefect, the editor of the *Scotch Collegian*, he won first place in the Shakespeare Society's examination, won a scholarship to Ormond College at Melbourne University, gained first-class honours in history and Latin at the public examinations, rowed in the first crew, and in 1914 became school vice-captain. Burns became famous with his poem 'For England!' which he wrote and published in the *Scotch Collegian* and which captured perfectly the sentiments of many of the pupils, teachers and parents associated with schools like Scotch. It expressed the patriotism that these schools taught and demanded of their pupils. Unlike the rest of the literature poured out by Australian pupils, it was popular in other parts of the Empire and it endured and was used to stimulate recruiting in the early days of World War II. J. T. Laird describes it as the archetypal war poem of these years:

> The bugles of England were blowing o'er the sea,
> As they had called a thousand years, calling now to me;
> They woke me from dreaming in the dawning of the day,
> The bugles of England – and how could I stay?
>
> The banners of England, unfurled across the sea,
> Floating out upon the wind, were beckoning to me:
> Storm-rent and battle-torn, smoke-stained and grey,
> The banners of England – and how could I stay?
>
> O, England, I heard the cry of those that died for thee,
> Sounding like an organ voice across the winter sea:
> They lived and died for England and gladly went their way,
> England, O, England – how could *I* stay?

Burns went, reaching Gallipoli in August 1915; after three weeks in the trenches he was killed. Doubtless his poem and his life inspired many similar Australian boys to follow his example.[23]

The patriotism encouraged in schools such as Scotch affected the masters as well as the pupils and indeed, from the outset, there was a stream of masters seeking to enlist. One of the most controversial of such recruits was the Rev. P. Stacy Waddy, headmaster of the King's School, who sought leave of absence to join the AIF as a chaplain. Waddy was an outstanding headmaster, and as a young man looked set to serve King's for many years yet. The school council refused his application for leave, believing that his task was to remain behind to guide the school through difficult times. Waddy resigned, obeying, he said, 'the voice of conscience' that told him that love of country surpassed his love for the school. His resignation generated much discussion and such bitterness that when the replacement headmaster died after only a short time in office, the council refused to consider Waddy's application for his old job. He never worked again in Australia, serving his church in Jerusalem and England. The council was at least correct in seeing the war years as a time of trial for King's: so many of the teachers resigned to join the AIF that in March 1916 the school was compelled to appoint the first woman ever to the teaching staff.[24]

Other schools were also embarrassed by the shortage of teachers, none more so than the state primary schools. The education departments boasted of the loyalty of the teaching service so quick to respond to the call of war, but enlistment created problems. In 1915 in New South Wales the department adopted the expedient of 'inviting applications for temporary employment from qualified persons. Applicants were not subject to any entrance examination, but careful enquiry was made into their qualifications'. Such temporary teachers must have threatened standards in the schools but the enlistment figures indicate that the department had no alternative: 755 New South Wales Education department teachers out of a total male teaching service of 3,497 in 1914, enlisted for service, of whom 116 were killed in action. The Victorian teachers, uncannily, matched this figure almost exactly. Of the 1,500 or so men in the teaching service between 18 and 45, 752 enlisted for service, of whom 146 were killed. Undoubtedly, too, the Victorian schools suffered as a result of these enlistments; nevertheless the department boasted of the 'intelligent patriotism of our staff' and encouraged enlistment. Because of the deaths and casualties among teachers, and the altered ambitions of those who returned, children through the 1920s remembered their teachers as elderly: women and older men came to the fore in the teaching profession as never before.[25]

All this activity on the part of pupils and teachers demonstrated how the war dominated Australian schools, shaping the ideals and values of the children and to some extent, through them, of their parents. The Victorian Education department saw the 'world tragedy ... [as] the teacher's opportunity' because it gave the teacher a noble cause with which to stimulate and motivate his children and a vital role within the community as organiser and fund-raiser. The school became an important centre of patriotic endeavour. During the war new rituals designed to reinforce patriotism and love of Empire emerged such as in Victoria, where from late 1917 onwards children in government schools were required to salute daily 'either the Union Jack or the Australian

The Victorian State School Children's Physical Training Display, Melbourne Cricket Ground, December 1916

flag, whichever may be available'. Many of the private schools also adopted this practice, although at Geelong College the salute was taken only each Monday. In New South Wales the responsible minister directed that at the close of each day's work the national anthem was to be sung by all pupils. This would, he believed, impress upon the children the magnitude of the Empire's struggle and would help 'in inculcating a healthy national patriotic spirit'. Significantly, both these directives came as the polarisation within the community increased, as if ministers saw the schools as a part of the government's machinery of propaganda. Everyone was to be involved. We have seen how quick were the schools to erect honour boards. How telling then that the Rockhampton Girls' Grammar erected a board listing the enlistments amongst the boys who had once attended the kindergarten class, or that the North Sydney Girls' High and many others erected boards listing the names of the girls' fathers and brothers who enlisted.[26]

Given the intensity of this commitment and the central place the school assumed in the lives of pupils and community, it is hardly surprising that the schools abandoned their political neutrality on questions that seemed to have patriotic implications. As in the churches, so in the schools, patriotism overrode all other considerations and removed the 'politics' from the discussion of public questions, or so the patriots believed. Thus many headmasters and the schoolboy editors of magazines supported the introduction of conscription well before it became a matter of political debate. Speakers at the Geelong College annual prize-giving in December 1915 called for conscription as the only way of reinforcing adequately the Australian soldiers at Gallipoli. Without conscription, they warned, Australians would soon fall to the 'lash of Prussian taskmasters'. In August 1915 the captain of Scotch College, Melbourne, wrote that the school would 'look forward to the day when the Government shall proclaim conscription' which, in his proposal, would be sweeping:

> Those who are necessary for maintaining the country's business will be sent to the office; those who understand harvesting will be sent to the grainfields; the mechanic will go to the arsenal, the miner to the coalfields; while those who have no particular ties will be trained as soldiers.

These young patriots and their teachers saw the defeat of the referenda as an indication of the very poor health of Australian democracy. At Scotch the 'No' victory was ascribed to 'motives of self-interest, of religious and social hatred, of class passion, and in some cases of mistaken idealism'. At Newington the editor expressed his disgust saying that Australia had never sunk lower: he saw the formation of the national government as a 'clearer dawn'.[27]

The Catholic schools dissented from these 'patriotic' sentiments; indeed, particularly after the Irish uprising of Easter 1916, these schools had become quite critical of the Empire. The St Joseph's College Literary and Debating Society, for example, discussed during 1916 whether the British had erred in undertaking the Dardanelles campaign, whether the Irish should be conscripted, whether Labor had done its duty in the war, and whether enemy subjects should be interned. St Joseph's, one of the two Catholic members of the Sydney Great Public Schools' Association, was at the top of the Catholic educational tree and drew its boys from the homes of the affluent middle class. Nevertheless, the teachers, aware of their Catholic loyalties, encouraged an open, questioning spirit that was not found in the Protestant private schools or in the government high schools. The Catholic opposition to conscription is reflected in the schools as the boys no doubt accepted most of the opinions of their parents and church leaders. The senior debating society at the Christian Brothers' College, Victoria Parade, Melbourne, formally rejected conscription after an earnest debate only days before the referendum. Headmasters elsewhere would surely not even have allowed the matter to be debated.[28]

The sectarian hatreds aroused by these controversies carried over into the sports fields of the private schools, and doubtless on to the trams and into the streets, wherever schoolboys met. Describing a football match played in August 1916, the *Scotch Collegian* complained that Xavier, the leading Melbourne Catholic school, was 'at times rather vigorous' and congratulated their side on going for the ball 'instead of the man, even in rather trying circumstances'. Xavier won the football premiership in 1917 from Scotch, but the *Argus,* in reporting the match, managed to hint that perhaps the competition was unequal. Xavier 'were stronger, heavier and faster than their opponents, and, in addition, were the more seasoned, only five of the Scotch team having played last year'. Xavier boys, this implied, were perhaps shirking their duties elsewhere. The public school headmasters soon after abandoned competitive sport between the schools because of the rivalry that had grown up amongst the spectators. The *Argus* noted that 'parties of boys had shouted at each other after matches', but, coyly, no Melbourne paper reported what was said. Doubtless sectarian animosities were at least mentioned in these slanging matches.[29]

Despite these divisions, the private schools stood together in distinguishing themselves from the government schools. They assumed that their pupils shared common ideals and a common spirit, even if the Catholics seemed to have an insecure grasp of it. *Pegasus,* from Geelong College, announced that the Greater Public School boys at the front represented 'the very life essence of Australia', that they were 'the very cream of the country'. There had even been talk, in the early days, of forming a GPS battalion. In the letters old boys sent back to their schools, they insisted that the *esprit de corps* of the 'old school', or of the GPS in general, survived in the AIF, and that their ideals set them apart, slightly, from their comrades. Stacy Waddy, in particular, the ex-headmaster of King's, wrote to the college magazine at length about the GPS boys he came across in the AIF. 'What a glorious little world the GPS constitute', he wrote, 'robust and live and full of real comradeship'. The soldiers recalled some, at least, of the high points of the school calendar: two ex-Geelong Collegians cabled from Cairo wishing the school good luck at the annual inter-school boat race. On the other hand, the boys from the government schools gave no evidence of inter-school or even intra-school camaraderie. They did not see themselves as the representatives of a particular class as did the GPS boys, for whom class loyalty was an important element of their schooling.[30]

War tested all branches of the Australian school system. It tested the doctrine that had been propagated for a generation, the doctrine, as the Victorian Education department explained it, that 'education is the development and strengthening of the powers of mind, body and soul, to the end that they may be used in forms of service'. War demonstrated how well the message of service and sacrifice had been implanted in the minds of pupils and ex-pupils. Girls and boys contributed in a bewildering variety of ways to the nation's cause, and cheered on their predecessors as they fought with the AIF in Gallipoli and France. The schools had taught patriotism and devotion to duty and Australia reaped what they had sown. There is much that is magnificent and stirring in the response of these young Australians, girls and boys, and there is much that is sad, the sacrifice of so many promising young lives. It is sad, too, that their romantic view of war as the great adventure was shared by so many adult Australians, at least for the first few years. Their innocence and excitement might have warned the community that war was not merely 'the greatest game of them all' but adults too had to learn the horror of war. How moving to hear the assembled voices of the Armidale School singing with gusto the special war verse added to the school song:

> While we are with joyous quip and jest
> Our boys are fighting the foe;
> Be it Hun or Turk they will never shirk
> When the starter bids them go.
> In our thoughts and prayers they hold first place,
> What we want is British Rule
> Our freedom's prize for which they race,
> Old Boys of the Armidale School.[31]

CHAPTER FOUR

'TO WAIT AND TO WEEP': AUSTRALIAN WOMEN AT WAR

Enthusiasm for war may have been a necessary emotion for Australia's clergymen and a natural one for her schoolchildren; the response of Australian women was less inevitable. Some believed that women, as the source of life, would incline more to pacifism, others expected that the inherent tendencies of women directed them to the 'caring' areas of tending to the injured and providing comforts for the men. In Australia, particularly, there was no urgent task that awaited the women, indeed, given the prevailing opinions about the place of women in society it was not expected that any major task would demand their attention.

The Australian ideal placed little value on women as workers; those who worked did so beyond the public gaze, largely taking jobs scorned by men as 'women's work'. The majority of women in factory employment were found in a few specific trades, the clothing industry, the textile industry, the manufacture of food and drink. Other women worked as shop assistants, domestic servants, nurses and teachers. Their wages were roughly half those of male employees performing similar work. Few women worked after marriage at least up until the 1930s. The historian of women and work in Australia found that 'The high wages paid to men, the emphasis on the family in the wage structure and on children in the national value system, the suburban sprawl and the lack of child-care facilities all combined to keep married women with children at home'. Though women had voted at state and federal elections for the past decade or so the concession had been bestowed patronisingly, preventing that radicalisation that the suffrage movement brought to many English women. Women took little active part in the political process. The formation of the AIF caused no immediate disruption to Australian economic life so that women were not suddenly whisked from home to work-place as happened in Britain. While the level of female paid employment grew during the war, the growth was gradual occurring only in areas long held to be appropriate for females. There was no large-scale munitions industry in Australia to give Australian women

A soldier farewells his wife and daughter at the departure of the first troops for Rabaul, August 1914

the experience of factory work and no wholesale shortage of labour to force them into men's jobs.[1]

Therefore, if Australian women were to contribute to the war effort at all, they had to create their own opportunities. The extent to which they did so becomes a measure of their patriotism and enthusiasm for the war. Australian women worked heroically for a cause in which many of them passionately believed. They set up new organisations, managed them effectively, and in the process learned new and valuable skills. But in the long run it did them little good. They were not able to challenge the sex roles that dominated the thinking of Australian males, they won no more respect and no higher place in Australian society. Indeed, the stereotyped thinking which Anne Summers and others have classified as 'damned whores or God's police' accurately summarises much of the thinking about women in Australia during the war. We shall see how meanly men wrote and spoke of women's 'natural tendencies' despite the evidence of concern and commitment that many of the women provided.

During the war Australian women initiated what might be described with some exaggeration as a completely new sector of the economy, the provision of 'comforts' for the Australian troops and victims of the war. All such efforts depended on the voluntary labour of women, but since unpaid labour is rarely accorded any value in Australian society, much of this work went unnoticed. The first of the organisations, in time and in size, was the Red Cross, which Lady Helen Munro-Ferguson, the wife of the governor-general, initiated two days after the outbreak of war. From the start the Australian 'establishment' dominated the Red Cross and set the patterns for many other women's groups. The inaugural meeting agreed that the governor-general's wife, Australia's 'first lady', should be ex-officio president of the Red Cross and that the wives of the state governors should preside over each state division's activities. To emphasise their particular brand of patriotism the founders declared that the organisation should be known as 'The Australian Branch of the British Red Cross Society'. From the outset, then, the Red Cross embraced the twin ideals of Australian patriotism: it depended on the social elite for respectability and it proclaimed its British inspiration and parenthood. It is also revealing that a body which was to depend almost entirely on the unpaid labour of women should insist on having men in all the 'difficult' positions on the executive. Thus the Hon. Edward Miller served as treasurer and Dr J. W. Barrett as secretary. Those women who were included on the executive owed more perhaps to their husbands' positions in politics or business than to their own organisational

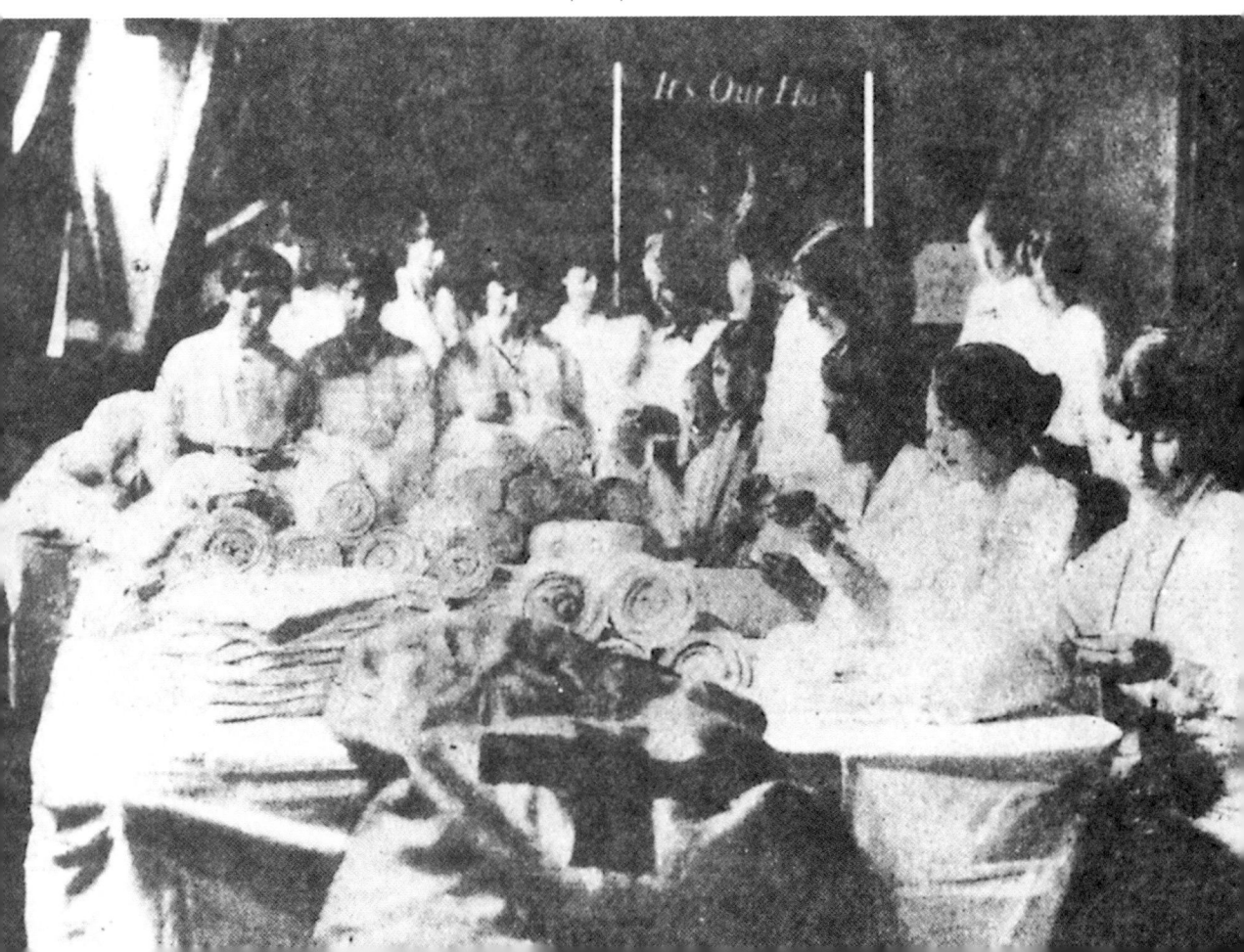

As the *Sydney Mail* had it: 'This picture is typical of what the women and girls are doing in every part of Australia'. These women were members of the Red Cross branch in Ashfield, a middle-class Sydney suburb

or entrepreneurial skills. Such male dominance of predominantly female organisations became the norm during the war years.[2]

Vice-regal patronage no doubt accounted for some of the phenomenal growth the Red Cross experienced during the early months of war, but a widespread desire to help shared by many Australian women was crucial too. Lady Helen called on the mayors of every municipality and shire in Australia to initiate a local branch of the Red Cross and few failed to act on her suggestion. Typically, the mayor published her letter in the local paper, convened a meeting at the town hall of all patriotic, loyal women in the district, gave the embryo society the use of rooms there, and then retired, handing over the day-to-day running of the branch to his wife.

In this way, by November 1914 in New South Wales for example, there were eighty-eight city-suburban branches and 249 country branches of the Red Cross where none had existed before. The Red Cross attracted widespread community acceptance from its inception. Thus the first New South Wales report indicates a wide range of supporters: the Australian Jockey Club donated £1,000, the Avon Lake Shearing Shed £3 1s 6d, the Enmore Loyal Daughters' Society 3s and the Waverley Methodist Literary and Debating Society £3 12s 3d. In such ways the New South Wales branch had received £35,310 5s 7d in its first four months. The Red Cross continued to grow. By August 1915 there were 337 branches in New South Wales and 462 in Victoria, of which fifty-four were in Melbourne. Membership of these branches is hard to assess. The first meeting invariably attracted an overflow attendance which was not surprising given the heightened emotions of Australians during the early days of war. But enthusiasm no doubt waned. Country branches tended to attract higher membership than suburban branches, indicating perhaps a greater drawing area, but their work output tended to be lower than city branches probably because fewer members were able to travel to the weekly working bees. The average membership at a productive New South Wales country branch was 130, while Sydney suburban branches averaged about fifty-five members. By the end of 1915 there were 11,531 members of the Red Cross in New South Wales.[3]

Successful in an organisational sense from the beginning, there was nevertheless a certain vagueness about what work the Red Cross could contribute. As the compiler of the Tasmanian story of war work put it: 'With the vague notion that Red Cross work had to do with nursing the wounded, special ambulance classes were started where women of all ages learned bandaging and other mysteries. Then the word was given that shirts, pyjamas and woollen socks were needed ...' Once pointed in the right direction the women of the Red Cross worked with considerable energy and enthusiasm. They made enormous numbers of garments for the soldiers, including knitted socks, vests, mittens and mufflers and for soldiers in hospitals, pyjamas, shirts, linen and specially designed medical aids. Each branch sent its weekly or monthly contribution to State headquarters, located at

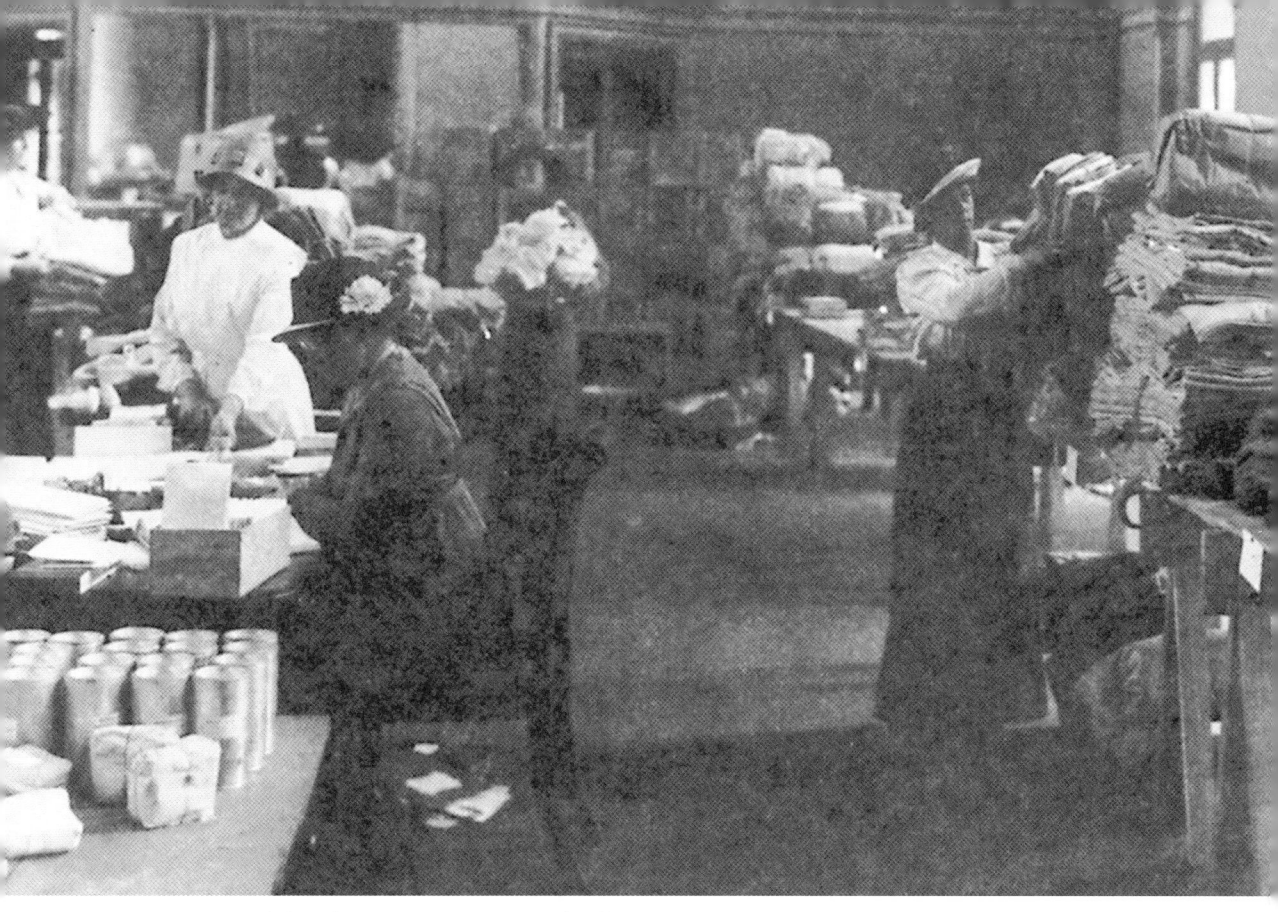

So enthusiastic did Lady Munro-Ferguson, wife of the governor-general, become, that many rooms in the federal government house, Melbourne, were taken over for storage of Red Cross goods. Given the restrictions on social activity it is unlikely that this room, the ballroom, would have been needed anyway

Government House, where articles were checked, packed and sent on to Britain or the front. Such was the scope of the Victorian undertaking that Red Cross stores threatened to engulf the federal Government House in St Kilda Road, the governor-general surrendering his ballroom, his dining room and, on occasions, the state drawing room. The various branches collected detailed statistics of the many aspects of their work which showed how devoted members were. They completed many hundreds of thousands of articles for the troops and for the injured, all of this at very little cost, as members, or the branches, supplied the raw materials for all goods made. Headquarters insisted on quality control demanding that 'all articles must be carefully cut, made and finished. Rough seams irritate the skin and bad finishing soon gives way and wastes material'. No doubt there were many stories of unflagging devotion to the cause of knitting, but few, if any, could have surpassed Ruby Wallace, a 13-year-old pupil of Edinglassie Primary School near Muswellbrook, New South Wales, who completed 100 pairs of socks, eighty pairs of bootees, twenty bonnets, three balaclava caps, four vests and thirty pairs of mittens, all in the space of a year![4]

Given the commitment demanded in terms of time and money, it is clear that not all women could have participated in the work of the Red Cross regardless of their loyalty or patriotism. It is hardly surprising that voluntary workers were more freely available in the middle-class suburbs than in the working-class ones, indeed, given the establishment image of the Red Cross, many working-class women, even if available, might have hesitated to join. Of the fifty-four Melbourne branches established by 1915, only fourteen were located in identifiably working-class areas and three of these were based on church groups. In Sydney, the middle-class dominance of the Red Cross branches is clearer still. Of the fifty-two suburban branches, only three were located in working-class suburbs at Annandale, Balmain and Erskineville and the membership of these branches, thirty-six, forty-two and twelve is below the suburban average. The Erskineville branch, in particular, displayed a rather casual approach to work, completing only twenty articles of clothing during the war years. Missing from the Sydney list of Red Cross branches are suburbs such as Auburn, Belmore, Campsie, Glebe, Granville, Homebush, Redfern, Surry Hills, suburbs all described by the 1917 *A.B.C. Guide to Sydney Suburbs* as 'industrial areas' 'inhabited mostly by the workers'.[5]

Of course, it would be ridiculous to draw conclusions about the loyalty or patriotism of the 'workers' from this evidence. Working-class women's concern with feeding and clothing their families left little time for other activities. Women whose husbands earned larger incomes and who had perhaps the advantage of a full-time or part-time domestic servant, were not tied as closely to the home. They were much more available for patriotic work. Unfortunately, however, as the nation divided over questions of loyalty from 1916 onwards, this evidence was called upon to prove the disloyalty or apathy of the working-class. Women who failed to contribute were as readily branded as 'slackers' as were the eligibles who failed to enlist. Undoubtedly this was part of the reason for collecting and publishing the statistics of branch activity: anyone reading such lists would be struck by the absence of working-class contributions. At the same time it might be appropriate to ask whether all of the record 10,100 articles of clothing despatched by the sixty-five members of the Vaucluse branch were made by the ladies themselves. Is it possible that some donated the work of their servants?[6]

The Red Cross society emerges as an establishment-initiated, middle-class organisation of loyal women devoted to the task of providing for the men of the AIF. As 'loyalists' it is only to be expected that the members should have followed closely the recruiting campaigns and the political turmoil of 1916–18. It is surprising, however, that the various branches of the Red Cross involved themselves officially in these controversies, showing again that patriotism, in the eyes of the middle-class patriots, overrode considerations such as the political neutrality usually expected of service groups.

The *Red Cross Record,* the official publication of the South Australian branch, argued unambiguously in favour of conscription in 1916 and 1917, stating that Australia's honour required a 'Yes' vote. The *Downs Red Cross Herald,* the monthly publication of the Darling Downs division, insisted

Prominent Workers in the Red Cross Movement.

MRS. RICHARDS (The Lady Mayoress.) *Photo: Falk Studios.*	MRS. GORDON WESCHE. *Photo: Falk Studios.*	MRS. C. G. WADE *Photo: Falk Studios.*
MRS. R. R. S. MacKINNON. *Photo: Judith Fletcher.*	MISS MARJORIE MORT. *Photo: Swiss Studios.*	MRS. JAMES ASHTON. *Photo: Kerry and Co.*
MRS. D. R. HALL. *Photo: Falk Studios.*	MRS. J. SPENCER BRUNTON. *Photo: Falk Studios.*	MRS. THOMAS HUGHES.

The leading lights in the Sydney Red Cross

that 'the voluntary system ... has had its day' and suggested that the only efficient answer Australia could give to conscription was a resounding 'Yes'. Alongside reports of war work, such as that from Oakey, Queensland, of a monthly total of six flannel shirts, thirteen tussore shirts, eight mercerised shirts, was an editorial expressing the hope 'that at the coming Federal elections the people will rally round the "Win-the-War" banner, and uphold it successfully until peace is made'. Apparently patriotism subsumed politics. As political controversy became more frenetic, the *Downs Red Cross Herald* became more partisan. The editor described the general strike of August 1917 as a 'rebellion' and delivered an unequivocal message during the second conscription campaign: 'The 20th instant will either be the birthday of the Australian Nation or it will be the day on which the free people of Australia voted away their freedom ... because they put love of self and hatred of England before their honor, their promise and their country'. It is little wonder that working-class women, whose patriotism led to different political responses, found little solace in the 'Australian Branch of the British Red Cross'.[7]

Important as the Red Cross became, it was only one manifestation of women's determination to participate, if only vicariously, in the war effort. As newspapers stimulated fervour with heart-rending propaganda about the

A street fair in Melbourne which raised money for the Red Cross. Such fairs were quite frequent and involved the organisers and helpers in considerable labour

sufferings of the victims of the callous Germans, women took to the streets to sell buttons and conduct fairs, to raise money in a variety of ways for the homeless. The French, Belgians, Poles, Serbs, Montenegrins, Syrians, Russians and Armenians benefited from this generosity. Parliamentarians and trades unionists complained about the multiplicity of the funds, calling for a centralised government agency to control the network of charity. But the range of funds gave everyone a chance to participate and even the outwardly idiosyncratic such as the Plum Pudding Fund of Northern Tasmania or the Tanned Sheepskin Clothing Fund doubtless did some good. Despite or because of this proliferation, the Australian people gave a total of £13,491,594 to the various funds which were largely initiated, organised and staffed by women.[8]

The appeals for war victims were often early emotional responses to the novel situation of war, made before Australia's own contribution of men came to be appreciated. Then the focus changed to collecting money and goods on behalf of the Australians serving abroad. In theory there was little need for such efforts as the members of the AIF were well paid and their accommodation and personal necessities were, of course, provided by the army. It was apparent, however, that the men missed many of the so-called luxuries to which they had grown accustomed in peace-time and that, in providing them, women found their greatest area of identification with the AIF. There simply was no other way women could participate in the institution that dominated Australian life: they could not become soldiers themselves. Thus organisations sprang up to provide tobacco, food items to break the monotony of army fare, such as cakes, puddings, condensed milk, biscuits and the like, newspapers and other remembrances of home. No other body of troops was so well cared for, but then none other was so far from home. From small beginnings these funds grew in size, amalgamating to form the Australian Comforts Fund (ACF) in 1916, which undertook to provide 'comforts' for all Australians abroad. It rivalled the Red Cross in the scope of its operations and the opportunities it gave to women to work and organise and to contribute in some tangible way to the war effort.

The *War Chest Review*, the official publication of the New South Wales branch of the ACF, gives a detailed picture of its operations, emphasising how large the task was and how devoted its members were. To overcome the problem of 'trench foot', a painful condition contracted by men standing for many days in wet and muddy trenches, the ACF organised the sock industry to give every man the opportunity of frequent changes into dry socks. The ACF provided the wool which it sent to the branches and then received back knitted and washed socks, which were shipped to the front at intervals of two to three weeks, when about 10,000 pairs had been accumulated. The New South Wales branch despatched 600,000 pairs of socks during the war years and the grand Australian total, culled from the various state reports, reaches a staggering 1,354,328 pairs! If it takes about ten hours to knit a pair

A mountain of socks

of socks, then the enthusiasm of the ACF is impressive – something over ten million woman hours. To this, of course, must be added the hundreds of thousands of shirts, pyjamas, vests and so on. Then to this we must add the great quantity of goods made by the Red Cross workers – evidence of a very great level of commitment and enthusiasm indeed.

Knitting and sewing are personal activities usually associated with love and concern. Undoubtedly many of the knitters in wartime Australia may have been similarly moved. Denied the opportunity to contribute directly to the nation's war work, women discovered that in knitting for 'one of the boys' they found a closer identification with his life and thus with the nation's sacrifice. Many thousands of them slipped notes and messages of encouragement into the socks they knitted, reminding the men of their high esteem amongst the women of Australia.

Beyond the symbolic importance of all this work there is the fact that much of it developed new skills in the voluntary workers. Quite obviously the clerical labour involved in running an organisation the size of the ACF was enormous, almost all of it conducted by unpaid women. The ACF's papers give an insight of the amount of paperwork involved. Take, for example, the difficulty in locating one of four cases sent by the Sock Society of Maryborough, Queensland. An error of loading at Southampton sent the case to Le Havre although it was intended for the base camp. The ACF eventually found the case but when it was discovered that it contained 152 cakes of soap it was sent on to the men at the front. Such oversight involved checking, packing, receiving, despatching and invoicing. The industry also, of course, cost a great deal of money – for raw materials and principally to meet shipping costs and the women became adept at raising money. Apart from house-to-house collections, 'doorknocks', which in North Sydney, for example, raised an average of £75 per month, there were garden fetes, button days, street stalls and even a flower shop and a cake shop in Sydney which sold donated goods for a considerable profit. The cake shop, so the ACF boasted, was one of the more inventive war work ideas in a situation in which just about everything else had been tried. The workers there collected about 1,700 dozen eggs during the life of the shop, which opened 17 May 1918; by the end of the war the shop had contributed £450 to ACF funds. The flower shop, begun in December 1916, collected flowers from as far afield as Michelago and Yass and raised £2,785. The ACF sent surplus flowers regularly to Randwick Hospital, Sydney Hospital and, revealingly, to 'the slums'.[9]

The obsession with figures demonstrated by the Red Cross also gripped the ACF, which kept detailed statistics of every phase of its activities,

Loading 8,473 cases from the Australian Comforts Fund

reporting, for example, that the Fund distributed twelve million cups of coffee free to the men in the front line. The ACF believed with some justification that warm feet shod in ACF socks and hot drinks from ACF coffee stalls contributed to reducing shell-shock and reinvigorating tired men or saving the lives of injured men. Behind the statistics lay, they believed, a vital aspect of war work. The final balance sheet in 1919 showed that the New South Wales branch collected £537,147 and that salaries during the war years amounted to only £2,382. The Victorian branch shipped goods valued at £328,444 to the men in England and France, including 194,704 Christmas Boxes and Billies which contained tobacco or cigarettes, handkerchiefs, writing wallets, chewing gum, pate, sausages and so on. The Victorian report modestly summarised its efforts:

> When one considers the vast amount of work involved to turn [the money raised] into various and varied comforts, one conjures up a vision of the busy fingers that knitted and stitched, the brains that planned and purchased food, smokes etc. and the clever hands and brains who were responsible for the packing, the shipping and the transport, one feels that the result is a creditable chapter.[10]

The various divisions of the Australian Comforts Fund were as firmly established in middle-class Australia as was the Red Cross, for much the same reasons, that is, that middle-class women had a greater amount of time available and the social status of the work appealed to them. The list of Sydney branches gives twenty-five suburban locations of which only two, Annandale and Auburn, were identifiably working-class. The North Sydney branch showed how thoroughly the social elite dominated. The Hon. Dugald Thomson presided, with Mrs Cecil Hordern as honorary secretary. In ten months the branch raised £1,590 including £300 from Lady Hay. A garden fete held at 'Tregoyd' the home of Lady Cullen in Mosman, made a profit of £1,485 12s 1d after expenses of £14 16s 11d had been deducted. Such a scale and scope exceeded the aspirations of the poorer sections of the community. Similarly in Melbourne, where the ACF began its life as 'The Lady Mayoress's Patriotic League'. All thirty-five suburban branches were located in the middle-class suburbs with the biggest branches established in suburbs such as Surrey Hills, Mont Albert, Kew and Fairfield. One branch even took its name from the stately home, 'Southesk', in Cotham Road, Kew, in which it met; at least one other branch met in a private home, Mrs George Kelly's 'Montalto' in Orrong Road, Toorak. Thus, while this kind of patriotic work was in no sense confined to the wealthier classes, it did find many of its supporters amongst these people who then puzzled over the 'apathy' or 'indifference' of the residents of the poorer areas.[11]

In their Red Cross or ACF work or in the work they did for hundreds of other organisations, these women demonstrated skills and abilities that

Working for the Australian Comforts Fund, Melbourne Town Hall. Groups such as this assembled at town and shire halls throughout Australia, but perhaps working in the centre of the city made it more likely that a photographer would drop in

few before the war had believed they possessed. Just as women in Britain or in Canada discovered that they could hold down men's jobs in factory, office and elsewhere and even discovered that there was a place for women in the army, so Australian women, in their unpaid work, learned that they could organise and manage. At first men were elected or appointed to the key positions on the committees of the various funds as if to indicate that women were incapable of undertaking the complex tasks of administration. The war work performed by women changed these beliefs, giving women fresh confidence in their abilities. Women were delighted to discover the new opportunities, delighted to be able to demonstrate that they, too, had been tested and not found wanting.

The editor of the ladies' page of the *Soldier* described an exhibition of women's voluntary war work and asked: 'Is all this energy and skill only to last while the world-war is being waged; or will women still be workers, and efficient and expert workers for all time?' By 1917 her page 'For Mothers, Wives and Sweethearts' printed a poem, 'The Awakening of Woman', as its constant banner: women, the poem suggested:

see the dawn is breaking, and they quiver with unrest,
As they see the work that's waiting to be done.
And the world shall quickly render to woman what is hers
As she typifies the race that is to be.

By October 1917 such radicalism seemed inappropriate and the banner became:

A mother's heart is always with her children
The wife is the key of the house
The sweetheart's counsel is certainly unselfish.

Gone, at least from the *Soldier,* was the suggestion that the experience and skill acquired by women through their war work might find an outlet after the war. But some remained hopeful as the editor of the South Australian *Red Cross Record* showed in 1918:

The end of the war is in sight. We women, as we knit and sew, while keeping all our energies still directed to war work, yet have time to let our minds go forward into the future. Even the least thoughtful of us cannot fail to see that feminine influence is going to be the greatest power in Australia after the war. In Victoria alone there are 42,000 more women than men. So our women must be taught much about the political situation, and also they have to learn a great deal of what is going on in the industrial world of their own country ... It will rest with the feminine vote what individuals will form the new governing body ... the petticoat power that is going to influence it must be devoted to "waking up" Australia ... Another good effect of this war has been the "waking up" of the womanhood of Australia; and finely the majority have risen to the trumpet call of patriotism.[12]

It would need another book to show how ill-founded was this optimism. Most of the funds, particularly the ACF, dissolved themselves speedily after the Armistice and much of the organisational skills were dissipated. The Red Cross endured, dropping its British title in 1928, but its activities, at the voluntary level, were much reduced. Women no doubt looked with pride on their contribution to the welfare and morale of the troops and gained satisfaction, knowing what they had achieved. But the mass of Australian women did not benefit from these advances as did women in Britain. Perhaps because the work was unpaid the achievement was not taken seriously.

Some women yearned to take a greater part in the 'real thing' as Defence department files, bulging with offers of service, testify. The first woman to request employment applied on 9 September 1914 with her husband. From that time onwards there was a stream of women willing to help the AIF but it should be noted that they restricted their requests almost entirely to 'women's work' such as nursing, cooking, sewing, washing and mending. Only occasionally did women depart from this pattern; these few offered to work as drivers, scouts or interpreters. These applications peaked in mid-1915 at the time of the first great recruiting campaigns which indicates that women were subject to similar pressures as the men to whom the campaigns were directed. None of the applicants was successful as the Defence department adopted a policy against the employment of females in any military capacity. Nurses were the exception here, of course. They did go overseas with the AIF, but there were few positions available and so competition for them was fierce.

From the outset the nurses saw their opportunity as Nurse Kirkcaldie recounted: 'The decision to organise an Australian army made it fairly certain that nurses would be required, and so the lucky nurses with official friends besieged them with anxious questions'. Kirkcaldie, lacking 'official friends', found it impossible to secure a berth with the Australians so she determined to travel to Britain to volunteer there: 'the thought of remaining inactive in Australia was simply intolerable'. Many, however, missed out. By 1917 only 1,757 nurses had been accepted to serve with the AIF, leaving many, doubtless, disappointed and frustrated and yet this was the only form of service possible at the official level.[13]

Melbourne 'volunteers' marching on Red Cross Day. As with so many groups of women they received no official blessing and could not persuade the authorities to give them 'real' work to do. Their persistence, and precision here, is a tribute to their enthusiasm

Not all women accepted these conditions complacently. Eleanor Jacob of Stanmore, New South Wales, formed a women's battalion at the time of the defeat of the first conscription referendum, on the principle that, 'If the Men Won't, I Will'. She appealed to single women between the ages of 21 to 30 to join her in the 'Australian Women's Service Corps' which would undertake any tasks the army might allot them, in Australia, Britain or France, to enable the soldiers in those jobs to take their place in the firing line. To demonstrate how useful the Corps might be, a member advised the public to stand outside Victoria Barracks in Sydney between 8.30 and 9 on any morning of the week and count the number of young men of military age arriving to work as clerks, most in uniform, many 'with chests thrown out as if they are the ones who are saving their country'. Freeing these men to fight would stimulate recruiting, the Corps believed, because many eligibles refused to believe 'there is so urgent a call for men when they see younger, stronger, better-fitted men being held back by the Defence Department on work which old men or women can do'.[14]

Miss Jacob's idea attracted many women, doubtless impressed by Hughes's conscription argument about the desperate need for men and more men. Within a month of its formation, 700 Sydney women had enrolled in the Corps; they spent their leisure time in a variety of activities. There were physical culture classes twice a week, a home nursing class, stretcher drill conducted by members of the St John's Ambulance Brigade, and a cooking class led by a Frenchwoman, Madame Sherwood of Double Bay. Meanwhile Miss Jacob conducted a lengthy correspondence with the Defence department, and various politicians. She offered her members for service in field kitchens, hospitals, laundries, offices or as drivers. The Defence department's first reply set out the position from which it never budged, despite repeated appeals from the Corps: 'I am directed to convey the thanks of this Department for your patriotic offer, which is highly appreciated, but to state that there are no positions wherein the services of your Corps could be at present utilised'.[15]

The Corps continued to meet, to drill, to prepare, in the hope of a change of attitude on the part of the authorities and, indeed, undertook peripheral tasks to keep its existence before the public and to maintain members' morale. The Corps provided a regular group of workers each Sunday to help other volunteers building 'homes for heroes' at French's Forest. This was one of many schemes to provide for the returned man, in gratitude, and no doubt to stimulate recruiting by demonstrating such concern. The women of the Corps laboured alongside other volunteers wearing 'large overalls, gardener's gloves, and sevenpenny stockings and boots, so that nothing is spoilt except our Monday complexions'. The Corps also took part in the 'Naval and Military Tattoo' held in Sydney on 30 June 1917; sadly, despite its grand title this affair comprised the women and naval and military schoolboy cadets. So, while Miss Jacob may have been the first woman to lead a 'march past' in the Commonwealth, the Corps may have demeaned itself by taking part in a 'children's affair'. Of course, there was no other outlet for their martial ardour and at least the women demonstrated that they could march.[16]

Like the other women's patriotic groups, the Australian Women's Service Corps seemed thoroughly middle-class. Their magazine, the *Despatch*, noted the addresses of training places and the home addresses of prominent members; without exception these were middle-class suburbs, Stanmore, Neutral Bay, Tamarama, Double Bay. Members unconsciously displayed attitudes consistent with the sheltered, respectable upbringing of middle-class girls. While visiting a returned hero in hospital, the AWSC members noticed that the patient 'had real tattoo marks on his arms' but reported that 'we were not in the least scared, we hadn't time to be'. Undoubtedly tattooed men were a novelty. The enthusiasm AWSC members showed as loyalist workers during the 1917 general strike in New South Wales is further proof of the class orientation of the Corps. Indeed, when the AWSC opened a register of volunteers, the office staff asked for the women's home telephone numbers in an age when the telephone was definitely a status symbol. Reports members sent to the *Despatch* indicate that the women found the type of work undertaken, mainly staffing canteens for the male loyalist workers, a distinct novelty, joking about their experiences of 'roughing it' as did writers in the private school magazines. Finally, the calm way in which AWSC members accepted government's refusal to use them in any

Some of the 1,200 women who registered in one week at the Department of Public Instruction in Sydney to serve 'in any capacity' during the 'Great Strike'

meaningful way typified their movement. Patriotism and frustration with the disloyal and apathetic had led to the formation of the AWSC and, while they cast envious eyes on the real contribution to the cause British women were making, the women's radicalism ended with its formation. Miss Jacob beseeched the government to use her Corps but could devise no strategy to bring her campaign to a successful conclusion.[17]

Given the limited capacity for women to engage in direct war work in Australia, the tag that in war women must 'wait and weep' was perhaps an apt description of the role of most Australian women. With 330,000 Australians abroad most women must have had a close relative or friend at the front, or be acquainted with many other women so situated. Enlistment accounted for 38.7 per cent of all males in Australia between the ages of 18 and forty-four. Dolly, in the *Soldier,* commented: 'You scarcely pass a woman in Sydney town who is not wearing an enamel brooch, representing the colours of the battalion in which someone belonging to her is serving'. Letters from parents to soldiers overseas indicate the extent of personal involvement and anxiety, but again it is the extent of the suffering on the homefront that is noticeable. A Healesville, Victoria, mother, Mrs Davies, wrote to her nurse daughter in September 1916 after the news of the losses on the Somme had reached Australia:

> I think I told you that Mrs Oliver lost her soldier son Lieutenant Oliver killed in France. They are in great trouble. Mr Milne was here last week. His son George is in France. Benton Farwell was wounded and young Bott. And a Healesville boy named Ellis killed.

Awaiting the arrival of a hospital ship in Sydney in May 1917. This must have been an anxious moment as only the permanently unfit were returned to Australia

Awaiting the arrival of the wounded in Sydney

As the war progressed Mrs Davies kept up a steady stream of names of neighbours, friends and relatives either wounded or, at least, abroad. Perhaps the casualties made a greater impact in a small country town like Healesville, but her correspondence is typical of the experiences of many Australian women.

> Do you remember Russell Barrett, Miss Collie's nephew? Well he is 18 now and has enlisted. It was only the other day he was a kiddee ... Fred Gaulton's three sons are at the front and John Gaulton's two sons are there too ... I have sent you a great many casualty lists. There seems to be one most days.

We can only really guess at the depths of anguish these women endured. In a land so far from the conflict relatives despaired of seeing 'the boys' again until serious injury or peace brought them home. Not for Australian women the comfort of a personal reassurance from men home on leave that conditions were not as bad as the papers reported and that each was sure 'to pull through'.[18]

Newspaper owners hoped to stimulate patriotism and recruiting by presenting the stark facts of war to their Australian readers but at the same time, of course, they increased the anxieties of those who waited. Thus 'Dulcie' writing a column, 'From the Girl He Left Behind', in the *Soldier*, explained how intense was the anguish of waiting as rumours circulated in Sydney that the Empire's personification of the manly spirit, its war minister, Lord Kitchener, had perished. 'Dulcie' complained that 'For some unknown reason the censor would not allow a special edition of the papers to reassure us one way or another. The suspense was awful. At last we realised it was all too true'. Perhaps a man in the front line would have realised how peripheral was Kitchener's contribution to the war effort, but to the inexperienced in Australia his loss seemed a tragic blow and a major setback. Before news became instantly available through radio and television, the public relied on the newspapers and, for matters of special importance, on the 'extra' edition. How gratingly must the newsboys' cries of 'extra!' 'extra!' have played on jangled nerves in the cities and suburbs of Australia and how eagerly were the 'extras' snapped up. 'Dulcie' resented the censor's prohibition on the occasion of Kitchener's death but he had acted to calm public opinion and not to give undue prominence to the event.[19]

Domestic political controversy also added to the tensions and anxieties of those forced to wait. Historians, skimming over the extremes of abuse and hysteria generated by increasing political division, have dismissed as fantastic many of the claims and accusations made; and so, in reality, they were. But many of these stories were believed at the time by anxious people confused by the unusual bitterness and the threats to their way of life, represented variously by the 'patriots' or the 'disloyalists'. Again, letters from Australians to the troops abroad demonstrate this point well. How many mothers would willingly deceive a hero son on active service about conditions in Australia, unless to pretend that things were satisfactory? Presumably, then, these stories of bitter division and evil were believed, at least, by those who reported them.

Evelyn Davies's mother wrote regularly, and for the most part happily, about life in Healesville but the 'disloyalists' in the community increasingly aroused her fury. In January 1916 she suggested that only conscription would make young men 'work or fight'. She worried about the pacifists, a small minority really, but led by Dr Charles Strong, a prominent Presbyterian minister who had left that church amid accusations of heresy in 1883, to found an independent Australian Church. Strong's church prospered until the war but then lost most of its members who rejected the minister's pacifism and his attacks on war hysteria. Mrs Davies was, in fact, remarkably sensitive to any opposition at all. By September she regarded the prime minister, W. M. Hughes, as 'the tool of the disloyal Labor party' because he did 'nothing but talk'. During the second conscription campaign she readily accepted the newspapers' proposition that 'No' voters were disloyal, informing a

These Tumut girls were trying to shame the 'slackers' into action. Given Australian opinion about women's role in wartime it is doubtful if they found permanent work

doubtless perplexed daughter that the 'R[oman] C[atholic] priests [were] at the head of the Sin Fien [sic]' and had organised elaborately to defeat conscription 'Just for hatred of England and to be "agin the Government"'. She worried, too, about the Germans in Australia 'holding good billets in the civil service' while 'Returned Soldiers do not get a fair deal. They have to join the Trades Hall [sic] before they are allowed a billet'. Mrs Davies had obviously absorbed the anti-German propaganda to be discussed below. She reported that the disloyalists so resented returned men that they singled them out for ill-treatment: 'it was dangerous for one to wear uniform as the hooligans set upon them, and the police refused to act. They had received their orders from the priests right enough'.[20]

Much of this reporting is, at the very least, vastly exaggerated but the letters do give a clear picture of how receptive an anxious woman could be to wild newspaper talk and how readily she accepted the idea that Australia was seriously threatened by the disloyalists. These anxieties helped deepen the divisions, which, in their turn, increased anxiety. Women tried to help one another to cope in those difficult times. A group of Sydney women opened the Centre for Soldiers' Wives and Mothers to help overcome the women's financial problems and to encourage them as they waited. The aim was to allow 'women [to] meet one another to share their letters and scraps of news from the front, and also to bring comfort to those who have suffered the loss [of a loved one]'. This was but one of many co-operative ventures: all reflecting the extent of the anxieties of the 'wives and mothers'.[21]

Many of these anxious women directed their energies to helping the social reform campaign put down gambling and drinking, activities alleged to be 'unpatriotic'. There were good reasons why women should join these campaigns. Perhaps the most potent inducement to reform and control was the largely unspoken suspicion about the likely behaviour of the large numbers of young men putting on the King's uniform. It would seem that the community developed an ambivalent attitude to the men of the AIF. As individuals, brother, son or husband each was loved and admired. The community carried this identification further, accepting warmly, from the heart, any man in uniform. 'Dolly' reported how frequently when she saw a group of soldiers 'almost involuntarily I waved my hand to them' because 'we [women] all feel a strong comradeship with any man in King's uniform'. But on the other hand it was generally feared that young men, removed from the constraints of home, mothers and sweethearts, living together and thirsting for excitement, might behave foolishly.[22]

Two events confirmed these suspicions. First was the report that the Australian troops had rioted in the Wazir section of Cairo. Critics, initially suspicious of the motives of men they dubbed 'six-bob-a-day tourists', seized on these reports to belittle the Australians and brand them as larrikins. Events in Sydney in February 1916 led many to believe that, noble as individuals, in the mass soldiers could be dangerous. A new training syllabus which increased drill for an extra four and a half hours a week, caused 15,000 soldiers from the Sydney camps to 'strike'. They marched on the township of Liverpool, broke into the hotels and drank whatever they found. Fortified, they swarmed on to the trains, which were still running to Sydney, and virtually took over the city for an evening of drunken hooliganism. At Central Station drunken soldiers hurled stones at the troops trying to round them up; eventually shots were fired: one rioter of 19 was killed and six others injured. The incident shook the city and the military authorities and tarnished the reputation of the AIF.[23]

Soon after the Sydney riot the New South Wales premier, W. A. Holman, announced a referendum to determine at what hours the hotels should be shut. Voters were free to choose any hour between 6 p.m. and 11 p.m. but they voted heavily in favour of 6 o'clock closing (60 per cent), with 9 p.m. attracting 30.9 per cent, 8 p.m. 3.6 and the remainder favouring either 7, 8, 10 or 11 or voting informally. This impressive rejection of extended drinking hours secured wide adherence throughout the state. Only in the inner-city working-class electorates was there any divergence from the pattern. These electorates favoured 9 pm. Women dominated the early closing campaign in two ways. Numbers of them took part enthusiastically, speaking at rallies, writing letters to the press and canvassing voters. They played a more active role in this campaign than women had ever done before in Australia and were blooded for the conscription campaigns that were to follow. Advocates of early closing seemed to presume that women naturally favoured the reform and that they had a particular interest in closing hotels. Much of the rhetoric was directed to women as 'God's police', eager to restrict the harmful pleasures of men. Thus Ethel Turner, the novelist, in a published appeal stated: 'I began with the words "Fellow Citizens", but I really only mean "Men Citizens". There is no need at all to speak to the women; their vote for 6 o'clock is a certainty'. Woman's role was to be guardian of the home, the natural ally of the anti-drink forces. In a peculiarly wartime analogy a prominent temperance campaigner for over forty years, Mrs Harrison Lee Cowie, appealed to all electors to:

> Vote for 6 o'clock to protect the women's homes from strong drink. Woman has a right to ask you to protect her home – her little kingdom. Sometimes the little kingdom has been, like Belgium, unable to protect itself against the enemy. But, as the British went to the rescue of little Belgium, we all plead for every man to come to the rescue and vote 6 o'clock.

The Liquor Trades Defence Union also accepted these sex stereotypes, the male as drinker, the woman at home caring for the family, and based its argument for 9 o'clock on the sanctity of the home. The Union suggested that closing hotels at 6 p.m. would encourage drinking in the home and that possibly women would drink with their husbands, causing them to neglect the children. 'There is a danger', warned an advertisement, 'that the bottle at the elbow will become handier than the bottle at the hotel bar shelf'.[24]

The need for women-only rallies – note the women largely confined to the balcony at this Brisbane pro-conscription rally. W. M. Hughes is speaking

A pro-conscriptionist making a last minute attempt to convince a voter

The success of the early closing campaign bore important implications for political life in Australia. It had been demonstrated that women were thorough, efficient campaign workers who could be trusted with work hitherto reserved for men. Furthermore, specific appeals had been directed to women, which they had answered, at least, so those who rejoiced in the 6 o'clock victory argued. Their patriotism, it was argued, lifted them beyond the plane of everyday politics. The temperance crusade, of course, had enjoyed only limited success before the war.

These lessons were not lost on the conscription campaigners four months later. Both sides believed that the women's vote would be crucial in determining the outcome of the first conscription referendum. Antis hoped that woman's natural reverence for life, as its progenitor, and her gentle susceptibilities would bring out a large 'No' vote amongst women. In their campaign the antis concentrated on this theme, summarised in the poem 'The Blood Vote'. The pro-conscriptionists concentrated on women's capacity for sacrifice as demonstrated in their enthusiasm for voluntary war work, failing to notice the middle-class nature of the volunteers. However, several of the women war workers' journals openly advocated conscription and the leading figures in the 'Yes' campaign drew on the organisational and entrepreneurial skills that women had developed in their Red Cross branches and comforts funds guilds.

The prime minister recognised the new conditions prevailing in Australia, directing a substantial part of his campaign specifically to women; he appealed to the patriotism of women at 'women only' rallies, a novel departure in Australian electioneering. 'Dolly', in the *Soldier,* described one such rally held at the Sydney Town Hall. Women arrived at 10 a.m. although the doors were not to open until 2 p.m. Every seat was occupied four minutes after the doors opened and, while waiting for the speeches to begin, the women kept up their enthusiasm by singing patriotic songs such as 'Rule Britannia' and the national anthem. When Hughes appeared on the platform, the women gave him an enthusiastic, emotional welcome, cheering, waving and singing. 'Dolly' admitted that she caught only one in ten of Hughes's words because of the clamour, nevertheless, she confessed that 'Not for worlds would I have missed taking part in this wonderful, thrilling, historical meeting of women of Australia'. This from a columnist who two months earlier seemed to deny that women could play an active part in politics when she claimed that most women, like herself, 'feel things rather than understand them' and that 'I am not very well educated in politics'. Patriotism and the assessment of national need had wrought a transformation.[25]

The opponents of conscription appealed to the supposed natural pacifist sentiments of women and they also related their general economic argument to the lives of women. Thus, while they maintained that the introduction of conscription would allow the ruling class to destroy unionism by importing cheap, coloured workers, they also argued that conscripted men's jobs would be filled by women and would thus overturn the supposed natural roles of the sexes. How strongly the sex roles were implanted in Australian society will be seen when we examine the reaction of the AIF to British wartime society where women increasingly found employment in traditional male areas. Members of the AIF expressed amazement that British women should work as porters, drivers, farm hands, labourers and so on, and they often expressed the hope that Australia would never sink so low. By playing on fears that conscription would require the full utilisation of female labour, the anti-conscriptionists showed how deeply ingrained these sex roles were. Australian male voters were swayed not only by the rumour that Hughes intended to import coloured labour to replace Australian workers, they also feared that they would lose their jobs to women.

In this climate is it any wonder that the government rejected offers from groups such as the Australian Women's Service Corps who wanted to contribute meaningfully to the war effort and that few new work opportunities opened up to women during the war? In the event, it is impossible to determine how effective was the propaganda directed to and about women in the defeat of conscription in 1916 and 1917. Sufficient to say that the campaigns were important because of the greater political role women developed and because campaigners had decided women might be influenced by arguments different from those used for men.

A contemporary postcard

If Australians believed that woman's natural role was to marry, keep a home and raise children then, cruelly, the war made this an impossible ideal for many women. The curtailment of social life and the reduction of the opportunities for marriage posed real problems for those who held traditional views. With 330,000 males, many of them single, absent from Australia for up to four years, obviously opportunities for marriage declined and this was reflected in the marriage statistics. At first, in 1915 there was an increase in marriages, up 4.42 per cent over 1914 figures, but by 1918 the number of marriages had declined by 23–48 per cent compared with 1914. Fewer women marrying and producing children disturbed the settled social patterns and no doubt increased the women's desire for worthwhile work, a desire largely frustrated, as we have seen. Particularly disturbing to Australian women were reports that large numbers of the AIF were marrying English girls. What hope had 'The Girl He Left Behind' of competing with the girl on the spot some 20,000 kilometres away?[26]

The problem was taken so seriously that the Hughes government tried to find a remedy. To ease the situation of the woman who discovered she was pregnant after her 'soldier boy' had left for the front, the Hughes government proposed that members of the AIF be allowed to marry Australian girls by proxy, that is, without being physically present at the ceremony. Such a scheme might encourage marriages between Australian sweethearts separated by the war and would legitimise those children conceived in the hectic days of an Australian's pre-embarkation leave.

The need for a marriage-by-proxy scheme is well illustrated by a pathetic file held at Australian Archives. A girl wrote to the Defence department requesting the return to Australia of her boyfriend because since his departure she had discovered that she was pregnant. They had been 'keeping company' for nearly six years and although she described herself as 'not a Girl fly about' she had yielded to him after he enlisted because he had promised to marry her and because she was so proud of him. Unfortunately, he was sent overseas soon after enlisting, at short notice, so that they were not able to arrange a wedding. The disgrace of an illegitimate child distressed her: 'I shall not be able to go through [with it?] I shall take my life ... I cannot tell Mother'. The department replied sympathetically regretting that the soldier could not be returned, suggesting that she travel to England to marry him there, but added, hopefully, that cabinet had recently approved marriage by proxy. She replied immediately asking for details of the proxy plan. Four days after she wrote this second letter, Hughes introduced the marriage-by-proxy scheme into parliament, to be greeted by a wail of united opposition from the churches whose spokesmen argued that the provision would encourage licence, that a girl would readily sleep with soldiers knowing that were she to discover a pregnancy after the soldier's departure, the 'mistake' could easily be rectified. Mr P. S. Cleary, a spokesman for Sydney's Archbishop Kelly, discreetly explained that 'Indiscriminate marriage by proxy would encourage the anticipation of that event'. He deplored this because 'The Church regards unwedded intercourse as possibly the worst of sins'. Even the *Soldier,* the self-proclaimed guardian of the AIF's interests, opposed the proposal because many of the soldiers' sweethearts were 'comforting themselves in the absence of their lovers with substitutes' and possibly thousands of them 'would willingly go through the ceremony to secure the soldier's allotment and separation allowance – often, too, in the hope that the "husband" would not return and that a pension would be the reward for their "sacrifice"'. Neither reaction paid any tribute to the honesty or generosity of Australian women, and shows, with brutal clarity, how dominant were the stereotyped images held of them. Hughes might have tried to refute these mean arguments but he chose the safer path and allowed his bill to lapse. This left the Defence department's troubled correspondent with no hope four months or more into her pregnancy. She asked plaintively: 'don't you think it is only fair to us Australian girls, if you are willing to let them go you ought to think of us, as my life has been one constant misery'. She confided that she had not heard from her boyfriend since he had left Australia and the department replied explaining in detail how to send him a cable. There was no other advice that they could offer.[27]

That Hughes sympathised with girls like this is apparent from his attempts to revive a marriage by proxy bill in late 1917 when he wrote to the leaders of the major churches asking them to withdraw their earlier opposition. In those letters he suggested that he was motivated solely by a concern to remove the stigma of illegitimacy from thousands of Australian children but as the illegitimacy rate declined in each year of the war and remained as a steady percentage of all births (5.26 per cent in 1914, 5.23 per cent in 1918) it may be that Hughes hoped for other benefits too, from marriage by proxy.

A highly romantic view of 'the girl he left behind'

Other results might have been to reduce the number of unmarried girls in Australia and the number of marriages between members of the AIF and English girls. Another benefit of great attraction to the Australian government might have been the effect of the scheme in reducing the very high rate of venereal diseases amongst the Australian troops. There is no doubt that the Australian government viewed that rate with alarm, making frequent representations to the imperial government about ways by which it might be reduced. Perhaps Hughes suspected that married men would be less likely to risk infection and wished to encourage marriage for that reason. However, he made no progress with church leaders; Archbishop Kelly explained his opposition saying that the scheme would lead to hasty, ill-conceived marriages and would co-operate 'with the seductive wiles of females'. Hughes again allowed the scheme to lapse, denying many Australian women the opportunity to fulfil the role society cherished for them.[28]

During World War II, if accounts such as that in the novel *Come in Spinner* are any guide, Australian women enjoyed increased opportunities for social life; indeed the bars and restaurants of the principal cities rang with the sounds of Australian and American laughter. Patriotic women enjoyed no such outlets during the Great War, on the contrary, patriotism required them to reduce their social engagements. If every man's place was in the army, how could any female patriot keep company with a 'slacker' and, as the army was overseas, few other men remained with whom the girls might socialise. Of course, such an exalted view of duty did not find universal observance and patriotic women had names for their sisters who entertained the 'slackers'. Mrs Davies of Healesville reported that 'It makes me sick to see a lot of girls making much of stalwart young men when they are just shirkers'. Because of such attitudes the social season in Sydney, Melbourne, or the small country town was cancelled – the big balls, the state levees and the church socials. For girls brought up to expect these few years of pleasure and excitement as a recompense for a life of subservience and duty, there is sense in the comment that 'It was really a tragedy when girls were debarred from dancing'. Indeed, much of the appeal of the 'patriotic movements' could have been as a compensation for the dull life war caused. Entertaining soldiers, organising and conducting fairs, fetes and button days, injected some excitement into an otherwise dull scene.[29]

But what are we to make of the members of the Women's Patriotic Club who met on the first Monday of each month at the Wentworth Hotel to 'pass a pleasant afternoon at either bridge or music'? If such gatherings could be passed off under the cloak of patriotism, what excuse had the patriotic classes to agitate for the closure of working-class entertainments, predominantly sporting? There were gradations, it would seem, in respectable social activities, only some of which might be seen as patriotic. On the whole, however, women's social life deteriorated during the war, another of the sacrifices expected of them.[30]

The war was not the watershed for Australian women as it was for women in other societies. The roles elaborated for them during the nineteenth century remained in force during wartime despite the intense patriotic feelings of many women. Denied access to important paid employment, women directed their energies to providing help for the victims of war and comforts for the Australian troops. Their zeal and energy created what might be described as a new industry in Australia but because the work was unpaid and not obviously vital, the workers in this industry were accorded little respect. It was dismissively categorised as the sort of work expected of women. To be at the periphery at a time of such crisis, adventure and excitement was, no doubt, frustrating for many women. There is little place for women in the great national celebration of Anzac. Instead women were required to 'wait and weep'. Some energetic women tried to expand this role but they received no encouragement from the government and little sympathy from other Australians. Only in the field of politics did women expand their position and functions and this only because stereotyped thinking made them the allies or opponents of conscription, tools to be used to achieve a result. The war experience of women confirmed rather than challenged their place in society.

CHAPTER FIVE

'MUDDIED OAFS' AND 'FLANNELLED FOOLS': SPORT AND WAR IN AUSTRALIA

Middle-class Australians with more time, money and an intense devotion to the ideal of Empire made far more open display of their patriotism than working-class Australians whose opportunities for parading their loyalty were far more circumscribed. Whether or not the absence of overt patriotism indicated apathy or indifference to the cause of Empire must be a matter for conjecture. Certain it is, however, that middle-class opinion-makers accused the working class of indifference, or indeed of disloyalty, and probably helped to foster at least a spirit of resentment and possibly a spirit of revolt. Doubtless the working class resented these attacks; they saw themselves as loyal, hard-working citizens, shouldering a disproportionate burden of the sacrifice through falling standards of living and a high rate of enlistment. By their bitter accusations, the middle class helped to foster the spirit they deplored, resentment and indifference.

The fate of organised sport in Australia during wartime provides an excellent example of this process by which the working class were alienated from the spirit of patriotism, which they came to see increasingly as a middle-class prerogative. The patriots threatened the very existence of organised, mass spectator sport during the period and, in doing so, aroused the antagonism of its most loyal supporters, working-class males.

Sport had assumed a unique importance in the lives of urban Australian males; the 'sporting revolution' witnessed in most Western countries in the late nineteenth century, was nowhere more evident than in Australia. Facilities were good, the climate kind, urban transport effective and leisure time available: in sum, the Australian male enjoyed every opportunity to devote himself to sport. Many played but more watched. They attended regularly and in large numbers – football, cricket, horse-racing, boxing, sculling – and yet few of the sports, with the exception of boxing, were thoroughly professional. Footballers and cricketers, even state or national representatives, only received expenses and some payment for working time lost. Sport was a sideline.

The Australian obsession with spectator sport invariably attracted the attention of commentators such as Anthony Trollope, R. E. N. Twopeny and Mark Twain. Twopeny believed that Australia could 'fairly claim to be the most sporting country in the world' with everyone 'from the oldest grey beard to the youngest child' taking an interest in it. Anthony Trollope found that 'There is hardly a town to be called a town which has not its racecourse, and there are many racecourses where there are no towns'. Commentators explained how the fact that the obsession knew no class boundaries, that middle-class and working-class shared the same enthusiasm for sport and rubbed shoulders at the same grounds, 'proved' the egalitarian nature of Australian society. These commentators who spent only a few hurried months in 'the colonies' failed to notice that a shared enthusiasm could derive from differing motives. Sport in Australia, in a very generalised way, meant different things to the different classes. The middle-class accepted sport because of the values it taught the young and reinforced for spectators of all ages: values such as loyalty, determination, unselfishness and the team spirit. Sport was a preparation, a training-ground for something higher; he who succeeded at sport equipped himself to lead in business, politics or the professions. Little wonder that sport attained such an exalted place in the private schools discussed above.[1]

The working-class viewed sport more pragmatically. Sport meant entertainment and pleasure, an exciting interlude in the monotonous round of the urban working situation; as such, sport needed no further or more serious justification. Gambling fitted in neatly with this view of sport, allowing the spectator to test his knowledge and judgement in the hope of making a 'killing', and an opportunity to break, even temporarily, the tyranny of wage slavery. Payment to the top players or contestants presented no problem in this account of sport so long as the money interests' did not dominate to the extent of rigged results. Competition must be real. Indeed, payment for outstanding skill was one of the rare ways a working-class lad might overcome the material handicaps of his upbringing and was a decided incentive for the years of sacrifice required in the fashioning of a top sportsman. Herbert Henry 'Dally' Messenger, a boat-builder, one of the greatest rugby players Australia produced, earned £350 on the first professional tour of Great Britain. Another rugby league footballer, J. D. Campbell, received what he described as 'a most satisfactory return' in 1915 of £4 per match.[2]

These divergent views of the meaning of sport in the very generalised terms described, obviously predated the outbreak of war but they became prominent quickly under the pressure of war. If sport suddenly had become less useful, a distraction from the real issues, then, in the middle-class view, it must be abandoned voluntarily or, if not, put down by government intervention. Middle-class patriotism and loyalty were jealous virtues

A STIRRING QUESTION

PATRIOTIC OLD GENT: "*You'll pardon me, but I couldn't help overhearing you. It does me good to find young men so interested in this mighty conflict. Now what, frankly, are your views about it?*"

GYP THE CROOK: "*Well, I was telling this 'ere bloke if 'Tornado' Tubbs can stop me cobber, Billy Walsh, inside er six rounds, then Billy's dead.*"

A stirring question. *Bulletin*, 1 July 1915

demanding the complete adherence of all Australians and it simply was not good enough that some should continue to play games at a time of national crisis. The debate about the place of sport in wartime Australia becomes a further link in the argument about the divergent views of patriotism. Because sport meant so much to so many Australians, the readiness to abandon it indicates the enthusiasm for a total commitment to the Empire that gripped much of middle-class Australia and the debate will throw considerable light on the responses of the Australian people to the challenge of war.

At first the followers of sport were no more perturbed by the news of war than other Australians: at worst war might involve a slight financial sacrifice and some small interference with the established sporting programme. The

Recruiting the 'sports'

slightly eccentric, deeply conservative sports writer in the *Pastoral Review*, writing under the martial pseudonym 'Fife and Drum', wrote about war in his August column but concluded complacently, 'next month, if all be going well with the Empire, we will talk horse again with a light heart'. Many of the sporting bodies' 'patriotic gestures' reflected this spirit. The Australian Jockey Club and the Victoria Racing Club both gave thought to cancelling their August meetings but decided instead merely to donate a proportion of the takings to the patriotic funds. The Victorian Football League determined to impose a 'patriotic surcharge' and lifted gate prices by 50 per cent; revealingly, football followers resented this imposition and the League abandoned its policy when attendances dropped sharply. The patriotism of one of the League clubs, St Kilda, was quite evident, however. When it was discovered that the club's colours were identical to those of Germany, the players decided to pin Union Jacks to the fronts of their jumpers to indicate their true loyalties. The club's colours changed before the beginning of the 1915 season.[3]

The news of war affected attendance at sporting events unevenly. In Melbourne crowds at the four VFL finals games declined by half, while in Sydney the Rugby League, whose patrons were even more firmly entrenched in the working-class than were VFL followers, drew very large crowds to the finals matches. The rising star on the Australian boxing scene, Maitland's Les Darcy, attracted 'a vast crowd' and 'half Sydney's police force' when he fought Fritz Holland in September at the Rushcutters' Bay Stadium. Boxing attracted few middle-class patrons. The four days of the Victoria Racing

The Bulletin's *view of Dr Lang who, as 'Fife and Drum', contributed a weekly sports column to the* Pastoral Review

Club's Spring Carnival saw attendance fall by 52,000 compared with 1913 figures; even the Melbourne Cup attracted 18,000 fewer spectators. A clear pattern had emerged: sports with a middle-class clientele declined while those which relied on the working class for support continued as before.[4]

Very quickly too, well before the adoption of recruiting campaigns, middle-class commentators suggested that sportsmen had a special duty to enlist in the AIF. No doubt this expectation derived in part from the fact that sportsmen were in good physical condition, but it also derived from the belief that sport had prepared them well for higher duties. 'Fife and Drum' called on the 'mudded oaf' and 'flannelled fool' to show that he had 'learned his lesson from his games', as if it were beyond dispute that games taught 'lessons'. When the recruiting campaigns began in earnest during the stalemate at Gallipoli, recruiters looked eagerly to the sporting bodies. English sportsmen, they claimed, had responded nobly to the country's call but in Australia the sportsmen had yet to appreciate the need. 'Fife and Drum' summarised the thinking behind these special appeals to sportsmen:

> What is the good of games if they do not provide a training ground for the sterner battles in our lives. If they do not give us men whose hands they have taught to war and the fingers to fight, then it would be better that we blotted them out from our daily lives altogether ... [5]

Enlistment from sporting bodies was good but the continuance of games at a time of crisis began to appear incongruous to those whose patriotism demanded a total commitment to the cause of Empire. As the recruiting movement developed, recruiters became increasingly concerned that sporting

Will they never come?

PUBLISHED BY THE PARLIAMENTARY RECRUITING COMMITTEE

Sport and recruiting

events hindered their efforts. This may seem fanciful but it should be remembered that many recruiters had developed the extraordinary notion that every eligible man ought to enlist. So intense was the concern for Empire and the Australian troops at Gallipoli that recruiters seemed prepared to accept few excuses from eligibles and could speak of the 'failure' of the Victorian recruiting campaign of July 1915 which added 21,698 recruits to the AIF. Thus they displayed particularly bad temper about crowds at sporting fixtures which consisted largely of young males with, apparently, time on their hands. The Rev. J. L. Rentoul, a fiery Irish Presbyterian, contrasted the heroes at Gallipoli with the youths at Melbourne football and branded the man who, though free to enlist, preferred football as 'a loon, a coward and a dastard'. Later, recruiters realised the good sense of not deliberately antagonising an audience but Rentoul's approach apparently received official sanction when a recruiting poster appeared entitled 'Will They Never Come': 'they' were pictured as a portion of the crowd behind the goals of the Melbourne Cricket Ground. *Sport,* a Melbourne paper, alleged that the poster had prejudiced footballers and spectators against the recruiting movement; they resented what they saw as 'class distinction' directed only against football.[6]

As the frustrations of the recruiters grew, a campaign developed to curtail or even to abandon mass spectator sport. L. A. Adamson, the headmaster of Wesley College, one of the great public schools in Melbourne, focused

A recruiting appeal at the Sydney Showground

SPORT AND WAR
N.S.W. RUGBY UNION TEAM, 1914—EIGHT ENLISTMENTS

Photographs such as this were common in Australian papers and were seen as a means of encouraging other 'sports' to enlist

attention on this campaign in its early stages in a speech he made at the school assembly which was then published in the Melbourne *Herald* and elsewhere. Adamson justified his well-known enthusiasm for sport because of what it taught participants; indeed, he claimed, 'the British love of games [had] proved a magnificent asset to the Empire' producing unselfish, devoted leaders, able to endure hardship and discomfort. Schoolboys might well continue with their games, even in time of war, because sport equipped them to take their places at the front if this was necessary. In the wider community in wartime, sport should be assessed from one standard only, namely, whether it hindered or assisted recruiting. Clearly, enthusiasm for sport so hindered recruiting in Melbourne that Adamson believed any patriotic German would pay well to have sport continue. The patriotic Australian, therefore, should devote himself to putting sport down. Adamson distinguished between amateur and professional sport indicating that he believed that money had corrupted the noble instincts of sportsmen and was incompatible with true sporting ideals and aims. He contrasted the performance of the South Yarra football club, the 1914 premiers of the Amateur Football Association, eighteen of whose players had enlisted, with the VFL clubs whose enlistments, he alleged, were not nearly as impressive. Perhaps VFL figures were not spectacular, but they were certainly good and deserved better than denunciations from the patriots. *Sport* published a 'Footballers Honour List' from 23 April 1915 onwards, which showed that by that date thirty-three VFL players and thirty-five VFA players had enlisted. By early 1916, twelve regular South Melbourne players and eight former players were in the ranks; Fitzroy had provided thirty-two present and former players. Other clubs seemed to have matched these tallies. Amateur football in Melbourne, like the Rugby Union in Sydney, drew a high proportion of its players from the ranks of the old boys of the private schools, and a higher proportion of spectators from the ranks of the middle class. Adamson warned his students that they could not remain true to the 'Public Schools' ideal' and continue to attend 'professional' football matches. His statement aroused considerable public controversy and perhaps, given his position, it was inevitable that some would see it as a class-based attack on the innocent amusements of the less privileged. However, the editorialists of many of the daily newspapers supported his views, although the Sydney *Bulletin*, a traditional opponent of the wowsers, rejected him: 'there's an hour for mourning and an hour for tears', the paper claimed, 'but there's also an hour for bucking up and belting despondency to leg'.[7]

The allegations of class bias in the campaign against the continuance of sport derived principally from the fact that while commentators and newspaper editorialists bemoaned the playing of football they directed few, if any, barbs against cricket or horse-racing, the traditional recreations of the social elite. Admittedly the campaign developed during cricket's off-season but even at this time the cricketers gave evidence of a good measure of the correct spirit. The president of the New South Wales Cricket Association,

Mr J. H. Clayton, made a special appeal to cricketers to enlist and instructed the clubs 'to make their annual meetings Recruiting Meetings'. The case for the continuation of horse-racing rested solely on the alleged utility of the 'sport'. Football served no useful purpose but the committees of the various racing clubs, comprising almost exclusively the wealthy members of society, alleged that horse-racing stimulated one of the nation's important industries, the rearing of high quality horses. 'Fife and Drum', who as Dr W. H. Lang was also the official handicapper for the Victorian Amateur Turf Club, argued that racing encouraged breeders to make sacrifices, to experiment in the hope of producing ever better horses. This, he further argued as late as August 1917, was essential war work because 'the nation which comes out on top in the end is that one which possesses the best horse supply'. Presumably Lang was dreaming of earlier campaigns in British history but unfortunately it seems there were similar dreamers in the British War Office. So racing's supporters, armed with the doctrine of utility, were better placed than the lovers of football to repel attacks on their sport; their views fitted in nicely with those who argued that all sport must have a higher purpose. 'Fife and Drum', indeed, scorned the mere entertainment value of racing and rested no part of his argument on the attraction racing held for the ordinary man. He suggested that 'those able-bodied men who frequent our suburban courses should be compelled to go into training ... The courses I am proud to say, will be pleased to see their backs'.[8]

On the argument of utility, therefore, the organisations controlling football in Australia found themselves very much on the defensive in 1915. In the face of a sustained campaign several of them decided to curtail the

A portion of the crowd at Randwick Racecourse on the day the 'tote' opened in 1917. Would the clubs have been happy to see the backs of *all* these people?

Football premiership final at which Balmain beat South Sydney five to three in July 1916, an early end to the season. Note the good crowd in the background, dubbed 'slackers' merely for their attendance

football season. In Sydney, the Rugby Union, traditionally a bastion of the amateur, middle-class view of sport, cancelled its 1915 programme because of the heavy enlistment of club players. Manly, for example, lost thirty-three of its players to the AIF and East Sydney and Annandale, with thirty-one volunteers each, were next on the long list. While the Rugby Union may have had no alternative, the Victorian Football Association's decision to curtail the 1915 season appears self-sacrificial in the extreme. Founded in 1877, the VFA was the senior body in Victorian football but was under the threat of being engulfed by the Victorian Football League which had been formed in 1897 by the strongest of the VFA clubs, dissatisfied with the parent body. Rivalry between the two groups was intense with the VFL gradually gaining the edge. To abandon its programme, although consistent with middle-class patriotism, was to hand football dominance in Melbourne to the VFL. Nevertheless, the VFA clubs agreed unanimously to curtailment at a meeting held on 14 July 1915, in the midst of the first Victorian recruiting campaign. It is fair to add that the VFA had a more conservative, middle-class image than the VFL, whose principal clubs drew their support from Collingwood, Richmond, Fitzroy and Carlton, suburbs with a large and often exclusive working-class component.[9]

If the VFA hoped that its demonstration of patriotism would force the League to follow suit, it was soon disappointed. The League met on 21 July 1915 to consider its position. Each club sent two delegates who were to vote in accordance with the club's instructions; the League required a three-quarter majority of delegates voting if there was to be a substantial change of policy. While it may be unwise to assume that a club located in a respectable middle-class area would adopt the ethos of that area, it is true that club membership was based almost exclusively on residence in the local area and that the clubs tried hard to maintain an identification with their suburb in order to encourage and to stimulate the recruitment of players. In the case of the Collingwood Football Club, for example, club membership lists show that the club fairly faithfully reflected the population pattern of the suburb: 'predominantly working class, but not exclusively so'. Indeed, 'eighty per cent of the Club's membership in the early part of this century was drawn from the local industrial wage-earning class'. While the club tolerated and even reconciled class antagonisms within its walls 'to the world at large Collingwood turned a resolutely working-class face'. It is interesting, therefore, that Essendon and the four south of the Yarra clubs voted to follow the VFA's lead and abandon the season, while the north of the Yarra clubs, located in the heartland of Melbourne's working-class, voted to continue playing. The motion was defeated as it did not gain the necessary three-quarter majority and games continued as before. Delegates in favour of continuation had argued that the 40,000 patrons who had attended matches on the previous Saturday had demonstrated that they wished the game to go on.

In Sydney, the Rugby League gave no evidence of even debating whether or not to cancel the remaining matches in the season. But then, the Rugby League, founded in 1907 because of exasperation with the amateur, gentlemanly spirit of the organisers of Rugby Union, to that point Sydney's football, was even more thoroughly working-class in its patronage than was the VFL. No doubt, too, the newly created Rugby League feared for its very survival were it to disappoint its followers by abandoning games for the period of the war.[10]

Although the patriots' campaign against sport concentrated on football, boxing, another favourite recreation of the working man, received some attention too. Boxing supporters attracted most unfavourable criticism when they counted out the New South Wales premier, W. A. Holman, who had attempted to make a recruiting speech at the Stadium before a title fight between Les Darcy and America's Eddie McGoorty. The newspapers denounced the apparent lack of patriotism on the part of the 16,000 strong crowd and the *Sydney Morning Herald* reported with approval the comments of a Presbyterian minister, the Rev. David Brandt, who called on the government to prohibit 'prize fighting' and 'to compel people [who attended such fixtures] to train for the defence of Empire'. Again, when confronted with apathy or a different interpretation of Australia's situation, the patriots' first response was to reach for the medicine of compulsion. Only one Sydney newspaper, the *Sportsman,* defended the boxing crowd. 'They counted out Holman the politician, not Holman the recruiter', the *Sportsman* claimed ingenuously, but the paper found safer ground in attacking Holman's unnecessarily provocative speech. The premier, apparently, had threatened his audience with conscription to compel the 'young loafers' before him to do their duty and it may be that he deserved a large measure of the blame for his recruiting fiasco. As the Sydney *Sportsman* was able to demonstrate, the Stadium crowd had warmly received and listened attentively to wounded men returned from the Dardanelles as they appealed for recruits only a week before. Unfortunately for sports lovers, this incident created a very unfavourable climate for sport in Sydney and won opponents of sport many new allies.[11]

Despite an increasing number of calls for compulsory government curtailment of sporting programmes, restrictions continued to be decided voluntarily by the various controlling bodies. As the 1915–16 cricket season approached the newspapers began to demand that cricket not be played and officials quickly decided against playing interstate cricket. By October both the New South Wales and Victorian cricket associations had announced that inter-dub cricket would be cancelled as well: only social games would be permitted. In New South Wales, at least, these were not easy decisions for the officials because cricket there was on the wane. Pessimists believed the survival of the game to be in jeopardy. In the year to 30 June 1914 the cricket association recorded a loss of £501 19s 11d, its third successive loss. During the following season, affected by the early months of the war, the association lost a further £835, heavy losses given that there was no prospect of a test series to refill the empty coffers. The officials set up a committee to examine ways of making cricket more attractive as a spectator sport which introduced novelties such as the eight ball over. The committee noted perceptively that the game depended as much as any other on a dominant personality to draw the crowds in and yearned for another cricketer in the mould of the great M. A. Noble. Despite the bravado expressed in the committee's claim that a game which had survived 200 years was unlikely to die out, especially as 'cricket in itself is [so] deeply rooted in the life of the Britisher', cricket was ailing. In such circumstances officials showed a daring commitment to the Empire's cause by virtually suspending the game throughout Australia. The Sydney *Sportsman* warned that the decision would give baseball, admittedly hardly a popular spectator sport, a big advantage and lamented that cricket 'already in a comatose condition could be killed off by its friends'.[12]

By the end of 1915 voluntary action had caused the cancellation of much of Australia's spectator and participant sport. A list of sports affected included rugby union, polo, interstate and inter-dub hockey, amateur athletics, cricket, interstate tennis, rowing and most of amateur and country football. It is not possible to estimate the amount of sport abandoned at club level but an occasional paragraph in a sporting paper indicates what may have been happening. Thus, in December 1915, the Sydney Swimming Club announced that in future competition would be restricted to the under-21 and over-40 age groups. Indeed, even in those organisations determined to continue to offer some form of competition, there were spectacular club failures. The *Bulletin* announced in July 1915 that the bottom had fallen out

Recruiting office, Melbourne Town Hall

of the Bendigo Football League when the Rochester club disbanded because of the enlistment of several players, followed by the enlistment of thirteen players from the Bendigo City club. In the north of Victoria, the entire Wodonga team, undefeated to that point, marched to the training ground and enlisted to a man. The opponents of sport overlooked such examples of patriotism in calling for the compulsory abolition of sport.[13]

Two episodes, one in Perth and one in Adelaide, demonstrated that the movement for the voluntary abandonment of sport had reached its limits. When the Western Australian Football League decided on 5 August 1915 to bring its season to a close by 21 August in the interests of recruiting, two clubs, Perth and East Perth, determined to test the legality of the decision in the Western Australian Supreme Court. The clubs lay fifth and sixth respectively on the competition table only one game each behind fourth place. Were the season to have been curtailed, neither side would have been eligible for a place in the finals game. The League declined to contest the action when it came up for decision before the chief justice because, as the president said, 'the members of the executive had not felt inclined to leave their occupations to go squabbling in the Law Courts over such a petty matter as a game of football'. Moreover, in law, the League's action was indefensible. The chief justice ruled that the season must continue as arranged and football continued in Perth throughout the war years.[14]

When the South Australian Football League announced that it would abandon its 1916 programme and hold no further football matches until the end of the war, a vocal section of the public began to demand that some football be played. The Port Adelaide League and Association clubs led the movement in favour of playing-clubs, again, based on a solidly working-class district. These clubs amalgamated to form the Port Adelaide Limited Patriotic Football Club, the first club in the proposed Patriotic Football Association, which hoped to continue where the Football League had left off. Significantly, after a preliminary meeting at a Port Adelaide hotel, subsequent meetings of the PFA took place at the Adelaide Trades Hall, headquarters of the labour movement. Clearly, the PFA threatened the existence of the SAFL which produced lengthy statements about the necessity to abandon sport and the disinterest in the issues of those who continued to play. The League's stand drew support from the South Australian Cricket Association, which refused the use of the Adelaide Oval, the best ground, and many of the local councils who also refused the PFA the use of ovals. Despite such handicaps the season began on 13 May 1916 with six clubs, West Adelaide, Norwood, West Torrens, Prospect, Port Adelaide and Railway. As the newspapers virtually ignored the 'outlaw' competition, it has been difficult to follow its history closely. But the fact that the game between Port Adelaide and West Adelaide, played under appalling conditions on the South Park Lands, drew a crowd of about 3,000 spectators, indicates that a section of the public at least, wanted some form of football. The Association arranged matches again in 1917 but interest appears to have been limited.[15]

While some sports enthusiasts were determined to work for the continuation of sport during the war and rejected the proposition that sport distracted Australians from the serious issues at stake, many commentators were increasingly puzzled by the apparent indifference or apathy of the ordinary Australian. The Sydney *Bulletin,* which in 1915 had argued that sport had a place in wartime Australia, by January 1916 proclaimed that 'War and football are rivals and there is no room for both of them ... Every footballer is a possible soldier, so the winter game will have no excuse this year for showing itself in public'. In February the Victorian Football League drew editorial wrath upon itself when delegates decided to press on with the game. As a concession the League determined to treat its players strictly as amateurs so that no one could say that a footballer had refused to enlist for fear of suffering financially. This decision recalled Adamson's statement that sports' officials who paid their players behaved exactly as would a patriotic German interested in restricting Australian enlistment. Money played an important part in the conduct of the VFL's affairs. Consider the plight of the Carlton Football Club which owed its bank £1,650. Naturally the bank wished to see the debt reduced and if football was abandoned Carlton would not have been able to pay off the debt which was guaranteed by the officers of the club: its officers faced bankruptcy. Other clubs experienced no such pressures. South Melbourne, for example, had assets of £1,750 with no liabilities: that club could take decisions independent of financial considerations. For South Melbourne, as for many middle-class individuals, patriotism was not expensive.[16]

Only weeks before the opening of the 1916 VFL season, the clubs which had voted to suspend the 1915 season unilaterally withdrew from the 1916 programme, leaving four clubs, Collingwood, Carlton, Fitzroy and Richmond, with an acute dilemma: should they follow suit or try to struggle on? Like many other patriotic actions the withdrawal threatened the existence of the sporting body. At the next League meeting, a Fitzroy delegate moved that the clubs which had withdrawn from the competition should also be asked to withdraw from the League. If this motion had succeeded, the way would have been clear for the four remaining clubs in the League to invite sympathetic VFA clubs to join them, thus completely restructuring Melbourne's football world. What was intended as a patriotic gesture by the affluent, middle-class VFL clubs, Melbourne, Geelong, Essendon, South Melbourne and St Kilda, might easily have resulted in their demise. Doubtless they accepted this risk when they staged their walkout.[17]

Despite considerable bad feeling, the four playing clubs met in private and decided to allow the others to continue to sit on the League. That body, representing all nine clubs, then issued a statement justifying the decision to continue playing. The League argued that despite the distressing times 'some degree of harmless and healthful recreation is both necessary and beneficial to everyone'. The League also stressed that the games would raise money for the patriotic funds and that few of the players were eligibles. The statement ended on a querulous note: why was football singled out for attack and other sports ignored? The answer may be two-fold.[18]

By 1916 football was one of the few branches of sport to attract mass public support; most other sporting bodies had voluntarily closed or restricted themselves. Furthermore, football drew much of its support from the working-class. As opinion-makers in Australia began to abrogate patriotism exclusively to the bosom of their own class, the middle-class, and to deny that the Australian worker was instinctively patriotic, they looked with increasing disfavour on his recreations. They implied that while such recreations might be innocent amongst a class which recognised its higher duty, they were definitely dangerous amongst people blinded to that duty. In the event the VFL struggled on with what must have been the least interesting programme in its relatively short history. Each club played the others three times before the finals began, in which, of course, all four were guaranteed a place. The walkout affected interest and attendance and for one winter at least football fever did not dominate Melbourne.

The Rugby League endured no such agonies and attracted much less newspaper criticism because in Sydney the campaign against sport concentrated on the evils of boxing. When representatives of the Council

THE SLACKERS ON THE BEACH
FIRST: "*Ullo! There's a chap out there in difficulties!*"
SECOND: "*By Jove, so there is. Oh well, I 'ope he pulls through all right!*"

Slackers. *Bulletin*, 4 November 1915

for Civic and Moral Advancement, a Protestant inter-denominational body, argued the 'case against the Stadium' they did so not only under the stimulus of the war. They had campaigned against boxing for several years because it catered, they claimed, to man's baser instincts. The war provided them with additional reasons for the elimination of boxing. The Council interviewed the New South Wales chief secretary, George Black, in July 1916 to demand that boxing be put down. Archbishop Wright, claiming to speak on behalf of the relatives of the dead, supposed that they found the continuance of sport an indication of the community's apathy to their sacrifice and suffering. Sir Thomas Anderson Stuart stated that he had observed the queues outside the Stadium and claimed that a large proportion of the patrons were 'hefty young men apparently militarily fit'. The Rev. Professor Macintyre, president of the State Recruiting Committee, supported this view: 'everyone was aware that the Stadium crowd contributed very few recruits in this national crisis'. This eminently respectable, middle-class organisation demanded that the stadium be closed forthwith and 'prize-fighting' outlawed.[19]

Unfortunately, as there were fewer boxers than footballers, the press could more easily investigate the private circumstances of the boxers to show eligibility and therefore disloyalty. The antagonisms expressed so forthrightly by the Council for Civic and Moral Advancement fell squarely on Les Darcy, Australia's most prominent boxer, who was constantly asked when he planned to enlist. Rumours and misunderstandings flew about. A report that Darcy had enlisted was amended: he had tried to enlist but his mother had withheld the permission he needed as a minor. In August 1916 his manager, R. L. 'Snowy' Baker, announced that Darcy had signed up for three more fights after which he would be barred from the Stadium until he had presented himself at the recruiting depot. This minor form of economic conscription was consistent with Baker's fervent patriotism. An ex-member of the New South Wales Lancers, Baker had three times tried to enlist but had been rejected because of a spinal injury. He organised fund-raising concerts, and took an active part in the recruiting movement, particularly the Sportsmen's Battalion. With a manager anxious to press his duty on him, with prominent citizens urging him to give a lead, Darcy was under considerable pressure. Apparently the patriots unnerved him. On his twenty-first birthday, which coincidentally was also the eve of the first conscription referendum, Darcy absconded to America illegally, without a passport. He went, or so he wrote to 'Snowy' Baker, because he saw 'a chance of settling my family on their feet for the rest of their lives ... the British Army wouldn't miss me for a few months'.[20]

The newspapers immediately vilified Darcy as a traitor, only the Sydney *Sportsman* daring to suggest that he be given a fair trial under the law rather than being singled out for special treatment. It was Darcy's fate never to undergo that trial and, unable to secure fights in America, he died, some said, of pneumonia, others said, of a broken heart. In death he became a symbol of the class conflict generated in Australia under the pressure of war. His body was returned to Maitland and its reception in Sydney and progress home became the occasions of demonstrations by those who had assisted in the defeat of conscription but who felt, nevertheless, alienated by the middle-class patriots. In his funeral oration Father Coady, a friend, showed how deep those divisions were when he contended that Darcy 'was a martyr to truth. His life was offered as a holocaust on the altar of prejudice, of jealousy and of avarice'.[21]

In this heightened, passionate atmosphere the opponents of sport now believed that exhortations and editorials would not succeed in putting down sport and calls for government restrictions became increasingly common.

Various Win-the-War Leagues and other patriotic bodies forwarded resolutions to the federal government such as this from Ballina: 'That as attendance at Race Meetings and Stadiums is detrimental to the Recruiting movement which should enlist the serious attention of the manhood of the Commonwealth the Defence Authorities be petitioned to close such meetings during the continuance of the War'. A brief reply from the Prime Minister's department claimed that 'it is not considered that the prohibition of the [sporting fixtures] referred to would be followed by any beneficial effect on recruiting'. Gradually this belief changed, probably because so many organisations and individuals argued the contrary position and also because the recruiting situation became increasingly desperate. A Sydney citizen somewhat implausibly suggested that if bars, race-courses and stadiums were closed, 10,000 policemen would be available immediately for service in France and that as the police were popular with youth, each would attract four or five boys to go with him, the addition to the AIF being, therefore, 60,000 men! In Adelaide, where all forms of spectator sport except horse-racing had been abandoned, a clergyman insisted that racing be closed too because the 'continuance of [horse-racing] is attracting large numbers of youths and others, who otherwise would be at the ovals and engaged in manly exercises ...' A member of the Tasmanian Legislative Council suggested that no man be admitted to a race-course, theatre or cinema unless he was in uniform or 'wearing a badge denoting that he is exempt from military or naval service'. Many of these extreme suggestions arose from the frustrations caused by the defeat of conscription but many, too, relied on a real contempt for the sporting community. A clergyman summarised feelings when he wrote of the cold-footed slackers at the Stadiums and racecourses': 'They are selfish, soulless degenerates, who were not fit to blacken the boots of the brave men in the trenches.'[22]

Prime Minister Hughes, believing he needed to placate this section of public opinion during the May 1917 federal election campaign, announced that his government would introduce controls on sport. When parliament reassembled in July after Hughes's resounding victory, the governor-general declared that: 'My advisers consider that action should be taken to curtail sport meetings throughout the Commonwealth, in order to concentrate the minds of the people on the more serious aspect of the war'. The government then waited until September before taking action so that football in Sydney and Melbourne emerged unscathed: what government would have dared to prohibit football finals in Melbourne, especially as in 1917 the VFL had returned to near full strength? The provisions against sport specified restrictions on horse-racing and boxing with more general powers to be used if required. Only one boxing contest was permitted in each state per fortnight and racing was severely limited with week-day racing almost totally eliminated. Editorialists in the metropolitan newspapers welcomed the restrictions. The *Sydney Morning Herald* rejoiced in the moves against boxing, a sport it believed 'serve[d] no useful purpose at any time', highlighting the middle-class view that sport must have some justification beyond itself. The writer complained of the 'love of sport and ease and luxury' that was 'laying deadly hold' of Australians and 'sapping the national character'. His hope that Australians would think 'less of sport in future and more of the serious things of life' showed that some hoped that the restrictions would endure beyond the war.[23]

As with other wartime victories against the recreations of the common man – the early closing of hotels and the moves against gambling – the restriction of sport, once introduced, was seen to have a general benefit beyond assisting the war effort. Temperance workers had argued for years that alcohol destroyed home life and led to crime. Working on heightened wartime emotions they persuaded governments and people to limit access to hotels and then suggested that the reform had been so beneficial that it should remain in force after the war. Because their campaigns had always been conducted with maximum publicity the community was in no doubt about their hatred of alcohol. Few Australians, however, had dared, before the war, to challenge the supremacy of sport. Only under war's extraordinary stress did the disquiet about the Australian emphasis on sport emerge. Some reformers hoped that sport would not regain its predominant place after the war.

Apart from demonstrating the antagonisms which some Australians directed towards the dominance of sport in society and the heightened patriotism of some, the restrictions on sport seemed to have had little other effect. Certainly their introduction did not lead to an increase in the number of recruits, indeed numbers continued to decline throughout 1917 and 1918. Paradoxically, boxing, which had suffered a slump following the departure of Darcy to America, now experienced another boom. Instead of leaving the Stadium in darkness on 'non-boxing nights', the promoters offered a vaudeville programme with a few rounds of boxing thrown in as part of the entertainment. Boxing was no longer sport but theatre. Possibly Captain Gallagher and Co. ('sharpshooters extraordinary') and Little Edith ('the child wonder shot') and Ford and Perrin ('expert dancers and comedians') were somewhat startled to find themselves performing in a boxing ring, but they proved enormously popular. The youths and other alleged eligibles who had flocked to sport at the Stadium were as much captivated by vaudeville. Many of the devotees of sport regarded it as a form of entertainment and freely changed their allegiance when circumstances required. Presumably now the patriots should have moved against the theatre and indeed any entertainment that distracted Australians from the 'serious aspect of the war'.[24]

The victims of the restrictions on sport quickly alleged class bias in the implementation of the government's decree. John Wren, the Melbourne sports entrepreneur, operated pony tracks in Brisbane and Melbourne which attracted an almost exclusively working-class clientele. Wren alleged that, although Brisbane racing as a whole was to be reduced by half, the State Commandant had allotted one of his courses, Kedron Park, six meetings in place of the scheduled fifty-six, while his other course, Goodna, had been closed altogether. Wren asked how owners and trainers could possibly make money on six meetings in the eight months to July 1918. Wren showed that the Queensland Turf Club, with a more middle-class appeal, had twenty-four meetings reduced to eighteen: hardly, he suggested, an equal sacrifice. An employee at one of Wren's Melbourne tracks supported the allegations of class bias: 'We that have permitted our flesh and blood to enter the battle resent the mouthings and feel the sting of the propagandists, leisured and dimpled who offer and suggest prohibition in regard to all things, but those directly affecting themselves'. The harsh treatment Wren received derived in part, at least, from the fact that the pony tracks operated frequently on week-days, but also because Wren prominently supported Archbishop Mannix, whose 'sordid trade war' jibe had infuriated the patriots and whose opposition to conscription was quite notorious.[25]

Wren found an unlikely ally in the former Liberal premier of New South Wales, Sir Joseph Carruthers, who warned his federal colleagues that the government's interference with sport had increased working-class antipathy and had harmed the recruiting movement. Carruthers alleged that 'the keen resentment felt . . . caused many people to cool down on their [recruiting] efforts'. As senior vice-president of the National Association in New South Wales, Carruthers felt he must also enumerate the political risks involved in interfering with sport:

> we have the liquor trade against us; we have also the Irish Catholics with few exceptions; we have the trade unions, very largely; and we are making bitter enemies of the Sporting Fraternity except for a favoured few.
>
> This latter class is more numerous than you imagine. Moreover it includes tens of thousands who are just as loyal as you or I.

It was this last point that the 'parsons, politicians and newspaper proprietors' refused to concede. The patriots' view of loyalty demanded that a man be so totally involved in the Empire's cause as to forego all other concerns. The restrictions on sport remained in force until the end of the war although there were no moves against the 1918 football seasons in either Sydney or Melbourne. Perhaps by April 1918 the government had come to appreciate the force of Carruthers's remarks and had also realised that the restrictions made no difference to recruitment.[26]

The various sporting bodies tried valiantly to prove their loyalty by publicising the number of men to enlist from their ranks. Like the churches or schools which indulged in this detailed record-keeping, the idea seemed to be that a man enlisted because he had imbued the patriotic spirit by associating with the church, school or club. The Victorian Cricket Association boasted

A recruiting meeting in Collins Street, Melbourne

that 2,854 of its players were in the AIF and the South Melbourne Football Club listed twelve regular players, eight former players and between 700 and 800 members who had enlisted; every other club or association could produce impressive figures. And yet, despite these lists, so long as any sportsmen continued to play their games, the myth remained that sportsmen as a whole had failed to do their duty. For this reason the recruiters directed specific appeals to sportsmen. In particular it became popular to recruit 'sportsmen's units' in which the incentive was to 'train together, play together and fight together'. Indeed, in New South Wales, a group of patriots formed the Sportsmen's Recruiting Committee, which was aimed directly at 'sports'. Surely there was confusion here; on the one hand damning sport as a check on recruiting and on the other appealing to the noble instincts sport had taught. Typical of the appeals used was that of Mrs Valentine A. Spence, who pleaded at a Sportsmen's Rally:

> A nation of sportsmen. We must all be sportsmen now for the sake of our future sport, and for the sake of the men. All are sportsmen, in the truest

sense of the word, who have made the great sacrifice that the freedom of the world may be maintained ... The rallying cry is ... 'Be a Sportsman'. No man who, being fit and able to serve his country, remains at home sheltering behind the heroism of his fellow men, has any right to claim the title which, more than any other, the Briton is proud of. This is the crucial test of sporting instincts.[27]

Apparently recruiters believed that the sportsmen's units attracted particular prestige and they utilised all sorts of novelties. Sporting heroes addressed crowds during breaks at matches and returned men marched through the suburbs in their sports' uniforms. In retrospect the campaign seems like one more gimmick in a recruiting drive which, as the years wore on, became increasingly gimmicky. The effort often far outweighed the result. A Recruiting Football Match held at the Sydney Showground in August 1917 secured only seven recruits and the organiser reported: 'I consider the match failed because the audience was antagonistic to recruiting and expressed itself so by counting out the Speakers'. Of course the match coincided with the great strike in New South Wales and increasing class bitterness.[28]

Many people, particularly recruiters and journalists, also used sporting analogies to make sense of the war to the apparently sports-mad Australian; it seemed as if some believed that Australians would understand the issues only if they were presented in the language of sport. Sporting terminology in fact helped to familiarise the people with the war but also to trivialise it. The *Sportsman*, lamenting the deaths of two former Rugby League footballers, announced that they had 'heard the final whistle' and then, congratulating six other footballer recruits, hoped that they might 'miss the ball every time it is passed to them, in this new game they are tackling'. Even Les Darcy's enlistment problems could be explained by recourse to sporting terms: 'Les will probably join in the sterner fight', a journalist wrote in the *Soldier* in 1916, 'where the gloves are off and there is no call to corners'.[29]

Such attempts to explain the war in 'the language of the people' assumed that sport dominated the lives of most Australians. Those who made these assumptions seem to have overestimated the grip of sport; for many sport was merely a form of entertainment and a pleasant way to escape the urban work situation. It was not a fixation with sport that brought about the indifference to the war of which the middle-class complained. Their simple remedy to this indifference of denying the sports' lover his weekly offering had to fail. The decision to enlist was not as simple or straightforward as some of the patriots seemed to believe.

CHAPTER SIX

FROM HERO TO CRIMINAL: THE AIF IN BRITAIN 1915–19

In seeking to recall the experiences of the Australian people during the war it would be absurd to leave out of account the story of the 330,000 men who served with the Australian Imperial Forces abroad. Of course their exploits as soldiers have been fully and fondly recorded in the *Official History of Australia in the War of 1914–18* and more informally in the numerous battalion histories and personal narratives. But no soldier, and particularly no Australian soldier, is a fighter full-time; he has protracted periods of leave and of training during which he can assess the society in which he finds himself.

Most Australians spent several months in training camps in southern England. Camp life gave them a chance to explore Britain in a physical and social sense. They continued these explorations when on leave from France. A significant number of Australian soldiers were British-born – as high as one in four of recruits to June 1915. Many of these men had relatives and friends to visit, although their attestation papers do not indicate how long each had lived in Australia. Doubtless their experiences differed from those of their Australian-born mates. There was an important sense, however, in which the Australians were 'tourists' and their experiences in themselves are informative and entertaining. Australian schoolchildren were inculcated with the importance of Empire and imperial achievements. Soldiers arriving in Britain for the first time confirmed how deeply that teaching had penetrated. They showed a special love and reverence for a land many of them regarded as 'Home'. But they learned too, what a difference there was between Britain and Australia and they came to understand and to value more highly conditions and social relations in Australia. They learned, in fact, that Britain was not 'Home'. In travelling, they had discovered themselves and Australia.

Members of the AIF were mighty letter-writers and diarists, eager to share their discoveries with the people at home. With that reticence others have commented on, they wrote little about battles and blunders at the front but when at rest they wrote of the people they met and the sights they saw. Fortunately, many of these observations are preserved in a superb collection

A general view of the Australian Base Post Office, London, showing the redirection of 750,000 letters from Australia. Such a mail was usually sorted in eight to ten days

at the Australian War Memorial in Canberra. The collection gives an insight to the reporting that many Australians received as a matter of course: those at home might not have believed their newspapers but they would accept without question what a husband, son or brother wrote. Many Australian perceptions about the war and the wider world beyond Australia were shaped by these letter-writers whose digest of news and views had a much wider readership than the loved one named at the top of the page: letters were proudly passed around so that all might share in the real 'news'.

From March 1916 onwards Australians were arriving in Britain with very high expectations of the land they had been taught to love. Gradually they learned how different Britain was from Australia and they grew increasingly uncomfortable. On the other hand, their hosts who had welcomed them as heroes at first began to tire of Australian colonial ways and became anxious to see the men repatriated. As reinforcements arrived in Britain even as late as 1918 there were some just as naïvely excited as the first wave had been in 1916. But much of the edge was taken off this excitement by the old hands.

Most of the Australians who enlisted after 1915 travelled directly from Australia to Britain, a lengthy voyage taking up to sixteen weeks, in tedious and uncomfortable circumstances. Their eagerness for landfall is understandable but to it they added a special excitement at the prospect of seeing Britain, a land so many of them had been taught to respect and even to love. Invariably, their approach became more dramatic when fast-moving destroyers picked up the convoys a few days before landfall to protect them from German submarines. Nurtured on tales of Britain's greatness, now enlisted to fight on Britain's behalf, escorted by the mightiest navy in the world, the men crammed the decks to catch the first glimpse of 'Home'. Norman Hale, writing to Australia in September 1916, expressed what many of the men felt:

> My first sight of England I shall never forget ... England's shores could be dimly discerned thro' the haze and it was sometime before I fully realized that I was actually going to land in the 'old country'. To a British Colonial it has a mysterious attraction, and as a boy at school I always felt that I would like to see England. There we read of England and her many wars and now today when she is in the midst of a critical struggle my wish is fulfilled.

They had been prepared, imaginatively, by years of schooling and private reading, to invest this moment with a sense of mystery and awe. G. H. J. Davies noted how 'green everything looked, how beautiful the trees were'. The little fishing villages along the Devonshire coast drew comment as 'the homes of England's bravest sons', the sailor lads who had won renown in days gone by. Occasionally a dock-side welcome put the final touch on these emotions. A. A. Cameron asked his wife to apologise to her father on his behalf for ever having dared belittle England from his Australian ignorance. As his troopship drew alongside the wharf a band played 'Land of Hope and Glory' and he thought he understood what it all meant.[1]

From the troopships the men 'entrained' for one of the many camps, usually on the Salisbury Plains, an excellent opportunity to observe rural England. Significantly, they recorded what they saw in the language their schoolbooks had used, as if that language alone was appropriate in expressing the emotions aroused. They remarked upon 'the quaint old houses, rich and beautiful farms with all and every tint of verdure'. A. E. C. Bray recorded that just the fact of being in England 'filled [him] to the brim with excitement'. For those who passed through Exeter there was a cup of hot coffee and a bun provided by women of the town which made the Australians feel wanted and welcome, adding to earlier emotions. The camps themselves rarely moved the men to much enthusiasm but they quickly reconnoitred the surrounding countryside, marvelling that the picture books and school papers had accurately described that countryside. Peter Callinan wrote of a 'typical old English village': 'narrow streets, old fashioned shops and houses, thatched roofs etc. and all the accessories we are familiar with in song and story'. Such immersion in a world once familiar in childhood caused many of the men to

England's 'storied temples'? Australian soldiers inspecting Salisbury Cathedral, July 1917

think deeply. E. J. Martin noted how 'the novelty of the surroundings [and] the sub-conscious whisper of heredity' kept in check 'the cheap vulgarity which is inevitably associated with the congregation of soldiers and members of Parliament'. Another, returning from the 'Plume and Feathers' along one of England's fabled green lanes, using borrowed language surely, described himself as 'full of happiness and thoroughly enjoying the mystic gloaming of a pleasant evening'.[2]

Of course, those who arrived in mid-winter gained a different impression complaining of 'the coldest [weather] most of the men had ever experienced', aggravated, no doubt, by the recent days spent in the tropics. C. H. Thorp wrote of waiting for their special train: 'we will not easily forget those two hours during which we perished with the intensely cold wind on that wharf at Plymouth'. T. Darchy, while admiring 'Ye Olden Village' with its many quaint delights, expressed surprise that the people had 'gone to so much trouble with this country. It has such a vile climate'. Malcolm Greig reported that the cold really depressed the men who were 'cursing England and saying they would never have enlisted if they had known this was the place they were coming to. If this is Merrie England then the less we see of it the better'. Doubtless such comments stimulated the fervour of those knitting at home but what are we to make of the indifference of W. D. Baldie quartered at Cambridge, who acknowledged the 'old air about the place' but complained that for 'all the history that its got ... its not comfortable or nice'.³

These were rare grumbles, however. Most of the men formed very favourable first impressions expressing amazement and delight that they had reached the land of their dreams: 'who would have thought that I would ever get so far round the world 2 years ago', was a typical comment. F. J. Brewer, attending a service in Salisbury Cathedral, let his thoughts wander along 'the realization of an ambition I had entertained and cherished from my earliest years – to wander through the storied temples of old England. I had accomplished it'. Where, we might ask, had he learned the stilted 'storied temples': from a school text? In some cases these first impressions were so overpowering as to impair the writer's affection for Australia, as A. A. Cameron demonstrated writing to his wife: 'We boast of Australia Liz but this is the land love ours is not in it'. Such enthusiasm proved short lived in most cases.⁴

When the Australians arrived in England they were welcomed as heroes because of the great reputation they had won at Gallipoli. Indeed the arrival of the main body of the troops by April 1916 enabled the Australian High Commission to plan an elaborate commemoration of 'Anzac Day'. On 25 April there would be a march of Australian troops through London and a service at Westminster Abbey attended by the King and Queen. No other body of troops, British, Colonial or Allied, was to be so honoured during the war. Pro-Australian propaganda prepared Londoners for the event: newspapers retold stories of the heroism and stoicism of the Anzacs. *London Opinion*, for example, told of the young lad from the western district of Victoria who, when he realised that his leg had been amputated, remarked 'Ah well, only one leg to be pulled now'. The newspapers exhorted Londoners to turn out in force to give the Anzacs a hero's welcome and asked women to bring flowers to throw at the troops: 'After all, we do feel deeply our gratitude and love for these brave sons of proud mothers across the seas. Why should we not let them see how we feel?'⁵

The reception of the troops rewarded these thorough preparations. So great was the crush of the crowds which lined the route that the Anzacs were unable to march in formation but walked in groups, acknowledging the affection and applause. This suited the mood of the day which was commemorative, not militaristic; the Australians carried no arms. The newspapers exulted in the Australians: 'Finer soldiers, men more resolute in their bearing have surely never been seen'. Grim and stern at the outset, they responded to the crowd's calls of 'Cooee' as they swung out of the Strand and laughed as they caught the posies girls threw at them: 'they were human, these gaunt magnificent spectres, after all!' *The Times* reported that the crowds were the largest seen in London since the King's coronation; two-thirds of them were women. At the Abbey 2,000 Australians gave full voice to the hymn 'For all the Saints who from their labours rest', bringing tears to the eyes of many observers. This reception at the heart of the Empire deeply impressed the Australian troops who hastened to report home how grateful the Empire was. The Australians at home, in their turn, basked in the reflected glory when they read accounts such as this:

> We were given the most magnificent reception from the population of London, who turned up in one vast crowd, and threw flowers and cigarettes and all that sort of thing at us and cheered themselves hoarse at us, and, in fact, we felt rather swelled headed at the way we were treated, and the way people shook us by the hand and women embraced us and all that rot, and attempted to cry 'coo-ee' and some very wonderful noises these attempts developed into ...[6]

Anzac Day, London, 1916

Despite the general approval and acclamation there were some voices of protest suggesting that the whole event, organised by the Australian High Commission, smacked of colonial swagger. *John Bull* presumed to speak for the relatives and friends of the men of Britain's 29th Division who had fought with honour at Gallipoli doing 'the work of demigods at the great landing'. It was only fair 'that they should have been represented in the recent grand parade on Anzac Day, and that the great ceremony should not have been confined to Colonial troops'. A survivor from the 29th Division contended, in a letter to *The Times,* that there were 'more British troops engaged [at the Landing] and their casualties were three times as heavy'. From the outset the Australians showed an insensitivity, at least, to the feelings of their hosts and a tendency to elevate their achievements far beyond those of other troops. From the High Commission's point of view the Australians deserved the acclaim of London, the more so because the Landing was seen as Australia's first test or 'baptism of fire', but such celebration was a sign, too, of Australian innocence, even immaturity.[7]

Soon after the London celebration the Australians were in the news again, this time in France at the Battle of Pozières from 19 July to 7 August 1916. Again sections of the press complained that the Australians attracted too much attention. *John Bull* 'groused' that 'official reporters at headquarters harp all the time on the Anzac string and say as little as possible about the remnants of the Old Army, the Terriers and the Derbyites'. Certainly the Australians received much praise. Philip Gibbs, one of the leading war correspondents, writing in the *Daily Telegraph,* claimed that not even the German machine-gunners could stop 'this tide of keen, ardent men, these clean-shaven, hatchet-faced lads who have brought a new type of manhood to France'. They deserved, he concluded, 'all the praise that can be given to them'. H. J. Greenwall, in the *Daily Express,* described how they repelled a German counter-attack with 'magnificent heroism': 'Like the Spartans of old, they never flinched beneath a hell storm of steel and fire, and never once ceded an inch of ground'. Lord Northcliffe visited them in France and reported that 'There is hardly one of them who has not patriotism burnt into his soul and burnt into his body'. The propagandists apparently hoped that by highlighting the bravery and patriotism of the colonials who had come so far to help the Empire, they would arouse renewed enthusiasm in those whose interests were so much more directly threatened.[8]

The Anzacs were at first surprised and then grew increasingly resentful at the concentration on their 'exploits'. C. E. W. Bean wrote from France that the Australians did not welcome the exaggerated attention given to them by the British press: 'Wherever one goes in the trenches', he wrote, 'one finds both men and officers very sensitive on this point'. An Australian, writing to the *Morning Post* from 'somewhere in France', complained:

You can't imagine how fed up we all are with some of the English newspapers and their infernal soft-soapy 'Anzac' articles. The way they record our little aches and pains – a petty raid on the Boche trenches, padded up with such rot as 'These giant athletes leaping the trenches' makes one sick.

But the constant propaganda ensured a warm welcome for the Australian soldier anywhere in Britain. They were easily recognised, being celebrated as much by press photographers as by reporters. For example, the *Daily Mirror* published a picture of an artillery crew under the caption 'Anzacs Never Wear Any Superfluous Clothing' for in the French summer they disposed of almost all their clothes except the famous slouch hats by which they were universally identified.[9]

So vividly did they capture public attention during Pozières that even the arrival of Australian wounded in London, a city well used to the constant stream of wounded at its railway stations, became the occasion of another celebration of Australian heroism. Again the *Daily Telegraph* led the way: 'the Australians are not ordinary fighters. They seem to be super-soldiers, who just go and do things and never talk … The Anzacs would face a wall of iron and go through it into the bargain'. To celebrate, again, Anzac heroism, sixty Australians received special leave to visit London and in June 1916

The Anzac in advertising

Dear Old Silly. "AND WHERE DO YOU TWO COME FROM?"
Wounded Australian. "WE'RE ANZACS, MADAM."
Dear Old Silly. "REALLY? HOW DELIGHTFUL! AND DO YOU BOTH BELONG TO THE SAME TRIBE?"

One view of the Anzacs. *Punch*, 10 May 1916

were driven through the city to receive the people's applause. Again this was a unique celebration, the only occasion when fit men were feted for their performance in a battle. The papers recreated the appropriate atmosphere, emphasising the 'huge-limbed, sunburnt Australians' and exhorting Londoners to give them a 'tremendous bush welcome'. The pictures, praise and celebrations bore fruit. The Australian became a special fighter in the minds of many, a peculiarly heroic figure, taller, stronger, fitter than his British comrades. This image began to appear in advertisements, perhaps the ultimate accolade of acceptance. The Anzac Motor Co. Ltd, specialists in GMC trucks, used a drawing of a particularly virile looking soldier in a slouch hat in its advertisements, with the slogan, 'Anzac Means Business'.[10]

No wonder, given all this propaganda, that the Australian found himself a very popular figure in England in 1916. The slouch hat quickly became his symbol and the Canadians, who adopted British uniform, learned to regret their lack of any identifying symbol to help them stand out from the general run of British soldiers. 'The Australian Hat does a lot', one soldier reported, 'because the fact of one being so far from home makes the people more interested perhaps'. But others professed to be able to spot Australians hatted or hatless; thus the bishop of Willesden, Dr Perrin, who, having explained that the Australian character was 'independent, democratic, easy-going' announced that 'Their very walk betrays their character'. The Australians delighted in the signs of a ready welcome. In small villages women and children emerged from their houses to stare and wave at them, as their trains passed through the towns people waved flags and cheered, the public seemed keen to listen to their stories, and seemed, too, remarkably gullible. Part of the attraction undoubtedly derived from the very favourable newspaper reports, but part of it derived from the fact that the Australians were a novelty. *Punch* exploited this aspect with cartoons full of 'dear old ladies' who had no idea of where Australia was or who the Australians were. The Australians enjoyed the notoriety and bragged in detail to their friends at home. One reported that while shopping 'the salesmen nearly fell over me in their eagerness to oblige and reduced their goods 2/6 because we had done so much for them'. Compatriots arriving in England after the *annus mirabilis* of 1916 would have had great difficulty in believing this report.[11]

Even at this early stage of ready and warm welcome, Australians were being identified not only by their heroism or their hats but by their capacity for making trouble. *John Bull* demanded that a sign 'No Australians are allowed in this camp' be removed from a British army post commenting

The Anzacs were easily identified. *Punch*, 2 February 1916

First Lady. "THAT'S ONE OF THEM AUSTRALIAN SOLDIERS."
Second Lady. "HOW DO YOU KNOW?"
First Lady. "WHY, CAN'T YOU SEE THE KANGAROO FEATHERS IN HIS HAT?"

that while it recognised the 'brave bushmen' were not exactly 'Cambridge Varsity Men' they were 'wonderful soldiers' and ought not be insulted. There were some tensions from the outset but at first these were subsumed by feelings of gratitude for men who had come so far to defend the Empire and by admiration for heroic Australian fighting qualities.[12]

While most Australians journeyed directly from the troopships to the training camps in the south of England the great ambition of all was to visit London, the city their teachers had always described as 'the heart of the Empire'. As C. A. L. Treadwell put it:

> Only a colonial can understand my feelings when the train arrived in London – London, the centre of the 'Home' we had heard of all our lives! It was our Mecca. London was the capital of the British Empire. London called up all the associations with the Crown. London housed the King for whom we had come to fight … It was clearer than any other place on earth. It has been the hope of generations of colonials – on many occasions gratified – to visit London. London, the throbbing heart of the Empire!

Most spent their first leave and much time subsequently in London so that the capital was swelled by an everchanging but large Australian population. Although the Australian Headquarters were in London, at Horseferry Road, Westminster, troops on leave were expected to look after themselves so that the Australians made all their own arrangements after an initial visit to headquarters for passes and money. Undoubtedly a large proportion of the AIF had lived in one of the Australian cities or towns, but the London press invariably described them as 'bushmen' and the Australians seemed stupefied, initially at least, by a city as large and as complex as London. T. E. Bradshaw, who, for the benefit of his readers, placed London '112 miles from Warminster' where he was billeted, was quite intimidated by the rush and bustle of it all: 'we were like country yokels at first until we sighted a Bobby who soon directed us to an exit', this to extricate themselves from the station on arrival! Many of the stations had 'moving stairways' as yet unheard of in Australia, and correspondents who wrote at length about them treated them cautiously. Typical of the reports is this from W. D. Gallwey:

> People were going down in hundreds and had no difficulty at all in getting on and off. I thought that if women could go down like that I could so stepped on to it. It was just like alighting from a tramcar while it was in motion. I swayed a bit but managed to retain my balance however the worst was to come yet for when it came to the descent I happened to be standing on the division between two steps and I very nearly went on my head. I clutched the rail but that was no good when I was moving so a girl standing near took me by the arm and told me when I got to the bottom to step off with the right foot. I stepped off with her and spun

A contemporary postcard

like a top. How she kept her balance is a mystery to me. An Escalator now is a nightmare to me.[13]

Intimidated thus at the start of leave, men joined together in small parties for protection and companionship. They diligently took in all the sights although one observer reported that they were more interested in the people than in the great buildings and monuments of history. They were by no means uncritical of what they saw. One reported that the Houses of Parliament 'wanted adjusting. Traces of the stones' original whiteness still show but it is mostly covered with soot and dirt'. Many others believed that London needed a thorough cleaning; 'Dirty and old with the queerest looking people in it' was a typical comment. Others could not resist comparing the sights with what they had known at home, perhaps for the benefit of their readers who would thereby have a better idea of things. A required landmark, St Paul's, failed to move one visitor: 'I stood under the dome and on looking up was only the more impressed by the size of the dome of the Melbourne Public Library, of which I was reminded'. Another declared that 'the Sydney G.P.O. clock is just as interesting as Big Ben to look at and I suppose just as accurate'. A third critic found little of interest in the British Museum: 'I cannot say a piece of broken stone with a plate on it saying it was someone's Venus is of much interest'. Moreover 'if there [is] more than one statue of the same man they are quite different so they are not much in the way of artists'. Many found real art in the theatres which abounded and thrived during the war. Almost every diarist and letter-writer saw Oscar Asche in 'Chu Chin Chow', a musical extravaganza based on the pantomime 'Ali Baba and the Forty Thieves', which opened at His Majesty's theatre in August 1916; the 'Zig Zag Review' was also very popular.[14]

Homesickness and loneliness accounted for many of the criticisms and the excessive enthusiasm for the theatre. Despite its size, London struck them as a friendless place. One writer contrasted the loneliness of London to that of the Australian bush: 'In the bush at least you are familiar with everything about you ... in London everything is strange and new ... [and so] the lonesome Australian is standing on the kerb wondering how he is going to spend the twelve hours which separate him from another day of visiting famous buildings and other unattractive things'. Another described it as a city which 'seemed to crush in its greatness' in which one was too rushed to have time to stop and think. Many Australians were bored which explains the tendency to congregate at Nelson's Column, aimlessly watching the passing throng. The majority had no relatives or friends whom they might visit where home cooking and home comforts might revive men too used to the taste of food cooked for the mess. The search for relatives became a hobby, although one with a serious purpose. Some men arrived equipped with lists of names or localities where relatives might be found, others placed notices in newspapers, while others again combed telephone directories looking for

Australians in London – where are the pigeons?

likely names. One inventive soldier advertised regularly in a matrimonial paper, seeking to acquire a whole set of relatives at once. He sought a 'Young Lady up to 23 years of age, widow preferred, one child not objected ... to go back to Australia after the war ...' Another discovered the family name in plenty in the telephone directory and wrote home for further particulars about his grandfather: 'I may find some *rich* relations, a good number live in the West end, and one in a *big* Club at Westminster'. He visited two of the places on his list but without luck.[15]

Despite this loneliness many Australians returned to London when other leave accrued, although they visited other parts of the British Isles, too. On longer leaves a man might spend a few days each in Edinburgh or Glasgow, perhaps make a brief trip to Ireland, but invariably most were drawn back to London for part of each leave, at least. Undoubtedly many felt more at ease with closer acquaintance. As Boyce reported on his fourth trip: 'I'm beginning to feel quite at home in London. I know my way about it so well now'. But in many cases, by this time London seemed so attractive simply because it was not France. As A. A. Barwick wrote: 'you have no idea of the relief it is to us to be among such beautiful and lovely sights, such a contrast to the torn and battered battlefields'. And another Australian agreed: 'Once back in London one feels that one has never left it so completely does it banish France from the mind'. These men continued the explorations they had begun on their first leave, visiting the churches, public buildings and museums of fame, making a second or third call at Madame Tussaud's waxworks and revisiting the theatres and pubs. Glad to be back after the horrors of warfare and now well used to English ways they sent back much more favourable reports to their Australian readers. Now time seemed too short, as one tourist announced: 'I could do a month there, sightseeing etc., if I had the necessary'. Some remained unashamedly overawed by it all: 'Everything was an eye-opener to me and freely I will admit it'.[16]

One aspect of London life caused the Anzacs considerable alarm, more so than the traffic, the crowds or the size of the city; they were amazed at the extent and scope of female labour. The letter-writers disapproved of working women. Their initial patronising attitude may have changed to respect for the achievements of women, but they nevertheless regretted that the war had forced such measures on society. Their reaction is testimony to the extent of the Australian sentiment that women should not accept paid employment. Part of the reason for this was the belief that women could not succeed at even simple tasks. Thus, one correspondent admitted that he 'was much amused at the women porters' on the railway stations while another conceded that the women on the buses seemed to be efficient, indeed 'they never failed to collect a fare'. This patronising note remained even when the Australians came to understand that women could be efficient and that work did not necessarily corrupt them. All this is neatly captured in a letter from W. D. Gallwey.

A tram driver and conductor in Scotland – such sights unnerved the Australians

> To my dismay a charming young lady dressed in a smart looking uniform came from carriage to carriage collecting our tickets. Such pretty and fascinating ladies to be doing this kind of work I never expected to see. I just felt like squeezing her hand when she took my ticket. Afterwards I saw ladies dressed in overalls cleaning engines. Some of them have very hard work to do and I take pity on them. I thought that these girls coming in contact and working with men would become bold but no they are quite the opposite. They keep themselves as ladies should and do not converse with everybody they meet.

While conceding these points almost every Australian remained adamant that Australian women must never be forced out to work. In this, as in many other aspects of their London experience, the Australians learned to be tolerant of a society with different standards and values, but it also reinforced their belief that Australian ways were superior and must endure. The people in Australia to whom these letters were addressed doubtless shared the vicarious thrills of being in London, 'it is simply stupendous, marvellous, and amazing, and other words that I can't think of at present', but they enjoyed too the comparisons and criticisms of London which showed that Australian life was unsurpassed. The letters, on the whole, reinforced Australian patriotism and the determination that what was best must not be changed.[17]

One aspect of a soldier's life on leave that he rarely wrote home about concerned his relations with women. However, enough correspondents discussed the behaviour of their fellows to allow some comments to be made. The Australians undoubtedly suffered from a lack of female companionship and many saw their leave in England as a chance to meet women and to resume as normal a life as possible. Far from home, with no prospect of return until serious injury or peace should intervene, trying to remain faithful to wives or girlfriends, strangers in a new land and often lonely, the Australians had to balance their need for female companionship against their duties to the army and to their friends and families at home.

Hospital provided the best opportunity for meeting English women and the speed of hospital romances was astonishing. One Australian, reporting a very restless night, wrote that he 'did not mind this for the night nurse and I are great pals and she comes and sits on my bed and yarns for an hour at a stretch'. N. G. Ellsworth observed that the nurses gave patients 'very broad hints' that they would like to be taken out and that 'a certain amount of jealousy exists between the Nurses on this account'. Other Australians met girls more casually. A wounded man noted how well the girls on the buses cared for him, '[I] am getting to know one of them on the Charing X run'. Even on picket duty patrolling the village pubs, soldiers found that they could strike up friendships with girls asking questions about Australia and the war: 'not a few friendship sprang up in this way'. Obviously, too, the Australians became adept at finding those places where girls congregated. Barwick reported that an ice-skating rink provided a good opportunity: 'there [were] plenty of girls here and we had a fine time with them'. Half the pleasure, at least, of many of these chance encounters was the opportunity of being taken to the girl's home to enjoy home cooking and the relaxation of family life, of meeting, seriously, English people at home. The Australians were lonely and genuinely wanted to make friends. Very often after a visit to an English home the Australian would write to his parents suggesting that they write to his new friends, thanking them for their kindness and saying how much their son enjoyed the visit. As these visits were so highly prized it was important that the Australian maintained a respectable reputation so that no girl need hesitate before accepting an Australian's friendship or admitting to her father that she was 'walking out' with one.[18]

Unfortunately, the Australians' reputation with women deteriorated rapidly and largely accounts for the overall rejection of the 1916 image of the Australian as hero. These new perceptions became increasingly common from 1917 onwards although, of course, the brash, confident ways of the Australians had offended some from the first. The *British-Australasian* mentioned, with concern, the case of a hotel proprietor who refused accommodation to an Australian in uniform, as early as March 1916. The heroic image overcame these tensions at first, but as it wore off, complaints increased. Comments such as 'Met Milly and friend at Trafalgar

Square. Got bus to Hampstead Heath. Fine place for a spoon. Left there late and had a rush back', indicate how simple the pleasures could be. Notoriety fed on different stories.[19]

Prostitution grew enormously in wartime London. The Home Office could not assess how many new prostitutes took up the trade during the war because so many of them were 'amateurs': 'many young women not formerly known to the police as prostitutes have been led to adopt this mode of life, or at any rate to be guilty of immoral conduct with soldiers'. While the women themselves received much of the blame, a magistrate of the Westminster Police Court identified the high wages prostitutes earned, 'notably from the Colonial soldiers who are often in possession of considerable sums of money', as an important factor explaining the increase. The Australians, not surprisingly, blamed the girls and many correspondents viewed the situation with alarm and disgust, again reinforcing their readers' regard for Australia where such conditions were unknown.[20]

The YMCA tried – but the Strand was a notorious place for prostitutes

W. D. Gallwey, an 18-year-old, sent lurid descriptions home of the difficulty he experienced in shaking off prostitutes. He claimed to have been propositioned on buses, in theatres and restaurants, as well as on street corners. At the pictures a girl offered herself to him for 10s and when he rejected her, she pleaded with him because the woman she worked for insisted that she bring an Australian home every night. Waiting for a bus in London after the theatre, Gallwey and his mate were pestered by prostitutes, 'one of [whom] had the audacity to put her hands on my face and stroke my cheeks'. On another occasion a fashionably dressed lady sat beside him in a restaurant:

> By her manner I could tell at once what she was. She ordered champagne for two and offered me a cigarette. I declined both so she had to smoke on her own. She seemed surprised at me and asked me if I was an Australian … I did not wait any longer but walked out and left her to any other Australian who might be looking for something in her line of business.

Gallwey's impressions may be exaggerated, deriving from his naïve and complacent views, but they give some idea of the extent of prostitution in London. Things were not much better in the provinces. At Weymouth and Salisbury, the centres of the biggest concentrations of Australians in England, police waged a constant battle against prostitutes and brothel-keepers. Newspaper reports of the court cases often singled Australians out as prominent patrons of these houses, damaging their reputation and inflaming opinion against them. So intensely did respectable people feel about prostitution that in Salisbury in 1918 a crowd gathered to hoot the owners and inhabitants of a brothel. There was pressure, too, to change the law which penalised the girls but took no notice of the patrons. The Australians continued to blame the women and some became suspicious of any advances from women. One correspondent reported that when a woman and her two daughters stopped him in the street to ask questions about Australia, he suspected at first that they might proposition him. One result of the prevalence and notoriety of prostitution in England was to lead Australians to think piously of the women they had left behind and of how innocent they were. In many ways Australians developed greater respect for their own women by comparing them with English women subject to wartime stresses and demands. Indeed, many Australian men began to idealise the women they had left at home.[21]

Given the extent of prostitution, it is hardly surprising that some of the troops contracted a venereal disease, despite the fact that, because of the loss of efficiency involved and because of the effect on morale at home, the AIF did try to encourage the men to take precautions. A correspondent reported that 'We got a great deal of advice from our officers and all over the walls of our huts are printed placards warning us of certain danger'. Such measures failed and by the end of 1917 the same man explained that 'Before we leave camp to go on furlough every man is given a certain outfit and is furnished with the addresses of certain houses of ill-fame. These houses are looked after by the military authorities and kept for the troops. There is less risk by going to these places'. If the 'certain outfit' was a prophylactic, known to the troops as 'dreadnoughts', then in providing them the AIF was ignoring the explicit instruction of the Army Council which had determined that they should not be issued to troops. Had the existence of the AIF brothels been revealed in Australia there would certainly have been an outcry. The risks involved in adopting both these measures show how concerned were the AIF and the Australian government to combat venereal disease. The attempts to introduce marriage by proxy were further evidence of this concern. The figures showed why. An army report stated that while the general British and colonial admission rate for venereal disease to June 1917 was thirty-four per 1,000 per year, the Australian and New Zealand figures were 144 and 134.2 respectively. Officials blamed these extraordinary figures on the high rates of pay, the absence of wives and families and the innocence of troops, unfamiliar with big cities. While reformers proposed draconian measures such as prohibiting colonials from entering hotels or imprisoning infected women for six months, the Imperial Conference which debated the problem at length found that there was no satisfactory solution.[22]

The problem aroused great concern in Australia, to the extent that it may have caused parents to withhold the consent potential recruits needed. Reference to these dangers in newspapers and in letters increased anxieties in Australia. How comforted can a wife have been whose husband wrote: 'I am glad I am going to Scotland [to visit relatives]... as if I went with some of them I would be uncomfortable if I didn't do as they did'. And what of the unfortunate soldier who somehow posted his mother's letter in an envelope designed for a different purpose:

> what you say about the French letter was an awful shock to me. I can only say I've never had anything to do with them or anything else of that sort and hope you will believe me. I may have borrowed the envelope with it in, anyway there were no doubt a lot of them about as we were just going on leave and the authorities make them available, to prevent Venereal Disease.

The effect of all this was to trouble those who waited at home in Australia and to create concern about Australians in the minds of many of their hosts.[23]

Because the Australians were mixing freely with English girls for an extended period, it is not surprising that there were frequent marriages. Indeed, many members of the AIF suspected that British girls were particularly eager to marry Australians, understandably as they believed, because the Australians were heroes, apparently wealthy, and physically superior to the British: 'the average Tommy', an Australian explained, 'is a miserable looking affair on the whole, and I don't wonder that the girls prefer our lads to them'. Indeed, so highly did they rate their attractiveness that something akin to fear crept into the Australian correspondence: 'I am not safe yet however for the girls are desperate. They are doing their utmost to get a Colonial before they all go home'. Others were less concerned, one soldier noting that 'it's really very funny how the girls are bestowing their affection on [us]' and while the joke was not appreciated in Australia it must be admitted that many Australians were 'highly susceptible'. They were, after all, many of them, single, of marriageable age, with little prospect of an early return to Australia. As one writer explained:

> You ruminate on this peculiar feeling of isolation which is gradually overtaking you, and after due consideration you find that it is sympathy that you most desire – the sympathy of a pair of soft arms around your neck and an understanding little soul to whom you can pour out all your troubles and doubts. This, you decide then, is the reason why so many Australians marry English girls.

Some of these marriages were hasty affairs as, for example, the case of the Australian who married his Dorset nurse whom he had known for only six weeks. Another girl married an Australian of only six hours acquaintance and she cannot have been encouraged by the telegram awaiting her when her ship berthed at Melbourne, informing her that he would meet her on the steps of the Sydney General Post Office. The *British-Australasian* lamented that 'By no means [have] all the men who have married here ... married wisely'. A correspondent showed how some of these hasty marriages were inevitable. He was single and unattached when he left Australia; had he been engaged to a 'nice girl' he would have remained single 'and as good as possible'. He had been away from Australia for nearly four years and he felt that he was 'getting on a bit', 'because war ages a soldier quickly':

> Now I can reckon on two leaves a year, each for 10 days or so, and a lot of damage from a matrimonial point of view can be done in ten days to a chap who hasn't heard decent English from a girl's lips for twelve months. Supposing the next time I get leave I go mad and get married; it simply means that before I get too old to make marriage distasteful, or before I go back to the line again, and get knocked, which is a mathematical certainty if one goes back often enough, that I have tried to propagate my species in a legal way ... but it also means another spinster in Australia.[24]

Others insensitively, even cruelly, played the girls along, with no thought of marriage, safe in the knowledge that one day they would escape to Australia. W. D. Gallwey reported: 'I have never yet contemplated matrimony but

A contemporary postcard tries to keep 'the girl he left behind' in mind

simply love for the sport of it. Where I have to laugh is to think I have them all on a string and they do not know it'. Some of the girls, however, viewed the game a little more seriously: 'The young lady of whom I told you, and who sent me a letter declaring her love, and all the rest of the rot, has written to me again ... anyhow, you need have no fears, and I can only affirm my intentions of *not* bringing home an English girl'. Thousands were less callous, 5,626 members of the AIF returning with English brides. At first, perhaps in an attempt to stem the matrimonial inclinations of the AIF, the Australian government refused to pay the fares of wives to Australia but eventually reversed this heartless policy. Many followed traditional courtship patterns:

> While in Hospital at Camberwell I met a very nice nurse, and naturally when on furlough I used to take her out to various shows and places. The affection has grown on both sides and when I was in London this week for four days ... I was surprised to find how serious we were getting. Instead of going to shows the nurse took me home and introduced me to her people ... There is nothing striking in her beauty and all that sort of thing, but I suppose it is just her way. She is a very sensible girl, or young woman as she is just on 25, and I think I have come across the right one. I have spoken to her about 'after the war' and she is quite satisfied to leave England and come out to Sydney. I told her straight that I would

not care to live in England as it was too cold. I informed her that you would all be pleased to welcome her out in Sydney and make her feel at home. I am sure you will all take a great liking to her as there is nothing flash about her, and when in mufti dresses very plain, although everything looks neat and natty.[25]

The men constantly discussed whether it was right or wise to marry English girls. During a formal debate at a south of England VAD hospital, a Tommy complained that 'them Colonials a' got more money to sport on than th' Tommies, and so the girls like to flash about wi' th' chap that 'as th' money ... Th' Tommy cooms first, after everybody else'. An Australian replied that origin should not influence whom one married and that, as he did not have a girl in Australia, he intended to look closely at the girls in 'Blighty'. Another speaker asked the Australians to think of 'the girls we left behind'. With a strong sense of justice he pleaded with the boys to remember 'those at home who made him socks and woollen goods of all sorts, who send him parcels by every mail, who worked so hard for him in raising money for field kitchens, etc.' and he suggested that they were the girls, 'we, as true Australians, owe a duty to'. It was a forceful speech on behalf of the devoted women of Australia but as another speaker explained: 'It is rather bad luck for the girls at home that so many of our boys are marrying abroad. Still we must look on it as one of the fortunes of war, for one must marry where one's heart is'. On such an eminently sensible point the general debate might have ended but so hard a fact was it for the Australians at home to accept that unease spread. Rumours reached Australia that many of the boys had contracted hasty, foolish marriages to women with an eye to the main chance. Many of the correspondents had sown the seeds for this view with their contemptuous descriptions of English girls.[26]

British people resented the Australian newspapers' depiction of the war bride as a low schemer and so, when a Sydney newspaper reported that the AIF were marrying a 'poor type of women in England' the English press reacted bitterly and again inflamed feelings when they reported how the ships carrying war brides were received in Australia. They gave extensive publicity to a story that one ship had been turned away from the wharf at Fremantle because of a hostile demonstration against the women. This may have been exaggerated but certainly both the Australian press and public were cautious, even sceptical about the women. The *Argus,* reporting the arrival of the first boat-load, noted that 'Critical eyes scanned the groups on the ship's deck, for everyone wanted to know what these conquerors of our soldiers were like. They were not all pretty, of course, but allowance had to be made for the effects of a long sea voyage', although, traditionally, this was thought to bring out the best in people! The *Age* noted that some of the women waiting to receive the brides 'betrayed some rankling feeling' and that a soldier threatened to deal with anyone who insulted his wife when

Australian soldiers and their wives boarding tugs at Tilbury Docks, London, before their departure for Australia

she arrived. In 1919, antagonisms were more pronounced. Those travelling beyond Melbourne from one 'bride ship' were taken to the Young Women's Christian Association rooms, in the centre of Melbourne, to rest. A crowd assembled to see them, some people cheered but others offered 'hoots and vulgar jeers'. The authorities must have anticipated some hostility because a police escort was provided. The *Argus* noted that when 'the policemen were withdrawn, perhaps a little sooner than they should have been, ... some girls and youths made merry in the street outside in what were supposed to be jokes at the English girls' expense'.[27]

If such 'respectable' marriages provoked tensions and anxieties on both sides of the world it is easy to see how the alarming increase of bigamous unions could further confuse the situation. At law, a bigamist could be prosecuted successfully only if both of his alleged partners were present in court. Thus, an Australian might be tempted to go through the forms of marriage with an English woman, confident that his Australian wife would not be brought to England should his bigamy be discovered; eventually he would be free to return, alone, to Australia. So while only those bigamists both of whose partners lived in England were likely to be prosecuted, their cases show how cruel the deception was.

There was the case of a Scot who saw service in South Africa, married in 1910 and migrated to Australia alone two years later. He enlisted in August 1914, was wounded twice at Gallipoli, fought in France and was discharged in 1917 with a very good character. He married in February 1916, having arrived in England only in the previous September. His 'wife', 19 when married, was described in court as 'respectable' of 'highly respectable parents'. By the time the case came to court she had borne one child and was expecting another. In summing up, the judge remarked how painful he found it to sentence a man who had served his country so well but who had also 'fraudulently ... obtained the possession of a young woman of 19 or 20 ... with the result that she was now burdened with an illegitimate child and daily expected to be burdened with a second'. He sent the man to prison for four months. After his release he lived with the girl for a short time and then abandoned her, although a court ordered maintenance of 5s per week per child.[28]

This case, and many others like it, received wide publicity in England causing widespread concern amongst the 'highly respectable' parents of girls 'walking out' with Australians. The press campaigned to compel the Australian Headquarters to furnish each AIF bridegroom with a certificate establishing his bona fides; Headquarters refused but promised to assist any enquirer. Such grudging assistance did little to calm prospective in-laws and apparently the problem remained. In April 1919, surely late in the day, a bill was introduced into the House of Lords 'to enable competent courts in the United Kingdom to entertain proceedings in respect of certain marriages contracted by Dominion troops'.[29]

Principally because of the problems caused by their relations with women in England the Australians found a change in the ready welcome and acceptance they had at first experienced. By 1917 they were seen, whether fairly or not, as amorous, dangerous, even lustful. Parents might be properly concerned to find a daughter on friendly terms with an Australian of whom it might be asked whether he was married, diseased or merely playing with the girl's affections. The Australians, too, had formed rather stereotyped views about English women: while they regretted that the women had been forced to accept paid employment, they found them less moral than their Australian counterparts and they derided their eagerness for marriage. By comparing conditions in England and Australia, the Australians elaborated a very rigid set of conditions to be applied to their women which considerably retarded the position of women in Australian society when the soldiers returned. And those who waited in Australia for the return of the men found reason for anxiety in the rumours that reached Australia. Each could only hope that her particular man would return unscathed.

The early favourable reactions of many Australians to Britain derived from the fact that they had been taught since childhood to expect a familiarity and a sense of belonging; but it derived, too, from superficial similarities between the two societies. As Coxhead, on leave at Brighton, wrote to his wife, 'You wouldn't know the difference here from a Sydney crowd, at, say Manly or Coogee ... The faces and clothing is similar, but perhaps the complexions are fairer here'. Gradually, or suddenly in some cases, the Australians became aware of quite profound differences between English ways and Australian, differences which, because so unexpected, antagonised the Australians and led them to reject much of what they found. In their rejection they gave offence to their hosts but increased their own self-esteem and their love of their own country. Members of other armies, particularly the Americans, experienced no such difficulty in adjusting to English society because they expected it to be different from their own. Australians, heavily dependent on Britain in so many senses, expected a very close affinity and were shocked by its absence. An early shock for some, and an indication of their innocence, occurred when they first tried to shop. They noted with disgust and annoyance that the English refused to accept 'Australian silver tended in payment'. Their parents, their schooling and all they had read about the close ties of Empire predisposed them to see Britain simply as an extension of their homeland. In no sense was it a foreign country – they expected to be at ease, at home. The rejection of Australian coins symbolised a larger issue; Britain was, in many senses, foreign.[30]

Such problems were a minor annoyance, akin to climate and landscape, but class differences profoundly affected the Australians. The first and most obvious evidence of class was found in the English distinction between officers and men. The Australians refused to accept that an officer automatically became a member of a class apart; indeed, because many Australian officers had risen through the ranks they retained close links with their 'mates', even when promoted. The Australians demanded that their officers win the men's respect by bravery or at least by competence; their refusal to salute

A point of view. *Bulletin*, 11 October 1917

TOMMY OFFICER: "*Aw! Er! Of course you come from the Antipodes?*"
BILLJIM PRIVATE: "*No, sir! I've come TO the Antipodes.*"
T.O.: "*Aw! You misunderstand me, you know. I mean you've come from down under.*'
B.P.: "*Wrong again, sir. I come from up over.*"

officers automatically was symptomatic of this. On leave, particularly, the Australians expected to be treated as the equals of officers which often led to confrontation.

In the English tradition officers and men were kept apart, the better hotels and restaurants reserved for the officers while the men ate and drank elsewhere. The Australians overturned such embargoes. Gallwey relates how, when he and a mate, both bearing the 'high rank of Lance Corporal', entered the Comedy, a 'high society' restaurant, 'it caused everyone in the room to draw their attention to us'. The two Australians remained, despite the stares, because they believed that they were entitled to go anywhere as long as they had the means. This seemed natural to the Australians but was bitterly resented by English officers, sensitive to every manifestation of Australian push and cheek. Their presence became a minor scandal in the restaurant: 'as we went out we overheard many funny remarks about us'. Similar problems arose on trains because soldiers were required to avoid compartments occupied by officers. Again Gallwey refused: 'In private life I am a gentleman so I do not see why I should not behave as a gentleman in the military'.[31]

Class distinctions also obtruded in civilian life to annoy and antagonise the Australians. Thousands of patriotic Britons welcomed members of the AIF to their homes to lessen the loneliness and to help them enjoy their leave. Often these were occasions of mutual enrichment and enjoyment

A picnic party at Harefield – the location of the first Australian hospital in England

but the Australians reacted angrily to any patronising attitude, any hint of a class line. Barwick expressed the common sentiment in condemning the 'tea fight given by some old society pot or other who would condescend with a lofty-air to give the poor soldiers some tea and cakes ... if I go to any of these shows it is an equal not as an inferior'. A hostess complained to the *British-Australasian* that it was difficult to find an Australian willing to accept her invitations to tea, leading her to conclude that the Australian 'prefers wandering the streets in company with female rubbish'. An Australian lady defended her countrymen suggesting that English women did not realise how often they patronised the Australian soldier: 'among the Antipodeans at least one cannot tell a gentleman by his tunic'. Mrs Jean Murray, from Cheshire, wrote to the *Daily Mail* asking why soldiers who had endured the horrors of war should also have to endure the 'tea-time nonsense' many hostesses provided. She described one party at which a 'visitor announced herself with the remark, "Oh I just came to see what you did with 'them', I am having 'some' to tea tomorrow. Can I have 'these two' as well?"' Mrs Murray reported that 'The men, not being addressed could only sit and look and listen. They were seldom spoken to, certainly never on equal ground – just spoken about as though they were some new novelty ... they were there as receivers of charity'. It would seem that many Australians who thought of themselves as civilised, well-mannered persons, eager to do the 'done thing' found themselves treated as inferiors by their hostesses, and naturally they resented this.[32]

Barwick reacted even more angrily to a manifestation of class distinction that would have been unthinkable in Australia, or so he believed. As a patient in hospital he discovered that one of the most popular nurses was to be married and in Australian fashion he organised a collection for a present and a tea party in the nurse's honour. 'They had big tables down the ward loaded with all sorts of things but I got a proper shock when they sat down for not a single nurse nor doctor sat with the soldiers, they had separate tables, I never saw a line drawn so fine'. Barwick reported that 'the Tommies seemed to take very little notice and they enjoyed themselves' but the Australians resented the insult and the snobbery. He decided against walking out because he was to make the presentation but he expressed his disgust to the matron, who, doubtless, resented his outburst.[33]

Perhaps the reaction against these English manifestations of class were stimulated by a war which reduced men to a rough equality. Certainly the Australians could not claim that theirs was a classless society; the rural workers, for example, had learned to tolerate the pretensions of the local squatter and his lady. But in wartime even this tolerance evaporated and the Australians, probably alert anyway to any hint of condescension, reacted angrily when they thought they found it. An Australian, writing in the *Spectator,* summarised the common attitude: 'When I came to England I had a shock ... I saw so much artificiality, so much convention that was empty and absurd... huge gulfs kept class from class, in spite of this horrible carnage in France'.³⁴

The Australians believed that the emphasis on class distinctions affected many areas of British life which they also condemned. They noticed and abhorred poverty: 'what did strike me very forcibly was the awful surrounding of the slums, the squalor – dirty children in the gutter'. Another correspondent, contrasting the two countries, claimed that his experiences proved Australia to be 'God's own country' because 'There is practically no poverty there, and I sincerely hope that it continues so for all time'. Such letters doubtless increased self-esteem amongst the recipients. The obvious poverty produced, so the Australians believed, a miserable type of man, 'poor undersized weavers from the Lancashire mills' who made bad soldiers and, as conscripts, convinced many of the Australians to vote against conscription. These poor, low-class men and women seemed to be unable to think for themselves or to challenge inefficiency or stupidity in the people above them. An Australian nurse complained that her English counterparts '[were] too polite to say anything [about military red tape] and [could not] fathom our calm independent ways'. But probably her 'reasonable', independent behaviour antagonised her superiors and more than likely she came to be regarded as merely another brash colonial.³⁵

As dislike of the English grew, the Australians insisted even more fiercely on preserving their separate identity. The slouch hat, as we have seen, set

Horseferry Road – the 'Australian end' of London

them apart. When hospitalised, however, they surrendered their uniforms in exchange for 'hospital blues', common to all patients. The Australians resented the consequent loss of identity and on discharge rejoiced that they could resume the Australian uniform. One correspondent wrote jubilantly: 'I have got my new hat now and feel a real Colonial again. I never felt so proud of being an Australian and native born till I came to England. There is something open and free about being a Colonial that is not found in the English soldier'. Even the King failed to impress. When he reviewed a grand march past of Australians at Salisbury in 1916, Thorp reported that 'there was obvious disappointment among them that he should be so small in stature and so worn of face'. Another remarked that 'really he is a very ordinary looking person'. For men reared on stories of the mightiest monarch the world had known, the reality came as a shock.[36]

In this growing mood of disillusion and disenchantment the letter-writers began to express themselves forcefully. 'I hate England', one of them wrote, 'a favourite saying amongst our boys here is that they ought to give England to Germany and apologise for the state that it is in'. A gloomy person, appropriately called Job, wrote: 'Australia will do me in the future. Next time England goes to war she can fight it on her own because I won't come over again'. Homesickness, the weather, and war-weariness, accounted for some of the complaints, but underlying them all was the realisation that England differed fundamentally from Australia. A resident of Salisbury asked an Australian acquaintance what struck him most about Britain. 'I imagined he would say something about the venerable appearance of the architecture, the closely cultivated appearance of the landscape, but no, he said what struck him most was the sight of women in public houses'. Thorp confirmed that this simple difference in social relations shocked and distressed many of the Australians. It discounted, he wrote; 'the general respect with which you were prepared to behold all English women'. Indeed, so unusual was such behaviour in Australian eyes that newcomers to England assumed the girls were 'of the kind who earn their living from the streets'. Presumably they learned otherwise quickly. The presence of women in bars was, no doubt, a small matter in itself but the extent to which it upset the Australians demonstrates how sensitive they were to different social customs. Australian customs about the place of women in society were apparently intractable; any departure from the norm appalled the Australians. Barwick wrote that the more he saw of the English 'the more I am beginning to hate and despise them, it makes me mad to see them calmly sitting down in the bus and women standing all around them ... Girls over here are not thought the same of as they are in Australia'.[37]

If the guests were disenchanted, the hosts, too, began to have second thoughts about the 'Australian invasion'. At first they had marvelled at the Australian's 'conscious self-importance, his disdain of the conventional, his free dare-devil manner'. Undoubtedly the Australians had played up to this brash self-image. Two Australians entertained a bus load of locals on the way to Euston station: 'We made out that we were real Australian bushmen and had some great fun. Elderly ladies were addressed as Mother instead of Madam ... We spoke to one another in real Australian slang'. Undoubtedly such fun occurred very often when Australians were together, but gradually such antics, such boisterousness and freedom, provoked more concern than laughter. The Australians realised that their British hosts had become wary of them and they resented it. Reports circulated that Australians in uniform were refused drinks in hotels, or accommodation, or meals in restaurants, service in shops, simply because of their reputation as troublemakers. Camps were placed out of bounds, nurses treated them circumspectly when they arrived at hospital, and the civilian population treated them cautiously. By February 1917, N. G. Ellsworth could report that 'the Australians have a very bad name in England now, and we get accused of some very terrible things at times'. Or, as Thorp wrote more dramatically, 'like a millstone round their necks has this bad reputation clung to them to such an extent that many an honest lad wearing the badge of the "Rising Sun" has been the victim of the grossest suspicions'. Such treatment hurt the innocent, increasing Australian dissatisfaction with British life. Thus, an Australian wrote of an occasion when he and his mates, fishing from a bridge, were ordered to move on by a woman from a nearby house. Her husband, she claimed, owned the water. 'She was told in a polite manner', the soldier reported, 'that it was hard lines to an Australian soldier if he could not catch a few fish'. She replied that 'she would sooner have the Germans, or convicts, there than the Colonial troops'. To most Australians such comments, increasingly common, must have seemed not only unfair but also very ungrateful.[38]

If the Australians deserved such approbrium, their behaviour must have exceeded mere 'good fun', officer-baiting and colonial swagger. Were they, in fact, criminals? Had their relations with the civilian population encompassed crimes that would have encouraged householders to see them as a more dreadful threat than the Germans? Court reports from both Weymouth and Salisbury, the areas of the greatest Australian concentration, show that this was not the case. Criminal activity by one soldier against another, or breaches of discipline, was, of course, dealt with by courts-martial. Soldiers appeared in civilian courts only when they had offended against civilians or local police. Overall, Australians appeared before civilian magistrates on petty charges of no great consequence, as the Weymouth and Salisbury records show. Even in London, with its greater temptations and possibilities for crime, the record is good, as a close reading of *The Times* discloses. Because of the size of the metropolis, however, Australians were not as obvious as they were in their smaller garrison towns. These two towns differ in character. Weymouth, a small seaside resort, 'Budmouth' in the novels of Thomas Hardy, had no previous experience of large military encampments, while Salisbury, the traditional headquarters of the Wiltshire Regiment, was familiar with soldiers and their ways. The magistrates at Salisbury inclined less to leniency from the outset. In Weymouth, in the beginning, the Australians received a hearty welcome and early arrests were treated in an embarrassed, light-hearted fashion.

One of the first Australians to have come before the court in Weymouth was charged with the theft of a horse and wagonette valued at £20. He claimed that he meant no harm and at the urging of the police the magistrates dismissed the case. The local paper headed its report 'A Colonial's joke'. The bench viewed crimes against the person and riotous behaviour much more seriously, but even so, at first, Australians were treated lightly because they had travelled so far to fight for England. In a case where eight Australians had bashed a cab-driver in a late night brawl, the victim himself appealed for clemency on their behalf because of their generosity in enlisting to fight for England. The magistrates sympathised with his point and commuted the expected prison sentence to a fine of £5 each. But they remarked that they 'would much rather see that such splendid men should not appear as frequently in the local courts as they did'.[39]

In the early part of 1916 the lenient attitude prevailed in Weymouth. When an Australian 'who looked little more than an overgrown schoolboy' despite his eight months at Gallipoli came before the bench charged with stealing or 'borrowing' a bicycle from an English soldier, the magistrates appealed to the Tommy to drop the charge. He refused, indicating, perhaps, the tension that already existed between British and Australian troops. Forced to proceed, the bench joked about the matter before fining the boy £1. Other petty crimes provoked amusement, too, as in the case of two Australians caught in possession of a cask of stout. In their defence they claimed that they had been 'minding' it for two other, unknown, Australians. The magistrates advised them not to be so silly in the future and dismissed the case. All enjoyed a good laugh, except, perhaps, the publican who was inconvenienced. This lenient policy may well have encouraged the Australians to disregard the law. That, and their increasing antagonism towards the English, brought about by 1917 more serious crimes which forced the magistrates to act more severely.[40]

In August when the police arrested an Australian for using obscene language and assaulting police, about a hundred of his countrymen came to his rescue. The magistrates described the attack on the police as one of the worst ever in Weymouth and fined the original offender £10. On Christmas Eve a riot between three or four hundred Australians and civilians caused extensive damage and when arrested the Australians continued to riot, virtually taking control of the police station until the military police intervened. The magistrates sentenced the ring-leaders to three months' imprisonment and the mayor explained that the Australians were quickly losing friends. Although other riots further damaged the Australians' reputation, their behaviour, on the whole, in Weymouth, was good. The crimes, apart from these riots, were of a petty nature, annoying, no doubt, to local residents but more evidence of high-spirits and thoughtlessness than of criminality. As Chaplain Jenkins of the AIF said when he farewelled Weymouth, on behalf of his men: 'I think the fact that 127,000 men have passed through the town without a great crime staining their honour is something to be said in favour of our own Australian people'.[41]

The record was not quite as good in the Salisbury Magistrates Court but again petty crimes predominated. At first, too, the bench inclined towards leniency, reluctant to 'send to prison a man who had been fighting for his country'. At the same time, however, the magistrates placed limits on their tolerance. When fining an Australian £3 for stealing £8, the chief magistrate explained that 'They were glad to see Australians here but it must be clearly understood that they must behave themselves'. Thefts and brawls arising from drunkenness dominated the list of Australian crimes. Increasingly, the Salisbury magistrates used a prison sentence as a means of deterring others, not always to good effect. An Australian sentenced to nine months in prison for stealing a horse and harness, thanked the bench, remarking 'that it is better than being at the Western Front'. Acts of ingratitude attracted the local paper's attention as in the case of the man who stole a £5 ring from people who had allowed him to stay in their house for the night: 'Anzac's Ungrateful Act' was the headline. There were some serious crimes, too. At least one case of attempted murder, one case of attempted rape against a VAD, and one case of murder in which the accused received the death sentence.[42]

By 1919 the Salisbury magistrates had quite lost their earlier patience with the Australians; they saw harsh penalties as a means of restraining the Anzacs, whose frustration at the delay in returning them to Australia led them to drunkenness and crime. An Australian fined £5 for stealing a £3 clock was told that 'when he came to this country he must respect [its] laws' and another whose defence was that he had been drunk received twelve months' imprisonment with hard labour for stealing clothes and other goods. Even souveniring, surely a typical AIF trait, incurred the wrath of the Salisbury magistrates, as in the case of the private fined £2 for stealing an officer's coat. Crimes against English soldiers increased, a symptom of Australian jealousy directed towards men more easily demobilised.

Riots, too, became more common. As in Weymouth many riots began when mobs of Australians attempted to rescue one or more of their mates from arrest by the civilian police. Occasionally these developed into pitched battles such as when the Australians attempted to wreck the Salisbury police station, throwing bricks, stones, bottles – anything they could find. When Canadians rioted at Epsom and killed a policeman, early newspaper reports labelled the affair another Australian riot – so synonymous had the two words become.[43]

It would be fair to conclude that most cases involving the Australians arose from drunken or boisterous behaviour rather than from evil or criminal intent. But as the general reputation of the Australians worsened, the Salisbury

Her hero returns – a scene outside the Anzac buffet, Sydney

magistrates treated them much more harshly as if they were determined to prevent serious crimes being committed by men they had learned to fear. The last Australian sentenced in Salisbury in 1919 typified the great majority of crimes in that town and in Weymouth: he had stolen a bicycle. Unlike many of his countrymen dismissed with a few words of praise or exhortation but was fined £3. Magisterial tempers had shortened considerably.[44]

In the British imagination the Australians had been transformed from heroes to criminals during their stay in Britain from late 1915 to late 1919. This transformation affected thinking at the highest levels, prejudice though it may have been. At its first meeting after the signing of the Armistice, the war cabinet discussed the Australian 'rowdiness' with Lloyd George leading the discussion. Waiter Long, colonial secretary, advised that it was necessary to remove the Australians from London as soon as possible. Even better, he implied, when he mentioned that they were also a nuisance in the country, would be to return them all to Australia posthaste. The Australians did not really deserve such harsh judgements. Of course, neither their behaviour in London nor in the garrison towns had been perfect, but it was far short of criminal. Their unpopularity had derived more from differences in temperament between host and guest than from really wicked behaviour.[45]

For most Australians the land they had come to fight for had ceased to be 'home' once they experienced the reality as distinct from the myth they had learned at school and from their parents. They enjoyed themselves and they wrote at length about their discoveries but their home was elsewhere where they were still heroes, still loved and, above all, understood. The growing disquiet about the war noticeable in Australia in 1917 and 1918 proceeded from many complex causes; one of them may well have been the disenchantment and dissatisfaction of the troops themselves, stimulated by their unhappiness in England.

All the diaries and letters reflect the mounting excitement as the return to Australia comes nearer. J. O. Maddox must have felt he was almost home when he saw the Southern Cross again in the night sky as his troopship steamed beyond the Equator. Nearly two months later, he was even more excited: 'After slow voyage we arrived inside Sydney Heads at 7 a. m. and there I saw the best sight of my travels. The beauty of the harbour improves after nearly four years absence'. A. E. C. Bray's troopship reached the heads late at night and dropped anchor at Watson's Bay, rather than proceed to the wharves. 'The feelings of being so near home was quite indiscribable [sic] for I knew that barring accidents it would not be very long before I was among my people ... As I waited my turn to go off the ship the inward excitement grew until it was practically unbearable'. Many of the diarists had written with almost as much enthusiasm as they awaited their first glimpse of England. Their experience of war and of what they found eventually to be a hostile society made their enthusiasm for Australia all the more intense. Most of them discovered an even greater love for their homeland because of their service abroad. A. E. C. Bray wrote that he 'realized more than ever in my life before what "Home" in a free country meant'. Another moving, yet typical, conclusion to a war diary records the arrival in Sydney: 'motored to East Hills. Decorated with Flags, the fatted calf was bubbling in the Pot. Realized dimly that I was a hero. Finis'.[46]

CHAPTER SEVEN

MANUFACTURING THE WAR: 'ENEMY SUBJECTS' IN AUSTRALIA

Apart from the men who enlisted in the AIF most Australians experienced the war vicariously, at a distance, relying on the letters from the front and on newspaper reports for a feel of the 'real thing'. Many Australians seemed to regret that the battles were fought at such a distance; they longed for direct experience and meaningful war work, as the enthusiasm and frustration of Australian women showed. Exaggerated patriotism, impossible demands, flowered in this climate of unreality. The Australians needed to manufacture threats and crises to make the war real and immediate; the claim that Australia was to be the 'first prize' of a victorious Germany was a product of this atmosphere. The political turmoil of referendums and elections grew out of the need to manufacture enemies, thus Australia, it was claimed, lay at the mercy of International Workers of the World agitators or Sinn Feiners.

The need to create a war situation, fraught with danger and uncertainty, affected the German residents of Australia most directly: they were the most obvious source of trouble if trouble had to be found. As a small group, they stood out and their separate identity was confirmed by the Australian habit of labelling all persons of German descent, whether born in Australia or not, as 'Germans'. In this chapter they will be referred to as 'Germans' or 'German-Australians' to distinguish them from descendants of British stock, styled, on their own terms, 'Australians'. This is not meant disrespectfully but emphasises the distinction universally applied during the war years. The process of naturalisation, even being born in Australia, made little difference to the perceptions of the dominant majority: German blood, however diluted, earned the pejorative title 'German'. While damning the recipient during the war years, here it is used only for purposes of differentiation.

The potential for disruption by these people was limited. There were few 'foreigners' in a remarkably homogeneous population composed almost entirely of people born in Australia or the British Isles. In the Commonwealth census of 1911, 33,381 persons living in Australia were German-born and their presence was diluted as they were spread fairly evenly through the four

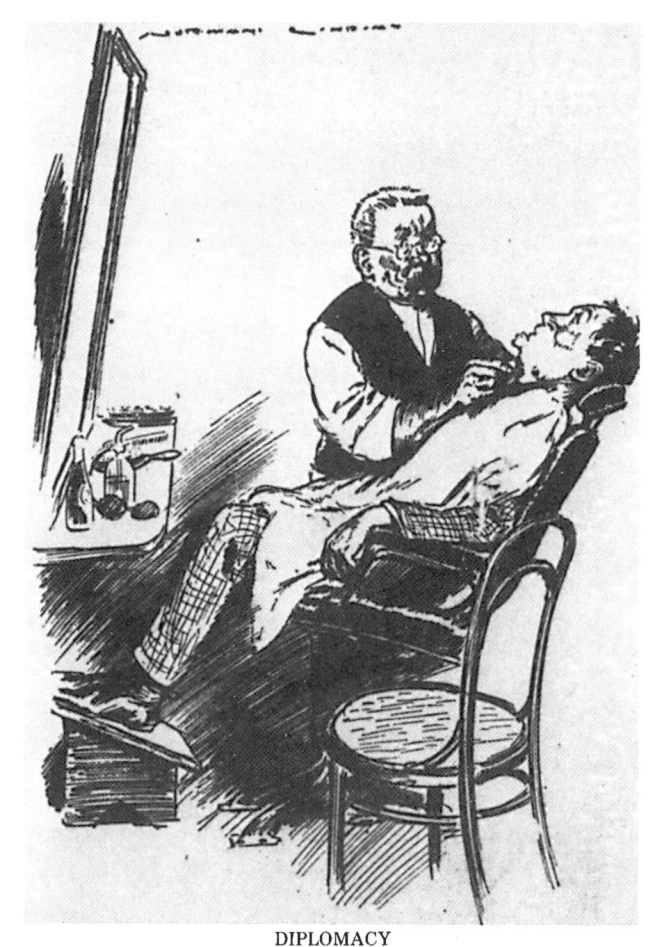

DIPLOMACY
PATRIOTIC AUSTRALIAN: *"Vell, I dink ve beat dose Germans easy, eh! vat?"*

An early humorous version of relations between 'Germans' and 'Australians'. *Bulletin*, 11 March 1915

most populous states. Unfortunately, the census did not show how many Australians there were of German descent but the numbers of adherents of the Lutheran church provide a rough indication of German background. There were 74,508 Lutherans in Australia in 1911; the greatest number (27,794) were in South Australia, then came Queensland (24,843), Victoria (11,906) and New South Wales (7,177). As many German settlers tended to form colonies in the rural areas, there were, in each state, identifiable 'German' areas. In South Australia they concentrated in the Barossa Valley, at Kapunda, Tanunda and at Mount Barker. In New South Wales they were strongest in the Riverina around Wagga Wagga, in Victoria in the Mallee district and in Queensland on the Darling Downs. As country-dwellers their potential for disruption and sabotage was even further reduced; in no real sense could the German-Australians be seen as a threat to Australia's national security.[1]

In areas containing significant numbers of Germans the immediate reaction to the news of war, on the part of Germans and Australians alike, was to stress the loyalty and patriotism of the Germans, and their happy integration into the general community. The editor of the *Barossa News* maintained, with some allowable exaggeration, that Australia '[was] a community of peoples of all nations and tongues' in which all were bound by the duties of loyalty and their oath of allegiance to the King. He appealed to 'Britishers' to 'show our brothers in adoption that we accept and place with us their patriotism and love for the British Crown'. Similarly, at Kapunda: 'we do not for a moment question the loyalty of our fellow colonists who have become naturalized British subjects'. And in Adelaide the editor of the *Advertiser* expressed sympathy for people potentially divided by twin loyalties:

> For them it is a cruel situation. Australia has had long experience of the estimable qualities of her German citizens, and knows that they have the strength of character which will enable them to adopt absolutely the right attitude ... every instinct of chivalry and good feeling should be invoked to secure the tenderest consideration for the lacerated feelings of these respected fellow citizens.

The editor of the *Daily Advertiser* in Wagga made much the same point: the Germans in the area had worked hard to develop their farms and, although they might feel some sympathy for the land of their birth, their interests lay in the land of their adoption and they would be loyal and show their devotion to it. Correspondents reinforced these magnanimous sentiments. Ernest W. G. Bagner of Norwood wrote: 'I therefore pray, I beseech, I implore the people of Australia to treat with equality and to honor those who loyally swear by ... the Union Jack'. John Blacket, also of Norwood, asserted that 'No South Australian, worthy of the name, will question the loyalty of our German brethren' and H. A. Holthouse of Kapunda reminded readers of the *Kapunda Herald* that 'We are all Australians although we may not have sprung from the same nation, and I do urge my fellow-citizens to remember this fact'. Such sentiments, no doubt genuine, rolled easily off the pen at a time when all Australians believed that the Empire would win a swift and decisive victory.[2]

The Germans, too, quickly asserted their loyalty and commitment to the Empire. Almost every Lutheran community seems to have passed a resolution pledging loyalty to the Crown and often they forwarded these resolutions to the state governor or governor-general for official recognition of their loyalty. The honorary consul for Germany in South Australia, Mr H. C. E. Mueke, a resident since 1848 and a naturalised citizen since 1866, personally called on the governor to explain that his office did not affect his loyal citizenship. A German member of the South Australian House of Assembly, Mr O. H. Duhst, was a prominent exponent of the loyalty of the

MANUFACTURING THE WAR: 'ENEMY SUBJECTS' IN AUSTRALIA

THE HUN'S CHRISTMAS DINNER—THE UNINVITED GUESTS
By December 1915 humour was no longer a factor. *Bulletin*, 23 December 1915

German people, explaining again and again how they could be relied upon in the crisis not to do anything that would arouse suspicion or alarm. The 'Liedertafel' in Adelaide likewise pledged loyalty, but, prudently, decided to postpone further meetings until after the war. From Germans everywhere in Australia, and from prominent Citizens, the first response had been to minimise the distinctions between the two 'races' and to stress their common membership in the Australian community.[3]

Such brave words and happy sentiments derived from a rather complacent view of the likely progress and outcome of the war, common in Australia in August 1914. The realisation of the 'seriousness' of the war brought about a change which was also prompted by an awareness that the Germans naturally felt sympathy for the sufferings of their own kind at home and at the front.

A South Australian German confronted the situation dramatically when he wrote to a newspaper stating that he could never fight against the German people, his own close ties with them prevented that. His letter aroused enormous hostility in Adelaide because it made people aware that the Germans could not simply shrug off their ancestry to cheer on the Empire as enthusiastically as British-born Australians. Increasingly, too, Germans in Australia suffered from the reputation fostered by British propaganda experts who portrayed the enemy in the worst possible light. The Germans, or 'Huns' as they were universally called, were accused of the most atrocious war crimes such as the butchering of Belgian babies, the raping of women, particularly nuns, and the looting of shrines and churches. Cartoons depicted the German soldier as a depraved, lustful animal of hideous proportions. The Australian press repeated all the excesses of the British press, indeed, Norman Lindsay's cartoons in the Sydney *Bulletin* translated the worst the British achieved to an Australian setting. The propagandists intended to incite the people to a hatred of Germans and they succeeded; the fate of the German-Australians indicates the extent of their success.

The Australian press, at first so dutiful in fostering good relations between both sections of the community, by October 1914 encouraged the growth of antagonisms. The *Advertiser,* for example, reported with approval the behaviour of an Adelaide crowd who thrashed and ejected from a picture theatre a German who, allegedly, muttered 'Glück für Deutschland' (Good luck to Germany), while watching a film of the German army entering Brussels. On the other hand, it may have been that the crowd simply wanted a scapegoat on whom to vent their frustration after a film showing a German army triumph. The South Australian newspapers published in predominantly German areas reflect a deterioration in relations between Germans and Australians. The *Barossa News* deplored the 'bitter lies and rumours' which circulated about German residents, an example of which was the rumour that the German consul, whose loyalty had earlier been the subject of public testimony, had been arrested for carrying incriminating papers. Another rumour asserted that a Patriotic Meeting at Tanunda had begun with the crowd singing 'The Watch on the Rhine'. Coincidental with these press reports of 'suspicious behaviour' was a spate of letters to the editor questioning the loyalty of German fellow-citizens. In September the Adelaide *Advertiser* published fourteen 'anti-German' letters, eleven in October, twenty-three in November and thirteen in December. Taken with the hostile news reports this represented an extensive coverage of the 'anti-German' viewpoint. Typical of anti-German letters was that from T. Scott of Murray Bridge, published in the *Mount Barker Courier,* who asked why so few German-Australians had enlisted with the 1,700 South Australians soon to depart with the first contingent of the AIF. The proportion of German-Australians was, he alleged, 'microscopic', a fact which accounted for the mistrust and suspicion in the air.[4]

Unfortunately, it is not possible to guess what personal impact this first wave of anti-German feeling had on the lives of the German settlers in Australia. However, an occasional grim incident appears, to remind us of the cost of this campaign to German-Australians, the first Australian victims of the war. In October 1914 the *Barossa News* reported that C. B. Kliche had left Tanunda for a few weeks for a complete rest because he was suffering from 'broken nerves'. In November the same paper reported that one of its own directors, Adolph Schulz, who was also Chairman of the Tanunda District Council, had committed suicide because he was 'greatly worried over the calamities of the time'. Schulz, aged 33, left a widow and a young son. Earlier the *Mount Barker Courier* had reported the suicide of Franz Ernst Jahn, aged 60, who had been depressed ever since the railways had sacked him on account of his 'enemy origin'. Such tragedies are only recorded in the small country newspapers, more intimate than their city counterparts; a thorough search through their files would doubtless bring to light many similar stories. The newspapers revealed to the German-Australians the extent of feeling against them; unionists refused to work with them and people attacked and abused them in the streets. No wonder, in these circumstances, that many became depressed; they found themselves aliens in the land of their birth or adoption.[5]

Despite growing calls for government action over the 'German problem', at this early stage the government moved in only two directions. Immediately regulations were drawn up under the War Precautions Act to prohibit 'trading with the enemy'. Just before the war, Australian trade with Germany had increased considerably, so the government needed to exercise great vigilance to detect many Australian firms lost a great deal of money by the regulations, firms as loyal and reputable as Palings in Sydney and Allans in Melbourne, both of whom found themselves embarrassed by their large stock of unsaleable German pianos, many of them very expensive. Even so, alert members of the public reported breaches of these regulations. In October 1918, J. Watson of East Melbourne reported that all the pianos in the windows of Maples' shop in Swan Street Richmond were German. Concern about enemy trading was extensive. The manager of the Exchange branch of the Commercial Banking Company of Sydney wrote in August 1914 to enquire if the bank was in order in paying cheques drawn by persons or firms of enemy origin. He confided that the bank had many German customers and while he was anxious 'not to be in any way disloyal to the Crown', he felt he also had obligations to his customers. The attorney-general replied that private persons could continue to draw money.[6]

The second area of government action involved the registration of aliens, again under the terms of the War Precautions Act. Each 'enemy subject' was required to report to the military authorities or the local police and there to swear an oath not to take up arms against the Empire. Technically, he was then a prisoner of war, but, depending on his circumstances, he could

1917. Bulletin, 19 July 1917

be paroled and allowed to live a normal life. Should he, however, give any cause for suspicion, he would be arrested immediately and interned without a court hearing. Unfortunately, the regulation gave no clear definition of an 'enemy subject'. Most German-Australians presumed that the process of naturalisation removed them from that category but as the arrest of Pastor Th. Nickel showed, this was not necessarily the case. Nickel, president of the Evangelical Lutheran Synod of Australia, believed he was exempt from the provisions of the regulation because he was a naturalised Australian. When he was arrested in early 1915 for failing to register, he was informed that as the German government refused to recognise naturalisation, the Australian government had determined to do likewise. Nickel was interned, causing something of a sensation in Adelaide, and was released only after strenuous efforts by his local federal member of parliament, Patrick MacMahon Glynn. All naturalised Germans then realised that the law gave them very little protection. Long-standing residents in Australia had the threat of internment without trial hanging over them throughout the war years.[7]

By 1916 the definition of 'enemy subject' was further enlarged to include any Australian natural-born subject whose father or grandfather was a subject of a country at war with the King. The effect was to include the vast majority of natural-born Australians of German descent within the category 'enemy subject'. This gave the Australian authorities complete power over almost all German-Australians and must surely have heightened anxieties and tensions. One can imagine what feelings the sight of two soldiers in full equipment marching a civilian to the railway station in the quiet town of Kapunda caused Germans and Australians alike. Such sights were not uncommon. By March 1915 there were 1,930 Germans interned in the various Australian camps; their numbers grew under the increasing pressure of anti-German feeling.[8]

After a brief period of tolerance, therefore, the Australian people grew increasingly suspicious and wary of their German neighbours. Alert citizens uncovered plots, acts of sabotage and spies with such regularity as to keep the police and military authorities occupied busily pursuing their investigations. All of the allegations proved groundless. One concerned Melburnian even wrote to the Defence department about the wireless mast he had discovered at Bishopscourt, the home of Melbourne's Anglican archbishop. Captain C. F. Woodcock, visiting the predominantly German town of Eudunda in South Australia in December 1914, found it necessary to remark on Dr Kilmar who travelled 'in [a] 6 cylinder motor car 40 h.p.' and who visited many residents in the district; such behaviour might have been expected from a doctor![9]

Despite Australian fears that Australia would be the first prize claimed by a victorious Germany, there was no evidence of any real German interest in undermining Australian society or penetrating her defence secrets. The Defence department admitted as much when the Melbourne *Argus* asked for co-operation in preparing an article 'on the work of the German spy system in Australia'. Major Piesse, the Director of Military Intelligence, replied in March 1917 that no case of spying had been discovered in Australia, at least since he had commenced duty in November 1914. Nor had there been any 'hostile outrages'. Perhaps the department should have publicised such good news widely because the hunt for German spies continued unabated throughout the war years. But perhaps again, publicity would not have made much difference anyway, so intense was the Australian need to feel threatened, to manufacture war conditions in Australia. Many of these attempts were merely laughable as the defence of Murray Bridge shows. The residents there agitated, as early as August 1914, for a military guard for the bridge which constituted the main connecting link between South Australia and the eastern states. Warned of the passage of the second South Australian contingent, surely a breach of traditional military secrecy, members of the Murray Bridge rifle club turned out to protect the bridge from assailants. No doubt this show of strength calmed locals who were fearful for the safety of South Australia's best sons but it did not impress one young man wandering about the bridge's understructure. 'The gun's not loaded' he suggested and 'you wouldn't shoot would you?' he asked. The guards then 'forcibly impressed' him 'with the seriousness of the situation'. Finally, in March 1916, the military authorities acceded to continuing local requests and placed a permanent guard on the bridge. But they removed it in August when the state commandant reported that the district was quiet. The chief of the general staff observed that his main ambition was to limit the use of troops in Australia and furthermore that 'The Bridge will only be one of scores of vulnerable points unguarded [but] no outrage has been attempted in two years of war'.[10]

The 'Hun' is now a very powerful figure. Bulletin, 27 November 1917

While it would be impossible to list all the manifestations of hysteria caused by the supposed German presence in Australia because the concern was so constant and extensive, nevertheless some examples will give an idea of the alarm Australians felt. People regularly heard sounds or saw lights or found wireless aerials which they supposed gave clear evidence of a German spy network; they reported their fears to the Defence department which deputed the local police to make investigations, a task which must have wearied them. Detective Ramsay of Sydney sent to investigate alleged signalling from a house in Flinders Street, City, reported that the flashes occurred when a lady boarder, Mrs Bengard, used a kerosene lamp equipped with a reflector to light her room when her thrifty landlord turned the gas off at the meter each evening. 'All the inmates [of the house] are Britishers and there is nothing suspicious in the matter', Detective Ramsay concluded. In November 1914 the police spent two hours searching the premises of John Douglas Couling of Cronulla, acting on a report that Mr Couling had secreted a wireless in his home. A thorough search revealed nothing and the officer-in-charge objected to the 'fool's errand', as Mr Couling, well over sixty years old, was born in Australia of British parents and was well-known and highly respected in the community.[11]

Reports against Australians or 'Britishers' were a nuisance to the police and the persons investigated but, because loyalty could be assumed, they were not nearly as harmful as reports against German-Australians. It is likely that some, at least, of these reports arose out of dislike or jealousy, or from a crude attempt to do a business rival down. However, the penalty was often internment. Thus Carl –, an electrician, was reported as a German secret service agent because he lived at Rose Bay in a large house with servants and was seen very often at night in the city in evening dress: a life-style 'hardly compatible with an Electrician's pay', the informant complained. Another loyal citizen reported his grocer at Milson's Point when his laundryman heard the grocer and another chuckling over a reverse the Allies had suffered. The complainant concluded: 'Is it wise that such should be allowed to trade in competition with loyal subjects?' Even more direct was G. M. McKenzie, who wrote about an enemy subject, A. Marx. Before enlisting McKenzie had operated an estate agency in Katoomba and he feared that Marx, also an estate agent, would pick up all his business during McKenzie's absence with the troops. 'Should I come back after the war it will be to find that this German has got the whole of my former business ... My contention is that he should be interned which would not do him any harm'. Nowhere in his letter does McKenzie allege any personal disloyalty on Marx's part, merely that as a recruit he should be protected from a business rival. An anonymous correspondent warned the authorities to 'keep your eye on' a man named Phul who had travelled throughout Europe in 1914 with a member of the German secret service. Phul was Australian-born, a wealthy farmer of Sandycreek near Gawler, South Australia, with cousins in Queensland, one of whom was in the navy: 'But the whole lot are traitors, most disloyal'. Each of these letters, and there are thousands like them in the files, required careful investigation by the police or the military, resulting in the internment of many people. But no evidence of spying on Germany's behalf was ever discovered; there were no ships at sea picking up secret wireless messages or reading flashing lights from a thousand points along the coastline. In many instances Australian rumours merely imitated what the papers reported about German spy activity in Britain.[12]

Australians were also alert for potential acts of sabotage and frequently wrote to the department suggesting preventative action. In October 1915 D. H. Ryan, a farmer from Hay, suggested that all Germans and enemy sympathisers be interned until the crops were harvested and safe at the railways because of the danger of the Germans setting the wheat alight as it stood in the fields. Ryan's suspicions had been aroused when he heard of a man who, after a few drinks, expressed pro-German sentiments; this man had a German father. 'John Bull Junior' suggested that the government intern all the Lutheran missionaries at the Finke River Mission in Central Australia because, with a light machine-gun, a few of them could prevent thousands of Australians from passing through the MacDonnell Ranges. Thus, if the Germans invaded Australia, South Australians would not be able to retreat to the safety of 'the centre'. Such stupidity was not confined to individuals. The Adelaide *Advertiser* alarmed its readers with an eye-witness account of bombing in the South Park lands but later calmed the public, explaining that the explosions were the work of a soldier (an instructor in bomb-throwing) who had been developing his technique. In February 1915 the 'Joke of the Season' was the public alarm caused by the appearance of two German aeroplanes over the pier at Glenelg. They were, in fact, two aerokites used by the Viceroy Tea Company to advertise their tea.[13]

Australians feared the danger of German spies or acts of German sabotage; they also grew to hate their German neighbours as the level of violence against them shows. Although the newspapers treated much of this violence as mere hooliganism or larrikinism, it does seem to have derived, in many cases, from deep-seated antipathy. No doubt, regardless of the motives, the victims felt intimidated and alienated from the community of which they had believed themselves to be part. At Tanunda, stables and sheds belonging to G. Auricht, a printer, were destroyed by fire, the Jetty Hotel at Glenelg was bombarded with stones at 4 a.m. and many windows smashed, thirty bags of wheat belonging to Mr Mutter of Mt Templeton were deliberately ruined, while at Mt Gambier, two haystacks belonging to Mr Schleter were destroyed by fire. In the Barossa, when W. J. Offe tried to mow his field for hay, he discovered that someone had planted wire stakes in the field, fouling his harvester and preventing him from mowing. Many of the shop signs of German traders were smeared with tar and, of course, shop windows proved an almost irresistible target for anti-Germans. How intimidated was Mr Winckler of Mt Gambier when a crowd of twenty or thirty New Year revellers gathered outside his house to yell abuse? When he protested they began to demolish his picket fence and to throw stones on his iron roof. They smashed three windows and destroyed several ornaments inside the house but dispersed before the police arrived.[14]

Violence against the person was also common. Reports of riots and brawls by crowds against individual or groups of German-Australians appear in all Australian newspapers throughout the war period. Almost invariably a disloyal remark on the part of the 'enemy subject' was given as the reason for the brawl, but we might wonder at the constant stupidity of the German-Australians in offending the obviously sensitive Australians. The victims received little protection from the official guardians of law and order, as the case of Friedrick Willhelm Loeffler shows. Loeffler sued James Baird for £19 19s for alleged assault when Baird had punched him in the face calling him a German coward. While the court found in Loeffler's favour, the magistrate placed damages at 1s, as if inviting other Australians to do likewise. Often soldiers initiated the violence against German-Australians and often the violence involved large numbers of Australians as in the case of the fifty men who attacked, tarred and feathered Mr Katz, a native-born Australian. He had provoked them by urging unionists to ignore the enlistment cards prepared by the State Recruiting Committee. There are many reports of similar attacks on farmers taking their produce to market, shop-keepers and tradesmen, all of whom came to fear for their safety. These attacks taught the German-Australians how unpopular they were in the community.[15]

Particularly disturbing to the German settlers were the attacks on the property of the Lutheran church which held a special place in the affections of the German people; they regarded such attacks as sacrilegious. Included in these outrages was the complete destruction by fire of the churches at Edithburgh, Murtoa and Netherby. An unknown loyalist painted the doors of the Quorn church red, white and blue because the pastor conducted the services in German. The use of the German language also provoked a crowd at Barellan to throw stones on to the church roof during the service and to intimidate the worshippers with threats. The crowd was further provoked when the people locked the church doors but, in the circumstances, this seemed a sensible precaution. As with many other churches, the Lutherans depended on voluntary labour to build, equip and maintain their properties and it must have been heart-breaking to watch the fruits of community effort, over many years, destroyed or defaced by loyalist mobs goaded on by fear and hatred.[16]

German-Australians suffered, too, by the refusal of their workmates to continue to work with them and by the actions of employers who dismissed them. Some unionists initiated action against working alongside German-Australians. Hatred of Germany may have been a motive, while patriotism, even if misguided, may have been another. Certainly, propaganda had stimulated contempt for Germans, the murderers of nurse Cavell and the masters of other atrocities. There were some calls for restraint, however: the *Australian Worker* asked unionists not to interfere in the matter as 'the question of interning or not interning Germans is one entirely for the military'. Part of the antagonism may have derived from a desire to secure

Holdsworthy internment camp – many destitute German-Australians were forced to seek asylum here

jobs for 'Australians' in a time of high unemployment. To many unionists it seemed unfair that 'enemy subjects' should receive regular wages while mates tramped the streets looking for work.[17]

Whether antagonisms derived from patriotism or bigotry, the result was much the same. Those German-Australians not on farms or self-employed found it very difficult to secure a job. The Melbourne wharf labourers decided in November 1914 that they would not work with Germans, thereby throwing about 150–175 men out of work. The Melbourne and Metropolitan Board of Works determined that all Germans be dismissed because the state of war meant that 'no German should benefit by the civil advantages which were obtainable in Australia'. The Fremantle Lumpers Union announced in December 1914 that they would not work with Germans, whether naturalised or not; Sydney wharf labourers took similar action. Railway workers at Newport in Melbourne, workers at the Cockatoo Dockyards, Sydney, the Sydney coallumpers, miners at Port Pirie and Kalgoorlie, workers at the Sydney glass and bottle works, and at the Beale piano factory, all refused to work with Germans. In Melbourne the Carlton and United Company dismissed fifteen Germans from the Victoria brewery, bowing, they said, to the wishes of the public. Ironically, the chairman of the board, Mr C. L. Pinchoff, had recently resigned his position. This list of places where German-Australians could not work is in no sense exhaustive but it does illustrate the general mood.[18]

German-Australians thus dismissed had little chance of finding another job and, with no social security benefits to protect them, they faced a very bleak future indeed. Consider the fate of Charles Ludersen, a stevedore at Port Melbourne, as set out by his wife in a letter to the attorney-general of 20 October 1915. Ludersen lost his job when his workmates refused to work with him, although he had been born in Denmark and had lived in Australia for thirty years. He had been naturalised in September 1914. Even worse was the case of G. V. Wettel. The fact that two of his sons had enlisted with the AIF might have attested to his patriotism but nevertheless, as a German, he lost his job. Of his five children at home only one had a job at 10s per week; his landlord had given him notice to quit. He had, he wrote, 'the best of references, one also of eight years from Messrs. Bagshaw and Sons, and am barred on account of my birth, although I sent my two boys to the war. That beats anything'. Wettel presumed that his only hope of 'providing' for his family was to apply for admission to Torrens Island, the South Australian internment camp. The minister for defence, G. F. Pearce, agreed. His department, in response to many men in a plight similar to Wettel's, had adopted a plan similar to that in force in Britain. This allowed destitute Germans to be interned at their own request, and during their internment their wives would be paid at the rate of 10s per week, with an additional 2s 6d per week for each child under fourteen years. No doubt the temper of the Australian people would not countenance any more generous scheme

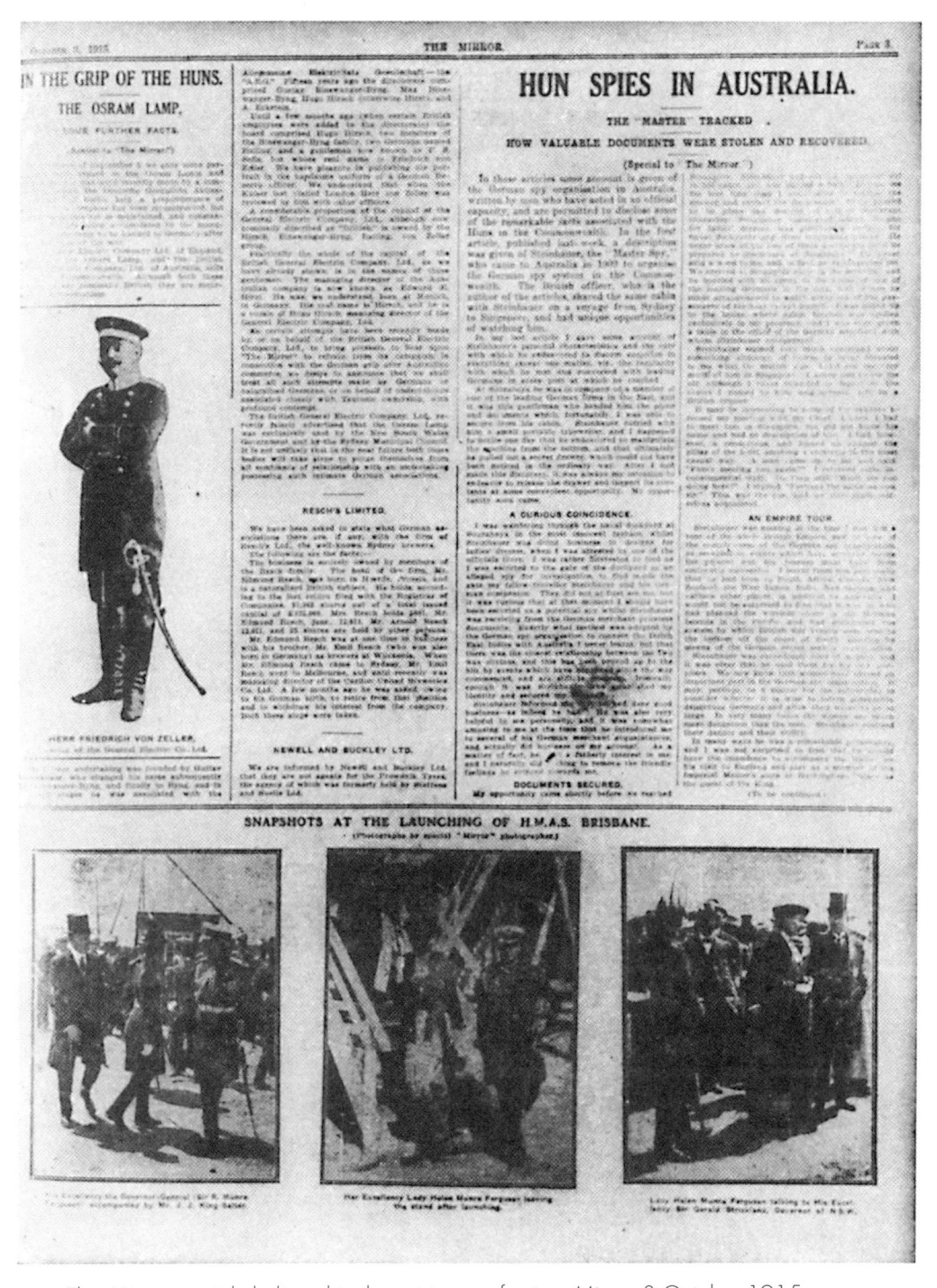

The *Mirror* certainly believed in the existence of spies. *Mirror*, 3 October 1915

for the maintenance of unemployed German-Australians and their families. But this was subsistence living, if that.[19]

The community was particularly agitated about the number of 'Germans' in the federal and state public service, possibly because of concern for national security but also because of simple jealousy as a public service post was regarded as a valuable sinecure. The matter first came to prominence in Adelaide in November 1914 when an unsigned leaflet called on 'British Australians' to awaken to the danger of foreigners in positions of trust in the public service. Agitation continued, particularly at parliamentary level, with members challenging ministers about the loyalty of particular officers. In September 1915, the New South Wales Premier Holman divided 'foreigners' into three categories: the non-naturalised, who were not represented at all in the New South Wales public service; the German-born naturalised citizens, of whom there were only twenty-five in the service; and 'Germans' born in Australia. He believed the latter should be allowed to remain in their jobs unless it could be shown that a particular officer was disloyal. Six months later Holman admitted that there were only sixty-four persons in the third category and that each individual officer had been investigated. At their 1916 Conference the premiers decided that henceforth no 'enemy alien' would be employed in any branch of the public service. The difficulty was to define who was an 'enemy alien'; Australian birth or naturalisation did not guarantee acceptability.[20]

Despite assurances such as Holman's, rumours spread about the large number of Germans in the public service. Mrs Davies of Healesville, writing to her daughter, Evelyn, a nurse with the AIF, referred in late 1917 to the Germans 'holding good billets in the civil service'. She added, 'I wish the Germans were all dead'. In February 1918 she returned to her theme, complaining that the 'Germans still hold good billets in the Defence department and civil service in spite of criticism'. Perhaps because of that criticism, the federal government appointed a Royal Commission in May 1918 to enquire into the 'origin of birth and parentage of all persons now in the Commonwealth Public Service'. The Commissioner, A. N. Barnett, made nineteen interim reports before delivering his final report on 30 May 1919. He compiled lists of all people investigated during the time covered by each report: in the second he listed 64 suspected persons, 50 in the fourth, 43 in the seventh and 31 in the tenth. He provided details of many of the persons listed. The investigation was quite thorough, therefore, and did attempt to encompass all German-Australians in the Commonwealth Public Service. During the year of the enquiry Barnett took evidence from those who suspected the loyalty of fellow workers, evidence which shows how cautious people had to be in wartime Australia. Thus to say, as did a Mr Polkinghorne, British-born with a German wife, that the newspaper accounts of German atrocities were 'tripe' was to lead colleagues to question his loyalty. In a long list of charges as superficial as this, it was also alleged against Polkinghorne that he had nicknamed his son 'Dutchie'. For these reasons he lost his position as acting secretary of the Commonwealth Naval Dockyard, Cockatoo Island.[21]

Few public servants lost their jobs. In most cases the Commissioner decided to retain the officer's services, although he often recommended that 'on the grounds of expediency' the person under examination be employed in a capacity away from contact with the public. It would seem from this that the public were highly sensitive to the position of Germans in the service. But the definition of 'German' was far from exact. In almost every case Barnett investigated he found the officer to be Australian-born of German parentage. Consider the case of Matilda Rockstroh, postmistress at the St Kilda Road Post Office, a public servant of thirty-three years standing. Her parents had migrated to Victoria in 1857 and 1863 respectively; she was born in Australia and might, with every justification, have considered herself Australian. The Commissioner found no trace of disloyalty or disaffection in her statements or actions but concluded, nevertheless, that:

> her close lineal connection with the German race, and her long social and domestic association with her own German relations and friends makes it unlikely that her inclinations and proclivities, if they could be discovered, and put to an enforced election, would tend towards the interests of the British Empire as against those of her own race.

After all this, Barnett decided that Miss Rockstroh might remain in the public service if she did not come into contact with the public. She lost her position as postmistress solely because of her misfortune in having German-Australian parents. Even worse, perhaps, was the Commissioner's decision about H. H. Clausen, a linesman in the General Post Office, Brisbane. Although Clausen had arrived in Australia as a child and was 41 at the time of the enquiry, Barnett found that 'Physiognomically his Teutonic origin [was] striking' and he recommended that on the grounds of 'expediency and in the public interest' Clausen be dismissed. That is, he lost his job not because he seemed disloyal but because he looked too obviously 'Teutonic' and the public would not tolerate the government employing him. Officers investigated resented the experience. W. H. Leek, postmaster at Leichhardt, Australian-born with two sons in the AIF, denounced the Royal Commission in 'a violent and unseemly indictment of the Government' at the conclusion of the interrogation. He spoke of it as 'a bitter outrage' and a 'gross scandal' and referred to himself as 'branded with shame for the rest of his life'. He referred also to 'the mental suffering of his wife while he was being subjected to such torture'. Barnett recommended that Leek retain his position but drew his attacks on the Commission to the attention of his superiors in Sydney.

Despite the harassment and the injustice to individual officers, Barnett's final report into the loyalty of public servants was an anti-climax. He had recommended the dismissal of about fifty officers in the interim reports and had nothing further to offer beyond suggesting that statutory provision be made for the future exclusion from the Commonwealth service of persons of enemy origin. However, this would have required the Commonwealth to predict who likely enemies were to be. Australian birth or naturalisation counted for nothing in Barnett's eyes, parentage, alone, determined loyalty. Should Britain have declared war on Ireland, for example, there would have been widespread turmoil in the Australian public service, on Barnett's principles. The Royal Commission arose out of public disquiet about 'Germans' in safe jobs and the Commissioner showed an appreciation of public hostility by removing 'Germans' from public contact. The whole exercise was a further illustration of the hatred Australians felt for their German fellow citizens.

In this increasingly hostile environment no German-Australian member of an Australian parliament could look to his electors with confidence. The career of George Dankel, a federal Labor parliamentarian for the Adelaide suburban seat of Boothby, illustrates how anti-German feeling grew in Australia under the pressure of war. At the general election in September 1914 Dankel increased his majority from 1,941 votes in 1913 to 3,442. With the war only a month old, commentators saw his victory as a happy augury for harmonious relations between the two races. By August 1916, despite the obvious patriotic pride he took in his son's enlistment in the AIF, Dankel was a most unpopular member. He faced meetings calling for his resignation from parliament and a petition circulated, eventually signed by 17,000 Adelaide electors, calling on him to step down. He retired before the May 1917 general election.[22]

The climate of opinion changed quickly after Dankel's victory in September 1914. The 'race question' became an important issue in the March 1915 South Australian State election. There were several German-Australian candidates on behalf of the ruling Liberal party, including Herman Homburg who had resigned as attorney-general in January because of anxiety about his loyalty. Homburg determined to stand for re-election to parliament to give people the opportunity of showing their confidence in him. He could not appreciate how his world had disintegrated. At an election rally he said:

> I think it is a great pity that at this time racial questions should be introduced. When I see the happy contentment in our settlements – many have intermarried and have lived on terms of friendship – I feel it is the essence of a maggot mind that could today suggest a difference between the two sections.

Homburg realised how intense that difference was as the votes came in. Candidates with a German background lost each seat contested; men like Homburg and O. H. Duhst who had spoken so handsomely of the loyalty of the German people and the integration of the two races, were dumped by the electors. The anti-German vote defeated the government and indeed, the premier, A. H. Peake, an outspoken supporter of the cause of the German-Australians, lost his own seat, one of the very few parliamentary leaders so to fall from grace at any time in Australia. The defeat led to bitter recriminations within the Liberal Union, the thinking summarised by one member who wrote that 'in the present excited state of public feeling it would certainly have been better if candidates of German origin had withdrawn from political contests during the war'. The result in South Australia hardened the attitudes of politicians elsewhere who found it expedient to follow the anti-German sentiment. German-Australians now had few friends in high places.[23]

Paradoxically, despite the decimation of the German-Australian representation in parliament, electors feared the strength of the 'German vote' which they assumed to be so disciplined that the 'Germans' controlled up to eighteen parliamentary seats. There were, therefore, various attempts to disenfranchise the 'Germans', notably in a bill introduced into the South Australian Parliament in 1916 which was defeated in the upper house. The defeat of the first conscription referendum in 1916 brought about a search for scapegoats, one of which was the 'German vote'. The Hughes nationalist government, as a consequence, prevented 'Germans' from voting in the 1917 general election and subsequently extended their definition of 'German' to include a naturalised subject born in an enemy country.[24]

This action, which gave official sanction to the view that the loyalty of German-Australians could not be relied upon, particularly distressed these embattled people and angered many of their sons fighting with the AIF. 'Private' wrote to the *British-Australasian*, protesting that his mother had been denied a vote because 'she descends from German descent' [sic].

> Now this has hurt me very much. She has two sons fighting for the Empire, one in France (myself) and one in Palestine, her brother also was refused a vote; he had two sons also fighting, one killed in action on the Somme last year, and the other serving in the -th Battalion. More[,] mother was bred and born in Australia and a more loyal woman never lived. She worked hard in every respect towards assisting the troops on this side, she paid particular attention to the Red Cross, and now all her work has gone by refusing her a vote. I am really hurt that much that I can hardly explain the position to you, to think that me and my brother are away fighting for our country and she treated like that.[25]

The restriction on the franchise denied the German-Australians one of the fundamental rights of citizenship and indicated to them that they had been effectively banished from membership of the Australian community. At best, now, they were tolerated within that community but were not full, participating members of it. Other niggardly, petty actions and restrictions

> **TWO BEAUTIFUL HUN HOMES AT NEUTRAL BAY.**
>
> WHERE GERMAN WOOLBUYERS ARE LIVING IN LUXURY.
>
> "Enoshima," Burroway-street, Neutral Bay, the beautiful home of P. Schlesinger, the German woolbuyer.
>
> "Marengo," Bertha-street, Neutral Bay, where L. Bersch, another German woolbuyer, lives in luxury and ease.

A typical *Mirror* story. *Mirror,* 6 November 1915

made the situation not only clear, but also deeply hurtful. Australians deplored any manifestation of German identity. Parliaments forbade the use of the German language in church services, in newspapers and in the German schools, which were eventually closed anyway. The prohibition of German church services distressed 'our dear old folk', as the Reverend O. Nichterlein reported. The Postmaster-General's department threatened to remove a telephone from any subscriber who conversed in a language other than English and, as we shall see, letters written by German-Australians were read closely for indications of disloyalty. The South Australian Parliament and public wasted a good deal of time debating whether to change German place names to patriotic English ones and eventually legislation was introduced to do so. On the other hand, in March 1917 it became an offence for an individual to anglicise his name. This had become common practice as Frances Phillips, formerly Kahn, had testified in a letter to her sister in the United States: she explained that she had to abandon the family name 'on account of the feeling that existed towards the Germans ... I could never have got a position with the name of Kahn'.[26]

Leading the campaign to introduce and to enforce these irksome restrictions on the German-Australians was a newcomer to the Sydney newspaper scene, the *Mirror of Australia,* a weekly. To make a mark on the very competitive situation in Sydney the *Mirror* adopted a stridently anti-German attitude, borrowing, perhaps, from Horatio Bottomley's highly successful, but repulsive, English newspaper, *John Bull.* We often rely on newspapers as the voice of public opinion but it is not always clear how far papers reflect the public's attitudes and how far they create it. Certainly the *Mirror* succeeded in stimulating people to sign petitions and join anti-German leagues but its concentration on anti-Germanism from its inception probably derived from a shrewd assessment of the public's mood. With a singular lack of taste and justice the *Mirror* published the names and addresses of prominent Sydney 'Germans' and then speculated about their probable disloyal behaviour. Typical of the *Mirror's* approach was this attack on Oscar Plate, an employee of the Norddeutscher-Lloyd shipping line:

> [He] is still at large and enjoys the hospitality of this city at his beautiful home at Elizabeth Bay, whilst his countrymen are poisoning our brave men in the trenches and are sending innocent women and children to destruction on the high seas ... This Hun can view every transport that leaves Sydney Harbour in comfort from his own verandah ... this representative of the nation of baby-killers can obtain an excellent view of Garden Island [naval dockyard] from his bedroom window ... The only safe place for Herr Plate is in the Holdsworthy Concentration camp, or some equally secluded abode, where a bayonet or a bullet will prove effective if any mischief is attempted.

It should be noted that here and in many other similar 'cases' the *Mirror* made no specific charge of disloyalty but merely combined opportunity and 'Germanism' to allege disloyal, treacherous action. The *Mirror* mounted a campaign to ensure that every 'Hun', as 'Germans' were invariably called, was interned. It congratulated the government whenever a prominent 'German' was arrested but listed the names of dangerous 'Huns' 'still at large'. The paper campaigned strenuously against the 'German' element within the public service which, as the Royal Commission showed, was largely mythical. The paper revealed the names of highly-placed 'German' public servants and warned its readers that these people represented a substantial security risk. And of course the *Mirror* concentrated on the 'German spy network' it supposed existed in Australia. It claimed that the authorities had traced the theft of valuable documents to a former German consul-general who, from his Sydney base, also had 'the means of furnishing the German Pacific fleet [sic] with coal, wireless apparatus etc'. The man must be shot as a spy, the *Mirror* thundered, but the whole story sat oddly with the subsequent claim that Australian intelligence had not uncovered one case of espionage in Australia during the war. The *Mirror* was borrowing too literally from its English counterparts.[27]

It may seem to us that the *Mirror* was written by cranks for a fringe element of Australian alarmists but it sold widely and was taken seriously to the extent that the censor sought to prevent the publication of the more hysterical stories for fear of over-stimulating readers and creating panic. Petitions organised by the paper invariably succeeded; for example, 21,000 people signed a petition to disenfranchise 'Germans' within two days of the paper opening the campaign, surely evidence of influence. The *Mirror* also sponsored an 'Anti-German League' which had thirty-two branches throughout New South Wales backed by a team of efficient workers. The *Mirror* focused and encouraged anti-German feeling; that its gutter tactics survived at all is an indication of the depth of that feeling.[28]

At the beginning of the war those who had called for tolerance and sympathy for the German-Australians had emphasised how severely they would feel the tug of divided loyalties. These calls fell on deaf ears. Although remarkably dependent on Britain themselves, Australians showed no awareness of how acute was the dilemma facing German-Australians who still had a lingering affection for the old homeland. In September 1914, a prominent South Australian-German, E. Elkan, posed the problem neatly when he wrote to the South Australian *Register:*

> If there were a call to arms against any enemy but Germany you would find every [German-Australian] respond heartily in defence of Australia. I would offer my services as one of the first; but before I would take up arms against the country of my birth I would rather put a bullet through my head, and so would many more. I would offer my services in an ambulance corps.

Elkan's purpose in writing was to show 'what a dreadful nightmare this war is to all of us German-Australians'. He had lived in Australia for thirty years, had married an Australian, but had at least eighteen relatives fighting with the German forces. He miscalculated badly in seeking sympathy. Within a week the *Register* had published forty-three letters of protest, such as the advice that he 'ought really go back to his native land, the land he would sooner shoot himself for, than fight for Australian freedom and liberty'. Undoubtedly there were many cases where the balance of the divided loyalty fell in favour of Germany but Australians seemed to believe that this would be true in every case: that the loyalty of every German-Australian, native-born with deep roots in the country even, lay with Germany. The newspapers encouraged this sentiment by reporting every 'disloyal utterance' alleged against a German. Who are we to believe in the case of Gustav Pischul,

A CAMPAIGN OF LIES.

Foul slanders and gross misrepresentation against the Government's scheme for Compulsory Service is being conducted by men whom Mr. Hughes described as "The Agents of Germany."

DO NOT LISTEN TO THEM.

Think of the Australians in France! Shall we leave them unsupported whilst shirkers crowd the Racecourses and the Stadium?

Do you want Australian Conscription or German Conscription?

If we lose this war, the Germans will dominate Australia. Let us make this impossible, and secure our liberties.

The British Government has appealed to Australia for more men.

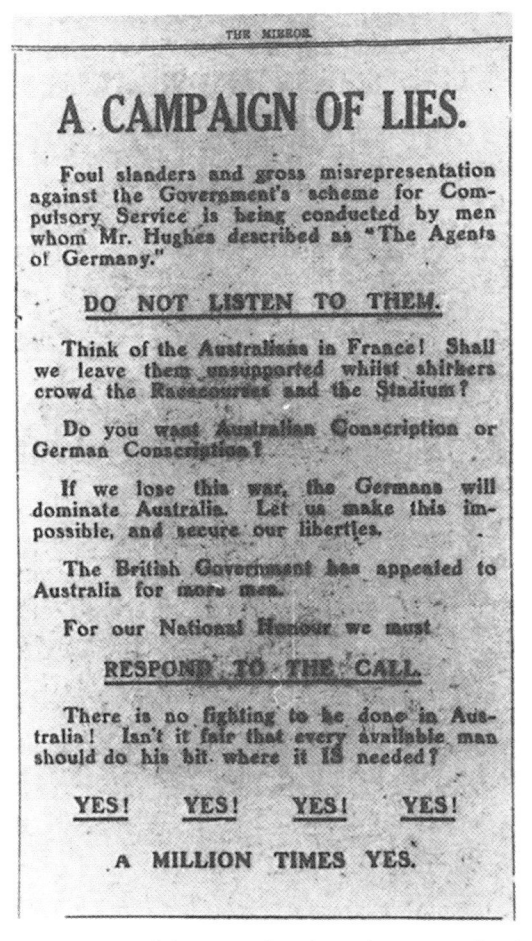

For our National Honour we must

RESPOND TO THE CALL.

There is no fighting to be done in Australia! Isn't it fair that every available man should do his bit where it IS needed?

YES!   YES!   YES!   YES!

A MILLION TIMES YES.

A clear expression of the view that Australia was to be the first prize of a victorious Germany. *Mirror*, 23 September 1916

for example? The complainant Ludovic William Grant, a soldier, claimed that Pischul said to him, 'I have got no time for the British nation, they are ratters'. Pischul claimed to have said: 'Good morning, Englishman', which would certainly have been a more prudent way of addressing a soldier in uniform. The court believed Grant and sentenced Pischul to one month's imprisonment.[29]

Under the stimulus of violence and insults, of reduced employment opportunities, of government actions designed to show them that they were not Australians, the German-Australian contempt and sense of alienation grew. The censors, who kept a close watch on Australian mail as well as on the newspapers, reported the extent of anti-Australian feeling amongst the German-Australians. The letters intercepted give no evidence of organised disloyalty, but they do show that some Germans hoped for a German victory. This sentiment was almost invariably associated with an increasing bitterness towards Australians who were seen as unjust, as a letter from

Holdsworthy internment camp

'A Lutheran' in the *Kapunda Herald* showed: 'Kapunda has raised in me bitterness almost beyond control to know that because I have German blood I am first branded disloyal then watched at every turn and looked upon with suspicion and mistrust ... Can anyone imagine the bitterness of it all?' A woman from Merbein, in Victoria, writing to her sister in the United States, complained of damage to the property of the German-Australians and the regulations preventing them from buying land or shares. 'It is', she wrote in February 1916, 'getting continually worse'. She also wrote, with evident satisfaction that '[the British] are sorry already for their smartness' and that the Australians, whose first response to war had been one of hysterical delight to be allowed to have a crack at Germany, were now 'beginning to know what war is'. Other writers, not so obviously influenced by the anti-German attitude in Australia, saw themselves as Germans-in-exile, with few ties in the land of their adoption. Thus, a man from Canterbury, Victoria, writing to his sister in Germany, rejoiced that the Allies were in trouble: 'That ought to be a warning to ... them to leave us Germans alone for all time'. And Christian Rowedder from St Kitts in South Australia, who was later interned, probably on the evidence of this letter, wrote to his father in Germany that:

I have only one single thought *'HOME'*. I wonder when that will come at last ... I still have the hope always that I may be of great service later ... [I] spend my time always waiting from one paper to the other in order to find among the lies a grain of truth.

Another correspondent, a woman, wrote more sensitively of the ambivalence many German-Australians experienced: 'I am, and remain, with every beat of my heart, a German woman, although I love this country and like living here'.[30]

So often the consciousness of being German, rather than Australian, was accentuated in a community increasingly hostile to the Germans in its midst. Banished from the community, the Germans' increasing dislike and contempt for the Australians was the natural outcome. Joseph Werner, writing from Sydney in 1917, complained of being 'insulted at every turn' and continued, 'I should be glad if I were not here, I would rather be in the South Sea Islands with the blacks and cannibals'. Pathetic as many of these letters are, there was little in them to worry the censors unduly. Even in the cases of disloyalty the only contemplated plan of action was to leave the country when that became feasible; the censors discovered no treachery or treason. The fears, expressed by the *Mirror* and shared, apparently by many Australians, seem to have been groundless.[31]

The only 'action' alleged against the German-Australians was that 'German votes' had been instrumental in the defeat of the first conscription referendum. Those who felt their dual loyalties most strongly no doubt wished to see conscription defeated lest some of their young men be faced

Sleeping quarters at Holdsworthy

with the awful problem of being forced to fight against their own kind. A somewhat disoriented German-Australian who admitted to having enlisted in a fit of boredom showed how terrible he would have found it to fight against his former countrymen: 'had I ever come into the firing line I would never have fired *one* bullet at a German'. Many German-Australians feared that conscription would force mutinous actions on their sons. Despite this motivation for a strong German-Australian 'No' vote, it is difficult to establish evidence of such a block vote at the first referendum. Kapunda, a solidly 'German' town, voted heavily against conscription in 1916 (523 Yes – 1,443 No); but the majority for No was almost identical in 1917 when the 'German votes' were specifically excluded (554 Yes – 1,331 No). Nor, given the atmosphere of late 1916, could any German afford to publicise his anti-conscription views; indeed, it is likely that many of them thought it wiser to avoid the booths completely on polling day as voting was not compulsory.[32]

Although no evidence of German disloyalty or treachery emerged during the war years, the Australian government organised an extensive internment system with large camps at Holdsworthy near Sydney and Langwarrin in Victoria, and smaller camps throughout Australia. Internment and imprisonment, let it be emphasised, were totally different. Internees were housed in 'camps', not gaols, and their guards were soldiers, not civilian officers. They were not subjected to normal legal procedures and so each was given no details of the charge which led to internment, had no opportunity to defend himself and could expect no public interest or awareness of his fate. The newspapers gave their readers few details of life within an internment camp: for the most part, internees simply ceased to exist for the community and they had few friends to plead their cause. Senator Pearce, the minister for defence, boasted that there were more aliens interned in Australia, proportionately, than in Great Britain. Nevertheless, he conceded, on the grounds of cost, selective rather than wholesale internment became the only feasible policy. Australia interned any 'enemy subject', a vague concept as we have seen, thought to be disloyal or dangerous, for whatever period of time thought necessary. As there was no trial before internment, it became very difficult for an internee to protest his innocence and the whole system of arrest and the length of imprisonment appears quite arbitrary. By March 1915 the authorities had 1,930 internees in the camps, by October 1918 this had grown to 3,135. Most of them were males; there were only fifty-eight females in the camps.[33]

Before America's entry into the war removed its neutrality, the American consul, Joseph I. Brittain, regularly inspected the camps for the German government to ensure that conditions were not too harsh. He suggested various minor improvements in administration from time to time but reported that, on the whole, the camps were quite satisfactory. At his visit in May 1916 the Holdsworthy camp held 4,299 prisoners and since it had opened in 1914 there had been only six deaths at the camp, including those

One of the victims after a riot at Holdsworthy, 19 April 1916. According to a guard riots were quite frequent because, confined in a small space with nothing to do, prisoners got on one another's nerves

of two men shot while attempting to escape. While Mr Brittain was happy with conditions, his reports make things seem primitive. For example, there were only six 'hot shower baths' in the camp and twenty 'cold shower baths'. There were forty-eight tubs and taps for washing but these were in the open; in winter, washing must have been unpleasant. The beds he described as 'a sort of canvas cot' with straw-filled burlap sacks 'constituting a sort of mattress'. Many of the prisoners slept without mattresses to be free of insects. While there were few complaints about food, the men did complain about the dust and the lack of anything to do. Only a thousand of them were employed at any one time, 500 in the morning and 500 in the afternoon, for which they received 1s a day. They worked for two weeks before being replaced by the next shift so that they were employed for only two weeks in every eight. We may doubt that conditions improved after Mr Brittain's visits ceased when America threw off her neutrality.[34]

The prisoners were not happy. They found the boredom oppressive, the conditions primitive and the mixing together of all classes and types of persons unsatisfactory. Because of this, and the tensions and frustrations of confinement, brawls, riots even, were frequent and serious. A guard, who invariably took a light-hearted view of the internees' troubles, recalled that 'After kicking and knocking their countrymen about, they threw them over the barbed wire; one man had 20 stitches put in his head'. The authorities allowed such outbursts to be 'fought to the finish' as the easiest way of maintaining order. Because they were interned without trial, internees bombarded the authorities with demands for full accounts of the allegations

'German' schoolchildren and their teacher at the Berrima (New South Wales) internment camp

of disloyalty against them or with petitions for release. Often they believed that the jealousy or resentment of neighbours accounted for their arrest rather than disloyalty. This must have increased the frustration. Certainly the policy of selective internment made abuses possible; the Katoomba real estate agent who had wanted a business rival interned to protect his own agency would have been better advised to have alleged specific disloyalty on the part of his rival in the letter to the premier. Selective internment angered many Australians, such as the editor of the *Mirror*, who believed that all 'enemy subjects' should be interned. Thus twenty-seven 'British subjects' from Binjour Plateau, Queensland, wrote to the prime minister just before the conscription referendum, asking that all Germans be interned. They lived amongst Germans, they wrote, and knew them to be disloyal so that should conscription be accepted the women and children of Australia would be endangered by the absence of the men. Were Hughes serious about conscription, he would intern all Germans first.[35]

Selective internment caught some odd fish in its net. Consider the case of Max Tannenberg, interned at Langwarrin in 1916. Aged about sixty-five, he had been naturalised for twenty-seven years and had lived in Australia for forty-two years. Very probably he thought of himself as an Australian. Even if his 'German' nature had endured during such a long time in Australia, it is not easy to imagine what harm a man of his age could do. He had no knowledge of the reasons for his internment and Frank Brennan, MHR, who made representations on his behalf stated that Tannenberg denied ever having done or said anything that would in the least compromise him. While the files do not allow us to follow the cases of men like Tannenberg to their conclusion to see whether he was paroled after a few months or endured years at Langwarrin, his case does emphasise how arbitrary the system was and how little protection it afforded a man who had laboured through his working life as an apparently loyal Australian. No doubt such men suffered deep shock to find themselves regarded as aliens, as 'enemy subjects'. Willi Horn, an internee at Liverpool, reported that 'many of the people are half mad' – to which we may add 'no wonder'. With good reason, a government memo suggested that internees be kept under surveillance after the war because they would probably harbour a grudge against Australia and Britain.[36]

German-Australians had worked hard to establish themselves within the Australian community before the war and, for the most part, they had succeeded. In South Australia particularly they had won a leading position in the political, commercial and cultural life of the community. They had been admired and respected. But the Australians, so heavily committed to the war emotionally, needed to manufacture a war close at hand lest their knitting and their fund-raising be their only real war experience. The German-Australians became the scapegoats for Australia's fanatical, innocent embrace of war.

CHAPTER EIGHT

THE OTHER AUSTRALIA?: WAR IN THE COUNTRY

As any traveller through rural Australia soon realises, the war was an event of momentous importance in the country, or so the prominent war memorials would have us think. Every town, no matter how small, seems to have erected a memorial, testifying to the high level of enlistment from rural Australia and the esteem the townspeople had for the recruits. Most of the municipalities within the cities similarly celebrated their young men, but these memorials seem less obvious, now blending in with a busy city landscape.

This difference in the impact of the memorials leads to questions about the possibility of a different impact the war may have had on city and country. Because they were smaller, more intimate communities, the departure of men from the country left a more obvious gap and any disagreement about the conduct of the war became more prominent. An examination of the impact of the war in rural Australia confirms many of the themes already explored. There was the same enthusiasm, the same emphasis on the central importance of the war to Australia, the same desire to make some contribution, and the same bitterness and frustration as divergent opinions emerged. There were different interests, of course, and country people believed that they suffered from the neglect of urban-based administrators and politicians, but fundamentally the response demonstrated how similar were rural and urban Australians. Indeed, the war developed this awareness and helped to make Australians think of themselves as one people, with common interests, rather than a loose connection for whom state and local-based loyalties predominated. Common issues confronted all Australians and their fortunes depended on that great national institution, the Australian Imperial Forces.

Rural Australia responded just as enthusiastically to the news that Great Britain was at war with Germany. Country newspapers served their people well, producing special editions, making the news as widely available as possible. Extensive railway networks also meant that the city papers, with their more detailed coverage of overseas news, were available quite soon after publication. The ready availability of the news allowed country people to regard themselves as directly threatened by the war and to be involved in it. They were enthusiastic and confident that all Australians had a role in the drama that was evolving. Newspapers published as far apart as Mount Morgan and Goulburn reported that the war had become the dominant, indeed the 'sole topic of conversation', and doubtless many weird theories drifted about. One enthusiast at Mount Morgan remarked 'haven't we got splendid weather for the war' and lest anyone miss the point, the newspaper added heavily 'as if the climatic conditions were the same as in Mount Morgan'. The newspapers stimulated much of the interest in the war and their offices became the town centre for the exchange of information and views. In the early days excited people 'dropped in' incessantly asking for fresh news, confident that a momentous and decisive battle would soon take place. The *Ballarat Courier* reported that a large crowd gathered at its offices on 7 August 1914 because 'special anxiety was felt as to the issue of the fighting in the North Sea ... the announcement of a British victory was received with great cheering'. If proof were needed of the strength of Empire bonds, surely it is to be found in the image of rural Australians, so remote from the conflict, rushing to the newspaper offices in the first days of the war, desperate to learn of the Empire's fate. All Australians believed that events in the North Sea had serious implications for Australia, so far away.[1]

These anxieties found expression in a wonderful variety of patriotic displays and impromptu manifestations of loyalty. The Inglewood Council adjourned for five minutes as a mark of its approval of Britain's entry into the war and at the conclusion of business, Council retired to the Pelican Hotel where 'the sentiment "The King and Empire" was honoured'. At Goulburn the mayor presided over a patriotic demonstration on 6 August 1914 which attracted over one-third of the town's entire population. He pledged that Goulburn would willingly share the sacrifice with the rest of the Empire: there was no sense at all of 'missing out'. Patriots at Murray Bridge also demonstrated their loyalty two days after the declaration of war. Railway workers, in their uniforms, and carrying the Union Jack, marched to the post office where they were joined by other civil servants, cadets and members of the civilian forces, to listen to a patriotic address by the chairman of the district council, Mr John Homburg. After an enthusiastic meeting, 'the gathering dispersed quietly as becomes sober members of a British community'. Less formal, but no less patriotic, was the demonstration late on a Saturday night at Naracoorte, South Australia, when some twenty young men, singing patriotic songs, induced a crowd of about a hundred to join them. Householders, aroused from their beds in the hope of fresh war news, swelled the chorus, beefing out patriotic songs until about midnight. One can but wonder if the original twenty retired as 'sober members of a British community'.[2]

One of the many rural processions, this one in Tumut, led by the Hibernians. Sometimes these began spontaneously, particularly in the early days of the war, but often they were organised to raise money or recruits

The urge to make some contribution to the Empire's cause gripped country people, building on the patriotism displayed in the more ephemeral demonstrations. While the Kalgoorlie Racing Club donated all the profits from their three day carnival, about £500, to the patriotic funds, the people of Yass, New South Wales, demonstrated a more cautious patriotism. Their desire for sacrifice on the Empire's behalf led them to cancel the town's annual show, a decision which the show president justified when he argued that the war would have a doleful effect on the national economy. He reported that he

> had been reliably informed that the war would last at least twelve months, and he could see that Australia was in for a rotten time. The war would cost £5,000,000 a day, as they fought on Sundays, that would mean £35,000,000 a week for which somebody had to pay. They all knew that they and he would have to pay it and the average man would have to exercise care in spending money.

The people might be glum, but they were prepared to accept the burden. In Ballarat the early movement of troops alerted citizens to the seriousness of the war and warned them of the sacrifices that might be expected. Ballarat, its people demanded, could not be a 'passive spectator' of the war and had already 'assumed its share of the responsibility on behalf of the Empire' by sending its reserve troops to Queenscliff, at the entrance to Port Phillip Bay, for garrison duty. Moreover, 'Ballarat was prepared to take a bigger share if necessary in that responsibility'. The movement of the citizen forces, the parades of the rifle clubs and then the rush to enlist, all warned rural Australians that her troops would be called on to fight the enemy. The sacrifice would be primarily one of men. But, as at Yass, other thoughts turned to the effect of the war on the economy, and on trade in particular. Trade was always a topic of concern for country people whose markets were predominantly overseas. At Bendigo there was optimism because 'gold becomes a great national asset in the time of war and is even more in demand than when the nations of the world are at peace'; gold-mining remained Bendigo's most important industry. But at Albury there was gloom because the war would disrupt shipping and therefore put the export of meat at risk: good news, perhaps, for housekeepers, but bad news for farmers. Other gloomy predictions about unemployment and hard times for country people abounded, but always fell within the context of an exhortation to accept the sacrifice in the spirit of loyalty to the Empire.[3]

In their initial enthusiasm and their acceptance of the war, country people showed how similar was the spirit animating urban and rural Australia: Empire patriotism knew no boundaries. There were indications that the country people were even more zealous on the Empire's behalf than the majority in the cities. The patriotic procession and demonstration started in the country towns and was often more enthusiastic and spontaneous than the city affairs which required organisation, police permission and considerable planning. 'Small town rivalries' and local pride stimulated patriotism in

A recruiting meeting at Harden, New South Wales, 1915

the country where no town wished to be thought backward in devotion to the Empire. Similar comparisons between the loyalty of the various cities, although made, had little meaning and little effect. But in the country, appeal could easily be made to local pride to encourage every form of sacrifice. Thus, at Yass, in soliciting funds for 'Belgian Day' the *Courier* stated that 'we confidently anticipate Yass taking equal, if not superior rank with any provincial town in the State of similar area and population. It is up to us'. This became a recurring, common theme in appeals for men or money, because country people identified closely with their local area. Rivalries emerged within communities too, the nuances often perceived only by those with a feel for local custom. These rivalries, unlike those between towns, sometimes hindered patriotic activities. Correspondents in the country papers were quick to see discourtesy and disharmony, pointing out at Kapunda that the mayor's place in farewelling the troops had been abrogated by the secretary of the Progress Association, or at Angaston how the Cheer-Up Society had fallen into disarray or, again at Kapunda, how the tone of a school's patriotic display was apologetic, 'more suitable for a girls' teaparty than an Empire demonstration'. While the country was loyal, local society was complex and successful patriotic activity depended on the gradations in society being given proper recognition. To overlook the mayor, or to confuse the social hierarchy was to court disaster. Recruiters from the cities often failed to observe the proprieties and thus failed to secure valuable local co-operation. A Sydney-based recruiting officer appealed for a local organiser in Wyalong as well as one in Temora, towns only 70 kilometres apart, because while visiting the area he discovered that 'Very little preparation had been made by reason ... of a local feud between the two towns'. Local sensitivities demanded gentle treatment.[4]

The willingness to enlist in the AIF quickly became the ultimate test of loyalty anywhere in Australia. Country people boasted that rural Australia provided many more recruits than their proportion within the total population demanded, that their patriotism was more intense and that their young men were more robust and more adaptable, that they made better soldiers. Thus, while the degree and extent of patriotic fervour might be similar between city and country, rural Australians believed their contribution to be potentially more valuable. While expressing delight in the enlistment of five farmers from the Mallee district of Victoria, the *Bendigo Advertiser* regretted that 'so many farmers and farmers' sons have had to take the place of city men, as labour will be scarce in the seeding season'. With a wonderfully dismissive attitude for the men of the city, the paper further regretted that the city men had cold feet because their work was 'work that girls do' and therefore their enlistment would not be missed in the way that the absence of farmers would be. London observers assumed that most of the Australian recruits were 'bushmen', as we have seen, and C. E. W. Bean in the *Official History* accounted for the unique skills of the Anzacs by explaining that many of them

Volunteers leaving Tumut for the wars, 1914. Note the band and, apart from a few girls, the absence of women

were the independent, manly types found on the land. However, the figures do not seem to substantiate these generalisations; rural Australians were not grossly overrepresented in the AIF. But the pressure to enlist bore more heavily on country people who could not hide behind the anonymity that the large numbers in the cities provided. In country towns recruiters appealed to individuals whose private circumstances, employment and marriage status would have been known to some, at least, of the other members of the audience. In the cities recruiters appealed to big rallies at sporting events, entertainments and on the crowded streets, where every 'eligible' could find refuge in his own private circumstances. Potentially, then, country eligibles had to withstand more pressure, which may account for the slightly higher proportion of country men in the AIF.[5]

By treating volunteers as heroes and by elaborately farewelling each contingent of them, the people of the country towns created a climate that would induce other young men to imitate the recruits. But rather than seeing this as a conscious recruiting device, it should be regarded, particularly before the need for recruits became intense, as a spontaneous demonstration of loyalty and goodwill. No doubt the recruits departing for the city training camps enjoyed the notoriety their sacrifice had earned. There was an almost classical Roman note to the farewell of the first seven Murray Bridge youths to enlist. Organisers planned the send-off only at midday but by departure time at 4.30 p.m., three to four hundred people had gathered at the railway station. Councillor Parish, the only member of the council in town on that day, was working at the time but 'Sliding from the scaffold he mounted his bicycle and was at the railway station in time to voice the good wishes of

A highly stylised version of a city farewell from a recruiting poster, 'The Strong Post', 1918

the people for the departing warriors'. Not all farewells were as informal. When Herbert Henningham, an employee of the Wagga council, enlisted, the mayor and councillors, assembled in the council chamber, farewelled him with speeches. Both these demonstrations show what an important part the local government officials played in the life of the community. An early recruit from Eudunda received a case of silver mounted pipes at an elaborate farewell, while 'thousands' of the people of Armidale gathered to send-off Lieutenant-Colonel Braund and sang patriotic songs as his train departed.[6]

Speeches on these occasions often developed the theme of pride that local people felt for their own kind who were prepared to play their part in the world-wide conflict. The war, they felt, placed their town on the map. As Captain Coen said when addressing his well-wishers from the balcony of the Commercial Hotel, Yass, 'he was glad to know his native town was represented in the great army of the Empire'. Often the women of the town contributed to these occasions by providing sandwiches and other refreshments for the trip and, invariably, 'smokes' to help the men enjoy the journey. The point was that everyone could be involved. The farewell was a ritual, sincerely meant, that gave importance to a sad moment but which also drew attention to the need for recruits. Such a personal touch was virtually impossible in the cities where a recruit might solemnise his enlistment privately at a party for family and friends, or on a huge impersonal scale with a very public procession of troops through the streets of the city. The recruit from Yass, from Stawell or Kapunda, probably felt more like a hero as the citizens of his district saluted him.[7]

Such intense community involvement worked against the man who refused to enlist, for whatever reasons. While it was probably reasonable to publish the names of local recruits in newspapers and on honour boards erected in parks and town halls, it does not seem fair to have publicised the names of men who had not enlisted. In the cities their circumstances would have been known to only a small circle but in the country an eligible's reasons for not enlisting might be open to public scrutiny. 'Loyal Worker' complained that speakers at a recruiting meeting at Kapunda had named families in the town which had not sent any of their eligible sons to the war. He regretted the pressure thus placed on those families. A meeting of 'patriotic fathers' at Murray Bridge agreed to 'march en masse to homes where boys had not left for the front to plead with the families to allow their sons to go'. Although the meeting deferred this drastic action until the results of the war census cards had been tabulated, one speaker, E. J. Harvey, regretted the delay, explaining that 'The Australians would have been in Constantinople that day if the cold-footed "men" of the district had not "hung back"'.[8]

Perhaps the sending of white feathers was as common in the cities as in the country, but targets in country districts were chosen more accurately. George C. Robbie, Murray Bridge's 'professional patriot', public speaker and inveterate contributor to the letters-to-the-editor column, justified sending white feathers to young men. He referred to the case of the man who said he would not enlist while people tried to force him, arguing that he was an appropriate target for a white feather. Worse, he claimed, was the man in the government service who laughed about enlistment, saying he would only join up when violet powder replaced bullets as ammunition. Such cowardice merited a white feather, in Robbie's eyes. It is interesting that Robbie presumed his readers would be able to identify the men to whom he referred, conceding that. 'The cases mentioned might appear to some of your readers a bit too pointed'. The point is that Robbie and other Murray Bridge residents knew the details of each of the town's 'eligibles' thoughts

Collections such as this were displayed in council offices and published in local newspapers to honour local heroes and to encourage recruiting

on enlistment, which gave them considerable opportunity to bring pressure to bear on them. Of course, these 'urgers' did not have things all their own way because the 'eligibles' were often emboldened to strike back. Robbie finally took his own advice and enlisted but when he tried to speak at a public gathering suggesting that others follow his example, he was 'howled down for about ten minutes'. Frequently letters appeared in local newspapers asking recruiters to refrain from exhorting young men to enlist when they themselves either could not or would not do so.[9]

Because some men in the country towns withstood the pressures to enlist, the recruiting meeting became as normal a feature of rural life as it was in Martin Place or Collins Street. At all such meetings speakers stressed the need for recruits, the duties of 'mateship' in assisting those already at the front, and the threat to Australia should the Empire succumb to the barbarities of Germany. In the country recruiters appealed particularly to a sense of local pride, as if a strong motive for enlistment were to uphold the honour of the district. Notes appeared in local papers to the effect, for example, that Renmark, with a small population, had secured 170 recruits, while Murray Bridge, a larger centre, languished with only ninety-nine recruits. Recruiters used such figures in an attempt to shame young men into enlisting. The recruiting officer for the Goulburn district freely admitted that he played on the rivalries of the towns within his area, publishing progressive tallies for Goulburn, Yass, Cooma and Bega and appealing to eligibles to uphold the honour of their birthplace. This was not simply a silly tactic because people did see enlistment rates as a definition of a district's loyalty. For that reason, towns erected honour boards and memorials listing the names of all who had joined up, as a kind of public scoreboard. We look at these lists today presuming they are commemorations put up after the war ended to remind people of their debt to the AIF, but very often the memorials appeared in 1915 or 1916 as an incentive for recruits.[10]

Recruiters used other methods, too, again appropriate to the greater intimacy and knowledge about one's neighbours. The Maryborough Recruiting Committee employed a lady, Mrs Mutch, to interview the mothers, wives or girlfriends of eligibles to try to persuade each woman to 'let her man go'. The Shire of Huntly sent personal letters to eligibles asking them to attend the local agricultural hall where each man was interviewed separately and 'privately examined as to his reasons for declining service'. Should the unfortunate man allege lack of physical fitness as his reason for not offering to enlist, he was immediately examined by the local doctor who donated his services for the day. Such an intense method of recruiting yielded ten more men for the AIF.[11]

While recruitment was undoubtedly a source of local pride, it is really very difficult either to find an accurate measure of the rate of enlistment in a particular area, or a standard by which to compare enlistment figures from different areas. In New South Wales, however, the government published, at the end of 1915, enlistment figures for each of the state's country electorates. By comparing these figures with the number of male voters enrolled in the electorates (enrolment, unlike voting, was compulsory), we may arrive at some sort of 'loyalty index' for the country districts of New South Wales. With some exceptions, the electorates fell within the mean established by the Defence department in 1916 of recruitment rates. This means that country enlistment was not substantially higher than that of the cities. In New South Wales, to April 1916, one in every 11.5 males had enlisted, or about 8 per cent; the country electorates fitted this pattern. Nevertheless, there were some perplexing variations. Albury clearly won the 'loyalty stakes' with 34 per cent of the males in the electorate enlisting; then came Lismore and Tamworth with 19 per cent each and three other northern electorates, Armidale, Byron and Castlereagh, at 15 per cent. There were fifty-three country electorates in New South Wales in 1915.[12]

If, in general aggregate, the country reflected city patterns, at least in New South Wales for which we have figures, the phases in the recruiting movement were similar too. There was a period of excitement and brisk business, during which time well-wishers could be heard to say that they 'hoped the men would see some fighting', then a period of steady but unspectacular enlistment with a few high points corresponding to significant action at the front, or the first great recruiting campaign, and then followed a long period of stagnation when recruits were very hard to come by indeed. Within two

The 'Kangaroos' en route to Sydney. They started from Wagga, 100 strong, on 1 December 1915, and hoped to gain recruits as they marched

weeks of the outbreak of war, about a hundred men had enlisted from Albury, about two hundred from Wagga Wagga, and over two hundred and fifty from Broken Hill. After this initial throng of men anxious not to miss out, the country then provided a fairly constant rate which the *Ballarat Courier* referred to as 'the measured pace of recruiting'. In Kapunda, for example, forty-one men had volunteered by May 1915, 104 by July (reflecting the stimulus of the news of the Anzacs' landing at Gallipoli), 171 by November, 200 by March 1916, 238 by May, 248 by October and 260 by December. The decline in the second half of 1916 at Kapunda was common throughout Australia and, ironically, coincided with the expansion of the recruiting movement. How frustrated were Kapunda patriots to net ten recruits in five months! At Mount Morgan a recruiting meeting in September 1917, which attracted a 'large gathering' to hear 'fervent, vigorous, powerful and pathetic appeals' for more men, secured only one recruit. Such results occurred so often that they seem to indicate that the pool of available young men had dried up. The figures from the Barossa area of South Australia tell the story. In August 1916, eighty-two men had enlisted from Angaston, by April 1918 only eighteen more had been recruited; in Nuriootpa, nine additional recruits enlisted in this twenty-month period, nine in Truro and twelve in Tanunda.[13]

By 1917 recruiting was in a very low state indeed in the country, as the reports of various New South Wales recruiting officers showed. Lieutenant W. G. Williams toured the Queanbeyan-Bega district and submitted a very gloomy report to his superiors in Sydney. He found it difficult to secure a hearing, let alone to win recruits. At Cooma, he saw 'plenty of eligible men' but believed that most of them were 'passive resisters', while at Queanbeyan, 'the tone ... [was] bad. There are over fifty eligibles in the town' many of whom were 'conscientious objectors and as a result [were] hard to approach and harder to convince'. At Nimmitabel, a small town high up in the mountains beyond Cooma, Williams almost despaired:

> We addressed a fairly large meeting containing many eligibles and also personally interviewed a few but without result ... we were constantly referred to their local honour roll containing one hundred and thirty names but that is not a fair index of what Nimmitabel has done. For some time after war was declared railway construction works were in progress on the new line from Nimmitabel to Bombala and on examining the roll I found a great many names were those of railway workers who had enlisted in Nimmitabel and not local residents ...

How many other towns 'poached' recruits to make their patriotism seem more impressive and thus take the pressure off their own young men? Perhaps Lieutenant Williams simply lacked enterprise, for a report of a tour by Fred J. Bohm showed how ingenious a recruiter might be. On arrival at Wellington, New South Wales, Bohm discovered that no arrangements had been made to draw attention to his meeting and that he would need to advertise extensively and quickly were he even to secure an audience. At the time the meeting was due to start, only six people had gathered to hear his appeal.

> After deep consideration we thought out a scheme. We arranged with the Fire Brigade to ring the Fire bell and run the Fire hose to where we were to speak. The police were at first against the proposition but we eventually talked them over. The result was a decided success. Every body in the town turned out to see the Fire but when they followed the hose it only led them to our platform and after apologising for the hoax we addressed one of the best tempered and largest audiences of our tour … Seven men were secured.

A diverting story, perhaps, but seven recruits was not a great response from a large, enthusiastic meeting. Lieutenant Elfield, in the Riverina, experienced the response that had so depressed Williams: he addressed fifteen meetings, sometimes two per day and gained a total of only fifty-two recruits. He was inclined to blame the people and reported that, for example, Junee 'requires to be wakened up to its responsibilities'. But undoubtedly by 1917 there were few real eligibles available, men whose circumstances allowed them to enlist. It will be remembered that by the end of 1915 the Albury electorate, based on the Riverina, had supplied an extraordinary proportion of its men to the AIF. An early patriotic response in some cases stirred the wrath of later recruiters frustrated at the failure of their own appeals.[14]

To stimulate recruiting the various State Recruiting Committees posted cards to eligibles asking them if they intended to enlist and, if so, when. Despite the pressure, country men were as ready to decline the invitation as were the city eligibles. Of 650 letters sent to men in the Korong Vale area, the recruiting sergeant succeeded with 119 men, of whom twenty-four were subsequently rejected as unfit. Only thirty others promised to enlist at some time in the future. In the Mount Barker area 175 cards were sent to married eligibles from whom twelve immediately enlisted and thirteen deferred; of the 167 single men whose intentions were sought, forty-seven offered immediately and eleven deferred. The remaining 109 were not interested. The reasons for these refusals are, of course, lost to us, but there is a hint that some of these country eligibles resented the city-based nature of the recruiting campaign. As the Gunnedah District Association put it in a telegram to the New South Wales premier, the failure was 'the result of having administration in the hands of men with an absolute lack of knowledge of country conditions and requirements'. It is interesting that the dichotomy between the country and the city which was used to explain the supposedly higher country enlistment rate could also be used to explain the failure of recruiting in the country. The Gunnedah Association did not explain how

Inventive fund-raising ideas were not confined to the cities. These women ran a tea-room at Glen Innes, New South Wales, the profits of which were sent to the War Chest, Sydney

country people should be appealed to and apparently none of the recruiters learned the art, as enlistment rates continued to fall.[15]

The intense desire to help the Empire, which stimulated so much of the early enlistment, also led country people to give generously to the various funds and causes associated with the war. Fed by that rivalry between districts and towns which we encountered in relation to recruitment, the funds demonstrated the enthusiasm and the generosity of country people. Money flowed freely. Goulburn raised £1,000 within the first month of the war and could be well satisfied with the result, until perhaps the townspeople learned that the people of Cootamundra had raised £12,000 within the first two weeks. People everywhere gave generously and then happily regarded the result as 'very creditable'; they continued to give because they did not wish their area to fall behind. Pastoralists, prominent in the subscription lists, also gave in kind, horses to the Defence department, free of all expenses, or mutton and beef to feed the troops at the front. In Maryborough the patriotic fund committee determined to provide all the volunteers from the area with acid drops, sticking plaster and Bibles: 'the latter to be worn next to the heart to stop the bullets'. While out of the line, presumably the troops might read their Bibles! Doubtless other committees had equally unconventional ideas of what soldiers might need. But all of them displayed that same eagerness to do something, that was found in the cities.[16]

Much of the fund-raising became an excuse for fun and a social life that wartime 'seriousness' might otherwise have prevented. The war years would have been drab indeed for country people except for the outlet that the patriotic funds provided. At Murray Bridge several dances had been abandoned early in the war because the organisers 'considered it would be out of place to indulge in such joyous forms of recreation in the circumstances'. The necessity to raise money lifted the gloom. At a farewell to three soldiers from the town, there were thirteen speeches, several songs and the dancing, conducted with spirit, lasted until 2 a.m. There were dances, concerts, parties, carnivals, race meetings and even more elaborate entertainments held throughout the war years – all in the name of patriotism. The Kapunda Tennis Club organised a 'patriotic tennis dance' and decorated the hall with patriotic bunting, a tennis net and the implements of the game. One may wonder whether patriotism was only an excuse for socialising. At Freeling, South Australia, the Red Cross members arranged for a 'patriotic football match' between the married and unmarried men of the town. Amongst the players in fancy costume were a cavalier, 'nigger minstrels', a dummy, a Russian, a doctor and an ambulance team. Yass observed Belgian Day with an elaborate procession consisting, among others, of decorated cars, Red Cross nurses, the King of the Belgians escorted by two lancers, John Bull, the Allies represented by girls in national costume, and 'a bevy of animated Union Jacks'; the whole affair raised £296 15s 6d. Miss Fosberry of Wagga Wagga arranged for a 'bread and butter' dance in aid of a fund to provide a travelling kitchen for the AIF.[17]

While country people gave generously to the plethora funds, some believed, in the early days at least, that it would be wiser to save their money and thus be in a position to alleviate the distress that the war would cause in Australia. Country people, particularly, feared that war would bring about large-scale economic dislocation. As soon as war broke out employers tended to fulfil this expectation by dismissing workers in anticipation of the crisis to come. The *Mount Morgan Chronicle* sought to calm public opinion by pointing out that only two hundred or two hundred and fifty men had been dismissed because of the war. And this by 7 August 1914 – cold comfort indeed. In Tasmania, unemployment quickly became a new anxiety. Because the west coast zinc mines depended so heavily on the German markets, many of them closed down when war broke out, throwing most of the employees out of work. Broken Hill, a city built on mining, suffered similarly. But fear of the economic consequences of the war affected less vulnerable areas too. The editor of Lismore's *Northern Star* advised his readers that the rush on the local savings banks and the panic buying of foods was quite unnecessary. Australia, he announced, was in no immediate danger. He regretted the evidence of hysteria in the town which arose because 'so much information of an unreliable and sensational nature' had been spread about.[18]

Unemployment caused much hardship even though it did proceed from theories about the war rather than from a realistic assessment of its consequences. Once dismissed, initially at least, men found great difficulty in regaining employment, as a letter from 'Rejected to Starve' shows. This man had tried to enlist three times but was rejected each time because of bad teeth, despite his excellent record of service during the Boer war. The recruiters advised him that he would not be accepted even with 'artificial teeth', showing how high early standards were. Because 'Rejected' appeared to be eligible, fit and unmarried, employers refused him work; when he tramped all through the Wilcannia and Hay districts looking for work, each of the 'squatter[s told] me to go to war'. He reached Broken Hill where there was no work and he tried for six weeks to find a job. So 'Rejected' wrote to the paper in a desperate situation, unemployed and apparently unemployable, reduced to suggesting that the government issue him with a rejection certificate to give credence to his story.[19]

Certainly, the need for recruits must have reduced whatever concern employers felt for the plight of the unemployed, who must often have been told to 'go to war'. But how many of the volunteers were 'economic conscripts', forced by circumstances to enlist, it is not possible to say. It is impressive that in spite of the economic hardship and some measure

Women at work at the Kalgoorlie Soldiers Institute — patriotism knew no regional boundaries. Some recruits or even returned men may have used the facilities but it does seem rather remote. Doubtless the women also raised funds for the Red Cross

of uncertainty, country towns managed to raise large sums of money for patriotic purposes. Later, however, prosperity in the country grew because the Allies needed Australian wheat and wool. Employment prospects similarly improved and farmers began to fear a loss of skilled labour which influenced their views about conscription. But while the country boomed, there was still a great deal of uncertainty. The drought had lifted and bumper crops were harvested but would Hughes take away the labour needed to consolidate, or would he be able to find the shipping to send Australian produce to Britain? If the worker suffered in the early years, the employer worried later: there was a good deal of unease in the country.

The principal focus of women's work, in the country as in the city, was the Red Cross Society, a branch of which opened in every town of any size at all. The procedures adopted in the country imitated the city pattern; indeed, the fact that, at Yass, the branch was to be formed 'under the auspices of the Liberal Association', suggested the link between the Red Cross and the middle-class discovered in the cities. Despite, or because of this, the inaugural meeting was 'the largest and most representative meeting of ladies, ever held in Yass' and within four days of its inception, the paper reported that the branch was in full swing: 'A casual visitor to the mechanics' balcony would be surprised at the buzz of sewing machines, the whirl of cutting out scissors, and the chatter of tongues'. Despite such enthusiastic, if patronising, reports of branches at town after town, the numbers of women attending weekly meetings really was quite small. A branch with seventy-five members was considered large, and many annual reports put average weekly attendance at about fifteen. The meetings provided women not only with an outlet for their creativity but also with an avenue for socialising, but only for the women of the towns. The more isolated women on properties collected material and deposited made-up goods when they came to town for shopping, but they knitted their socks and sewed at home.[20]

That the Red Cross was seen as an exclusively female concern is apparent from the fact that a small number of men's branches appeared. Thus at Mt Barker the men organised themselves into an entirely separate branch from the women to make things such as cupboards, stools and crutches. This branch did not succeed, with membership at around twenty, few of whom seem to have attended meetings. The enthusiasm and devotion of middle-class country women made the Red Cross one of the truly national institutions to emerge from the war. Of course, the tedium and monotony of the work depressed many of the women, who found it difficult to maintain their enthusiasm. Although 150 Goulburn women attended the first Red Cross meeting there, numbers of workers dwindled so that by 1918 only about twenty were regular attenders. It is doubtful if this kind of decline can be explained solely by disillusionment with the war, obviously organisations cannot expect to retain the enthusiasm of their members over a long period of time.[21]

By mid-1916 disillusionment with the war was growing as country people sensed how severe was the stalemate at the front and how intense were the political passions developing at home. The country was in no sense protected from the bitterness and the controversy of the conscription debate and it would be wrong to believe that only in the cities, where radicalism found a more congenial home, were the referenda fought with passion. Indeed, there was little observable difference between the urban conscription campaigns and those conducted in the country. Country newspapers were as much in favour of conscription as their metropolitan counterparts. Editorials argued Hughes' case, reports of meetings heavily favoured the 'pro' side and, as polling day came closer, large advertisements for 'Yes' occupied prominent positions in the papers. Rarely was there a specific rural element in the rural press campaign in support of conscription. Some papers tried to refute the 'anti's bogey' that conscription would rob farmers of the labour needed to harvest their crops and they did stress what loyalty rural Australia owed Britain in return for the sacrifices wartime Britain had made to buy Australian farm produce. Hughes believed this point would win the sympathy of country people for Britain and he developed it as he spoke in the country towns. At Wagga Wagga he claimed that Australian farmers had profited from the war but only because the British and the French had continued to buy from Australia. He asked how wheat farmers could expect 'Britain to finance next year's crop if we turn their proposal down on October 28'. Apart from the revealing slip that conscription was a British proposal, Hughes' argument deserves little attention because it was ignored by the editors of the country newspapers, who may have found it a little too crude to suggest that their readers trade men for wheat or wool sales. Instead, editors relied on the arguments in vogue in the cities, the need to reinforce the Australian troops at the front, mateship, the honour of Australia and the threat to Australia.[22]

This last point dominated much of the campaign, showing that rural Australia shared the urban dwellers' exaggerated notions of Australia's attraction for the enemy. As the *Mount Morgan Chronicle* put it: 'Australia more than any other place on the globe is the ultimate aim of Germany's dream of colonial expansion'. Such sentiments were almost universal so that the anti-conscription editorial was a rarity indeed in the country newspapers. In an admittedly random search of newspapers from all states, only one 'anti' paper, the Maryborough *Alert*, emerges. There the editor saw the question as one between enslavement and freedom, writing of Hughes as mesmerised by the 'debasing company of Kings and nobles and war-mad jingoes and swash-buckling soldiers'. Brave words, braver to the point of madness had he written of the debasing company of *the* King, which is presumably what he meant. But such an outspoken editorial encouraged no imitators. Even in towns with a highly unionised workforce, such as Broken Hill, the papers maintained the universality of the pro-conscription position. In Broken Hill an editorial called on the people to regard a 'Yes' majority as 'a Christmas box for the soldiers'![23]

The public meeting, the other great vehicle for the dissemination of views about conscription, was prominent in rural campaigns. Because the politicians were so anxious to put their arguments before the people, the country towns received a bewildering array of visiting speakers. Campaigning must have been exhausting. Hughes travelled extensively in Queensland, New South Wales and Victoria and members of his cabinet visited many of the centres he missed. No doubt many of the meetings passed off peacefully, without incident, with the mayor in the chair, the epitome of neutrality and fair play. But often, too, bad temper intruded with as much force and vigour at the smaller country meetings as at the larger metropolitan ones. At Tamworth in 1916, when the leader of the 'antis' provocatively mounted a pro-conscription platform to call for cheers against conscription, a 'Yes' campaigner pushed him off. This rough treatment caused a minor riot as the proponents of both views rushed to defend their leaders. Eventually, the police separated the two factions and cleared the hall, ending the fracas, in which, the report notes, women played a conspicuous part. The involvement of women in a public brawl is surely an indication of passion on both sides. At Binginwarri, in Gippsland, an 'anti' threw an egg during a 'pro' rally and was promptly invited to 'step outside' by the local Methodist minister, the Rev. C.J. Walklate. A crowd formed around Mr Walklate, jeering him, and more eggs were thrown: evidence of division and passion, surely hard to hide and harder to heal in as small a settlement as Binginwarri.[24]

When the editor of the *Alert* accused Hughes of sowing bitterness, hatred and strife among hitherto friendly people, of reaping a harvest of severed friendships and broken homes, he was reflecting on the particularly disruptive character of the country campaigns. It is difficult to assess just how deeply this bitterness cut into the social fabric of these communities. In the cities numbers gave anonymity and the class structure of the suburbs determined that like-minded people usually lived together and rarely came into frequent contact with their opponents. We know that the country towns afforded no such protection and separation and that opponents were forced to rub shoulders with one another, but we can only judge the impact of this imperfectly. Thus at Kapunda shopkeepers and other small businessmen who had identified with the 'Yes' cause, found that their businesses suffered as 'antis' refused to patronise them. An ex-teacher complained that at the government schools teachers had directed the children to tell their parents to vote 'Yes' and had asked the children to indicate which side their families favoured. Such incidents may have been rare and are likely to catch the eye, searching for 'colour' and perhaps should be discounted. On the other hand, given the fanaticism of proponents of both sides of this question, and the complexity and seriousness of the issues involved, it is likely that these incidents reflect the turmoil and the confusion that the campaign caused.

After all, most observers and participants mentioned the bitterness that the referenda aroused.[25]

We should beware, however, of exaggerating the impact of the arguments of the politicians and the newspaper men. Much has been made in this book of the exaggerated perception of threat that many Australians held. But not all Australians. When a pro-conscription speaker at Broken Hill claimed that in fighting the Germans in France the AIF were defending the integrity and liberty of Australia, the crowd broke into loud laughter. They laughed, too, at the suggestion that the lives of the children in the patriotic tableau were threatened by the Germans and they laughed loudly again at a speaker who tried to show that the war was not a capitalists' war. The meeting was also interrupted by a man imitating the crow of a rooster, by the counting out of the speakers and by the singing of revolutionary songs. On the next day, when an 'anti' appeared before the Broken Hill magistrate, charged under the War Precautions Act with behaviour likely to arouse disaffection, the magistrate remarked that he would like to turn a machine-gun on all such disloyal people. Of course, both viewpoints existed in Australia, that of those who laughed at the idea that Australia was threatened, and that of those who wished to shoot such traitors. Their existence in rural Australia, where differences were far more obvious, increased tensions and anxieties.[26]

Historians have emphasised the prominent part played by rural voters in the defeat of conscription, explaining that they voted against the proposal because they feared the loss of farm labour, in its own way expert, and therefore hard to replace. To overcome this fear the government insisted that exemptions would be granted to allow the work on the land to proceed. It was woeful timing that many of the exemption courts began their sittings in country districts in the week before the referendum. These courts were examining the applications of men claiming exemption from the September call-up, instigated because Hughes was so confident that the people would accept conscription for overseas service that he had 'jumped the gun' by calling men out for service in Australia. Again, because of the greater intimacy in country communities and because of the greater interest of country newspapers in local affairs, voters there were much more aware of the exemption courts than the people in the cities. The courts necessarily had to follow the government's rules and guidelines and because these rules were so strict relatively few applications succeeded in avoiding the call-up. Indeed, the magistrate at Mt Barker commiserated with one applicant who gave his severe domestic responsibilities as his reason for exemption. The magistrate explained that the rules did not permit an exemption but he expressed his genuine concern for the man's plight and wished he had the power to exempt him.[27]

As the call-up would have affected all single men between the ages of 21 and 35, there were very many applications for exemption. At Border Town, for example, of the 128 men who reported to the military authorities, ninety-four were passed as fit, of whom four immediately joined the AIF, while eighty-seven applied for exemption from the call-up. In South Australia as a whole, by 12 October, 14,000 men had been examined, 8,548 passed as fit, 6,065 of whom immediately sought exemption. Doubtless, most of these men believed that they had a valid reason not to go to war. We can understand why recruiting had so fallen away in the light of these figures and we can understand some of the pressures for a 'No' vote. The voting of the men who sought exemption, and that of their families and immediate friends, must have been influenced by expectations of their success in the courts, sitting only days before the referendum. And as the court reports showed, these expectations could not have been high. At the Mount Barker court, where twenty-two of sixty-three applicants succeeded, the magistrate ignored business or family commitments, except to give up to one month's deferment to allow applicants to put their affairs in order.[28]

Some examples show how strictly the magistrates interpreted the regulations. Samuel Hedley Phillips, 25, the main support of his two sisters, one delicate and the other at school, sought exemption because he had a brother at the front. Many families had made sensible, hard-headed arrangements like this, deputing one brother to represent the family at the war while the other remained at home to provide for the dependants. The conscription proposals threatened to overturn these generous family schemes. Phillips's application failed. Isaac Joseph Dunstan, a miner aged 29, also failed, although he was the only working son left at home and the sole support of his widowed mother. While the regulations did exempt only sons, they worked against those families some of whose sons had enlisted leaving behind one son of military age to provide for the family, as well as one or more sons below military age, and therefore, presumably, unable to carry on the family business. In many cases the applicant stated that he was the family's sole support and the only person capable of maintaining the farm, but the magistrates had to ignore such circumstances, so restrictive were the regulations. Thus, Arthur Ellis, the sole support of invalid aged parents, a farmer with seventy acres under crop, was granted only a three month deferment for the harvest. The fate of his parents and of the farm would have worried any reader of this court report. The activities of the exemption courts, on the eve of the referendum, gave voters a jolt and warned them that Hughes's guarantees about maintaining the supply of rural labour might not amount to much. Conscription could have had disastrous consequences for rural life and productivity.[29]

Observers have noted how the conscription debates showed a distinction between the interests of rural Australia, anxious about labour supply, and those of urban Australia. The more important point has often been missed. In fact, the war gave dwellers in the country and the city a common interest and brought them closer together. The war served to unify Australians and give them a sense of common identity. There was a new respect for one another. No longer would rural Australians sneer at their city counterparts who, they imagined, devoted themselves to 'girls' work' in offices, shops and factories. The urban dweller had shown himself to be just as efficient a fighter, just as adventurous, just as brave. There was only one type of Anzac be he a country or city recruit initially: that identity was lost in his common allegiance to Australia. Australians were at war together and would gain nothing by emphasising differences and regional loyalties.

Events within Australia emphasised how related were country and city interests, so that in this way both sectors drew closer together too. The country reaction to the great strike of 1917 demonstrated what an active interest country people now took in national affairs. It could not be expected that the strikes that disrupted Australia in August and September 1917 would find much favour in the country. The railway strike threatened a great deal of inconvenience to country people dependent on trains for the transport of most of their goods, including farm produce, and much of their information. The issue, speeding-up, or the introduction of high-pressure job techniques, would have meant little to a person with no experience of a large-scale work environment. Not surprisingly, therefore, the country press lambasted the urban unionists for their 'selfish' behaviour and complained about the threat to national security that the strike represented. They made much of the idea that the strike was a 'stab in the back' to the Australians fighting abroad: as the *Yass Courier* had it, 'While the brave sons of Australia were fighting for the safety of their women and children, those at home would see that they were fed'. In New South Wales, where the strike was most effective, some country people decided that they had a part to play in the crisis. Patriots from country towns banded together and journeyed to Sydney to help the volunteers keep the city moving.[30]

Naturally most of the volunteers came from the professional, affluent section of rural society, men whose class loyalties predisposed them to the patriotism of the middle-class of the cities. Working men had neither the time nor the inclination to try to break the strike. Indeed, in some towns they clearly resented any attempts to act against the strikers. At Lithgow, so intense was the feeling against the 'patriotic class' that a recruiter reported that 'The business people were totally opposed to identify themselves with any meeting or taking part in any rally at the present time'. Nevertheless, towns with fewer unionised workers did try to show their concern. Prominent amongst those in organising the volunteer movement at Goulburn were an auctioneer, a solicitor, a grazier and a bishop. At Yass the mayor called a meeting to ask residents to support all government attempts to end the strike: 'It was', he said, 'a question of who was going to prevail, the forces of dissension or those of law and order'. Shortly after his appeal a party of eighteen left to reinforce the volunteers in Sydney. Amongst them were pastoralists, orchardists, farmers, labourers and motor-drivers, although, unfortunately, the proportion of each group was not stated. In Tamworth, the *Observer* hoped that 'It should not be an impossibility for the country districts to send ten thousand or more men to the city ... It will be a great triumph for the country people if they can teach the Sydney union bosses that the rural population cannot be ignored'. In the event the number of volunteers fell below the *Observer's* hopes but even so, fifty enrolled at Inverell and twenty-eight at Oakwood. Alderman Sherwood, the mayor of Scone, led a party to Darling Harbour which included several graziers and country businessmen. This pattern was repeated throughout rural New South Wales, in fact, so many volunteers arrived in Sydney that the government opened a camp for them at the Cricket Ground, renamed by the strikers, 'Scabs Collecting Ground'. The country, it seemed, believed itself vitally involved in the affairs of the city.[31]

In this case, the great strike brought about a realisation of the close ties between country and city. The war had already demonstrated how false was an excessive reliance on regional distinctions and how close were the interests and ideals of groups of Australians wherever they lived. Country people had played a prominent part in the national institutions the war had given rise to, the AIF, the Red Cross and the patriotic funds. Country people had experienced similar emotions, too: enthusiasm at the beginning, confusion in the face of conflict, intolerance and hostility for 'enemies'. But, most important, country people were as subject to class tensions and divisions as were city dwellers; the war had shown that the city-country distinction had less meaning at a moment of national crisis.

CHAPTER NINE
THE GREY YEARS

Peace did not take the Australian people by surprise, although the year 1918 had been a hectic one. First the Allies had reeled under the impact of a German offensive so successful that the British commander, Sir Douglas Haig, had issued his famous appeal on 11 April: 'With our backs to the wall and believing in the justice of our cause each one of us must fight on to the end'. Dramatically, the tide soon began to flow in the Allies favour. Good news appeared consistently in the Australian newspapers and, at last, it seemed believable; the war, people hoped, might be coming to an end. But no one had dreamed that peace would come as swiftly as it did; the speed of events gave an air of unreality to it all. By November 1918, the Australian people expected peace, and yearned for it.[1]

There were false alarms. News reached Sydney early on the morning of 8 November, a Friday, that the armistice had been signed. People making their normal journey to work began to celebrate as the news spread. A newspaperman reported that 'Anglo-Saxon reserve for once disappeared and passengers [on trains, trams and ferries] formed themselves into groups and cheered, and sang patriotic songs, and cheered again'. By 10 a.m. the streets of the city were filled with people, shop assistants, office workers and suburban residents, all of them devoted to celebrating the Empire's victory. By noon people were marching up and down, singing, cheering, making noise just for the sake of it. The main object, in fact, was a desire to create an 'infernal torture to the ears', but there were no complaints. The minister for education issued a proclamation closing schools for the afternoon but pupils may have anticipated him.[2]

The frenzy continued in the city. There was little work done as everyone was intent on celebrating the good news. Class barriers collapsed as 'sedate businessmen were to be seen parading about with their employees. "Mafficking" like the rest. The enthusiasm infected everyone'. At the Central Police Court the magistrate celebrated by discharging the previous night's haul of drunks, without even so much as a word of warning. Their delight was, perhaps, shortlived: hotels were closed at 2 p.m. for the remainder of the day, lest the crowds go too far. The anti-German feeling of the past years

A tin-can band

was a prominent feature of the carnival. Several thousand people viewed 'with laughing approval' the hanging of an effigy of the Kaiser. They applauded and cheered when the effigy was burnt. '"That's what ought to happen to the monster in reality" exclaimed an old woman warmly. "You wouldn't burn him though" said someone. "Wouldn't I just", she answered, "No fate could be too bad for those responsible for the atrocities"'. It was, of course, all premature. As people stole their holiday and sang and shouted themselves hoarse, newspapers published posters announcing that an armistice had not been signed. The posters had no effect: the people 'would not believe that the basis of their gladness was the error of a journalist in Europe'. By late afternoon, surely, the message had penetrated that it was all a mistake, but, nothing daunted, crowds, cheering, 'music', continued late into the night. Reporters noted shrieking, exuberance, ecstasy; there was more than a hint of hysteria about it all. Eventually the celebrants drifted home but on the following evening the usual Saturday crowds were roused to further demonstrations of joy when again a rumour passed around that an armistice had been signed.[3]

It may have been thought, therefore, that Sydney had released its nervous energy in two days of hysteria and that the real thing would pass off peacefully enough. On Monday 11 November at about seven in the evening, news reached the city that the Germans had signed an armistice. In those pre-radio days news, even in a large city, travelled slowly. On that day, however, the good news travelled swiftly as trains and ferries announced it to all by blasting constantly with their sirens. Everyone rushed to the city. By 9 o'clock the crowds in Martin Place and surrounding streets were enormous: 'the people were simply wedged there in an upright mass, and to get in or out, or to proceed twenty yards in any direction, was a task of a quarter of an hour's duration'. The authorities added an extra 150 trams to the city routes to cope with the crush of people; even so, this was not enough. The noise was remarkable as everyone seemed to think it necessary to beat some kind of instrument, usually a tin-can. Conversation was impossible and thousands of discussions took place in pantomime. Returned soldiers were treated as heroes, 'hailed with expressions of gratitude and affection, and showered with confetti, which seemed to have been imported to the city in limitless quantities'.

There were no speeches in Sydney because the crowds were too intent on making their own noise, perhaps, too; because they had listened to so many speeches during the war years. It was no time now for the recruiter or the politician. In Melbourne, however, the press demanded a statement from the acting prime minister, W. A. Watt. He said that, 'There will go up from the hearts of the people of Australia a great sigh of relief that the dawn has come'. In Sydney, at least, it was more a shriek and a bang than a sigh. Again, in countless places around the city, crowds rejoiced as the Kaiser was burnt in effigy, or hung. Watt voiced the feeling behind such displays: 'the

'The Boys will soon be home'

Another group of revellers in Sydney

nation which hurls civilisation over the precipice ought to be made to pay for its awful criminality'.[4]

Watt decreed that the next day, Tuesday, should be a public holiday but the New South Wales government, in confusion, nominated Wednesday. The effect was that little, if any, work took place in Sydney from early Friday 8 November until the following Thursday 14 November, a remarkable break. Large crowds assembled in the city on both Tuesday and Wednesday, still singing, shouting, beating tin-cans, waving flags and throwing confetti. Hotels were again closed, the papers noting with satisfaction that there were no incidents to mar the joy. The *Sydney Morning Herald* tried to capture the mood of the people:

> One man decked his house out in bunting and went picnicking with his wife and children. Another stuck fifty little flags in his motor car, filled the vehicle with youths, girls and tin-cans and carried out a hilarious and disturbing circumnavigation of many city blocks.
>
> Another – and he numbered tens of thousands – tied a tricolour in his buttonhole, bought flags for the whole family and took himself and his dependants to the city, where he crowded the main streets all day, and seemingly tireless, cheered industriously and was most determinedly joyful.

It is a measure of the extent of war-weariness and frustration that these simple, unplanned and unco-ordinated celebrations could continue unabated across five days. There were few speeches, few ceremonies, no returning troops to march through the city, no official bands or processions, just merrymakers indulging themselves in an almost childlike fashion. A reporter remarked on this, lest his readers think his report exaggerated:

> In cold print there may seem a certain lack of intelligence and variety about this kind of rejoicing but it is cold fact that it engaged the attention yesterday of tens of thousands of young and old people of both sexes – none of whom seemed either bored or unhappy.

Even the inmates of Long Bay gaol celebrated, crowding the prison church to sing hymns and patriotic songs. The extent to which their patriotism was stimulated by the reduction in sentences that the attorney-general ordered is not known.[5]

The celebration of victory was no less intense, indeed hysterical, in the country than it had been in Sydney. News travelled fast. When a telegram reached Yass announcing the armistice 'no wild bushfire, even if helped by a hurricane spread faster than this intelligence . . . People flocked into Cooma-street, and every boy who was the proud possessor of a tin-can, and everyone who could rake up a bell or a whistle joined in the joyful revelry'. The tin-can band was as ubiquitous in the country towns as in the city. In Albury the crowd rejoiced by forming impromptu processions headed by bands of tin-cans, marching through the streets until midnight. When the mayor mounted a permanent recruiting stand in the main street 'to say a few words', the crowd simply howled 'We don't want speeches' and he climbed down. Instead, a noisy band of townsmen 'who, at other times, are amongst the most staid in the community', sang patriotic songs and cheered until their voices cracked. Over 5,000 people celebrated the good news at Albury but 'nothing unseemly occurred'.[6]

The commotion at Ballarat prompted a reporter to conclude that 'there never was such a night in Ballarat': the tin-can bands again predominated and to them were added the sound of fire-bells and 'penetratingly sustained' blasts from mining, locomotive and manufacturing sirens. At Ballarat, too, the Kaiser attracted a great deal of hostility. 'With remarkable frequency' crowds sang that they would hang him on 'a sour apple tree' and they burnt his effigy with enthusiasm. At Tamworth people seemed 'to have become intoxicated with excitement', they 'gave themselves up to the occasion and yelled, screamed, fired crackers and made as much noise as they could'. An effigy of the Kaiser was suspended from a high-wire and 'after being subjected to a bombardment of hungers' it was saturated with kerosene and burnt to the accompaniment of cat-calls and groans. Unfortunately, an old lady and a baby were injured by firecrackers in two separate incidents.[7]

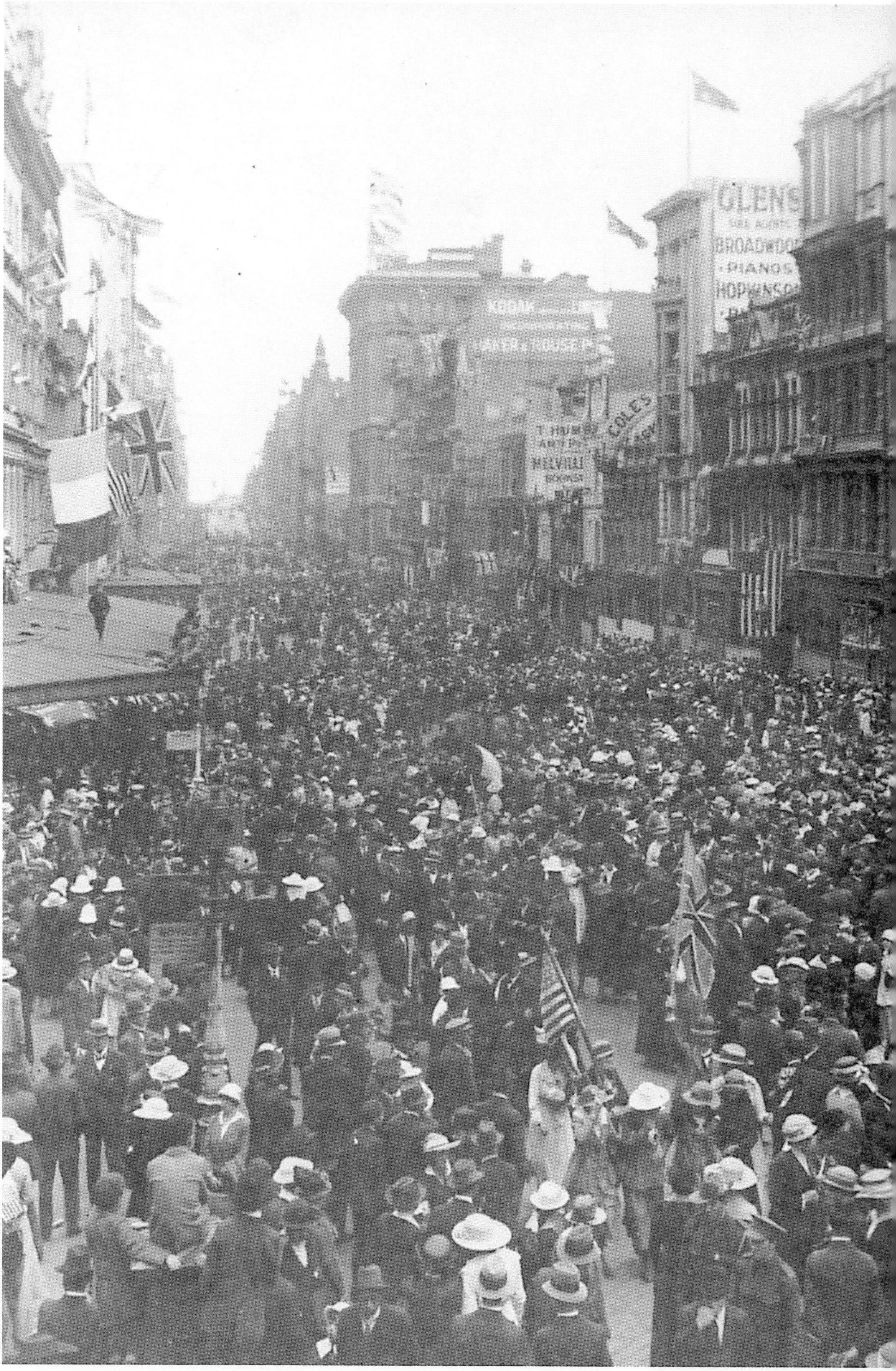
GLEN'S
PIANOS
KODAK
INCORPORATING
COLE'S

So Australians rejoiced. The speeches and sermons, the formal parades and processions, would come soon enough. The first spontaneous reaction was simply to let off steam, to shout and to make as much noise as possible. Exhausted and hoarse, many Australians, doubtless, went home from these celebrations, hopeful that the nation would return to normal, pre-war conditions. Now that the armies had secured peace abroad there were many who wished to find peace at home; they dreamed that the divisions and conflicts which the strain of war had caused in Australia would now dissipate.

The newspaper reports had highlighted how universal were the celebrations, involving all classes of people, despite the recent bitter disputes and eruptions of class antagonisms. 'No matter to whom one talked', a reporter wrote, 'road navvy or merchant, shop assistant or tram-guard, or trade-union official, one found a man delighted and satisfied'. This was despite the 'disloyalty' and 'war-weariness' 'displayed in some quarters on the occasion of the second referendum'. Some found the fact that 'disloyalists' and 'eligibles' seemed as exuberant as the patriotic classes, somewhat disquietening. 'Peggy', in the *Soldier,* disparaged the 'hundreds of hefty fellows who apparently had no thought of giving a hand in the war' but who shouted and cheered 'just as if they had a right to feel proud of our victory'. Ominously, 'Peggy' was suggesting that the divisions which had wracked Australia in 1916 and 1917 should be perpetuated into two permanent classes, the 'loyalists' and 'disloyalists'. An earlier article in the *Soldier* had made a similar point:

> The Australian people are going to be divided into two camps. In the one we will have the men who went, their parents, wives, sisters, sweethearts and brothers who were too young or too old to go. In the other will be seen a motley crew of able-bodied slackers and their supporters ... the country is too grand for the slackers to have a part in it.

But these categories were too simple. Loyalty was not only a question of family. There were many extreme loyalists who had no relatives at the front and there were others who had made little obvious contribution to the war effort in spite of the enlistment of a son or brother. Three divisions were to emerge in post-war Australia: the returned men, the so-called patriotic classes, and the rest. 'Peggy' would find that patriotism on the home front was not enough to win brotherhood with those who had fought. The returned men elaborated institutions and rituals into which no one else might intrude, however loyally they had contributed to the war effort. For the moment, however, these complexities were hidden from view. Some resented the right of eligibles to celebrate but most Australians overlooked such distinctions in a simple desire to rejoice.[8]

Opposite: Armistice day in Melbourne

Welcoming Anzacs in Sydney
Welcoming Anzacs in Melbourne

The adulatory treatment meted out to the few returned men in Australia at the time of the armistice gave good hope that their brothers in arms would be fêted when ships could be found to bring them to their homeland. Unfortunately, an influenza pandemic reduced the scope of many such celebrations and jolted those who had dreamed that the world would settle down after the war. 'Spanish flu', so called because the King of Spain was an early victim, had raged in Europe since April 1918 and had caused a terrifying death toll, killing more people than even the war itself. The pandemic reached Australia in January 1919, a delay which apparently diminished the virulence of the germ. Nevertheless, influenza caused the deaths of about 12,000 Australians in 1919. As doctors had no cure, it is hardly surprising that all sorts of precautionary measures were adopted. In New South Wales, the government enforced the wearing of masks and then closed public places such as libraries, schools, churches and theatres; it became an offence to remain in a hotel bar for more than five minutes. These regulations, introduced in January, remained in force until April, with some modifications. In Victoria schools did not resume from the Christmas holidays until 18 March and were closed again later in the year. The effect of the cancellation of victory celebrations, the effect of another tragedy in addition to the war, must have been most depressing. Even more tragic was the fate of some of the returning men who succumbed to the disease and died even as their ships were within sight of their cherished homeland. To have survived the horrors of war, only to fall victim to influenza, seemed so unfair. Relatives awaiting the return of their heroes must have felt the irony deeply.[9]

Nevertheless, throughout 1919, the troops did return, and their arrival gave some greater cause to hope that the shadow of war would be lifted, that Australians could begin again to go about the ordinary business of life. Simply to find the shipping to repatriate the Australian troops was an enormous task to which Hughes, the prime minister, again in London, dedicated himself with enthusiasm. He succeeded, perhaps even beyond his own expectations. There were 176 voyages required to bring the men home; the first ship sailed on 3 December 1918, the last on 23 December 1919. To find the shipping, to allot places on the principle 'the first to come out shall be the first to go home', to occupy the troops who waited in camps, required a prodigious effort of planning and administration. No wonder that General Monash regarded the repatriation as the best example of 'staffwork' with which he had been associated in the army. The voyage home was not always pleasant, as Angela Thirkell testified in *Trooper to the Southern Cross*. Discipline had been much easier to maintain as men had steamed to war; they had been eager to learn their drill, slightly apprehensive about the task in front of them. Now, returning home they were relaxed, proud of their efforts and their traditions, and eager to make their last days in the AIF memorable.[10]

The ambivalence of the Australians towards their troops, noted earlier, continued during this period of repatriation. As individuals they were heroes,

The hero returns

much loved, and eagerly awaited. As a group, as the Anzacs, they were also loved and respected, for had they not put Australia on the map and played a vital part in the Allies' victory? But they were also suspected, too, to be a large, almost alien group, whose cohesion and camaraderie might disrupt traditional Australian groupings and patterns. They were encouraged to melt back into civilian life, to leave aside the AIF and the war and to try to pick up the threads of earlier days. Obviously this would be difficult, because of their associations and memories, but also because Australia had changed.

Finding jobs for all the returning soldiers was well nigh impossible. Recruits had been promised that their jobs would be kept open for them but, of course, new workers had been taken on who felt entitled to retain their places. Few of these workers were women so there was little scope for automatic retrenchments as would have fitted the standards of the day. Some argued that 'slackers' should be put at the end of the queue as far as jobs were concerned and that ex-AIF men should have preference in employment. Employers, however, were not eager to replace well-trained, hard-working men with ex-soldiers whose skills were rusty and who often found it difficult to settle down into the old routines. Many ex-soldiers were reluctant to return to their old jobs. In some cases they had learned new skills but many thousands of them, too, now had higher expectations. They had tasted independence and excitement and wished to find a lifestyle in greater harmony with their recent past. Thousands, of course, were unfit for any kind of work; they bore the scars of war service visibly on their bodies, or invisibly in their minds.

The federal government set up a 'Repatriation department' to look after the interests of all returned men. One of its first tasks was to construct a scheme of 'soldier settlement' to cater for those men whose dream of independence and freedom from the drudgery of city life encouraged them to think that they could 'make a go of it' on the land. The scheme would also 'bust up the big estates', since the 1860s one of the ideals of Australian democracy, and it would extend land use. Soldier settlement was a disaster, ruining or breaking thousands of Australian heroes. The land chosen was often unsuitable, either for any kind of agriculture, or for the close settlement the scheme envisaged. A critic of the scheme wrote that 'the men who survived the hardships of the trenches tested again their physical endurance and their tenacity in adversity. For years, some struggled to clear blocks which were too small or too arid, to produce crops which the world valued little'. Many of the soldier-settlers simply walked off their farms, defeated

Reunion

after years of struggle. The various Australian governments which supported the scheme lost at least £23 million in its failure, but the hapless settlers lost much more, money, but more important, hope and meaning for their lives.[11]

The Repatriation department also handled the payment of pensions, gratuities and benefits, to the ex-soldier or his dependants, and maintained the hospitals needed to house or to heal war's victims. By 30 June 1935, £238 million had been spent by the department directly to assist soldiers and their dependants. Voluntary groups, particularly the Red Cross, assisted too, raising money and devoting great effort to help the returned man adjust. There was generosity and nobility in all these schemes; the annual bill represented only a fraction of the cost of the war to Australia.[12]

As soldiers returned to Australia throughout 1919 they were invited to join the Returned Sailors and Soldiers Imperial League of Australia, commonly known as the RSL, and they did so in large numbers. By October 1919 there were 114,700 members of the League, membership of which was open only to those who had served overseas. Although numbers of members fell away quite soon after reaching this peak, the RSL remained a prominent institution in Australia. It aimed to 'perpetuate the close and kindly ties of friendship created by mutual service in the Great War', 'to preserve the memory and records of those who suffered and died for the nation', to look after the needs of the sick and injured and their dependants and 'to inculcate loyalty to Australia and the Empire'. The League was successful in fulfilling all these aims, but especially successful in perpetuating the bonds that existed amongst members of the AIF. Returned men did not melt meekly back into civilian life but sustained one another with the friendships that had evolved abroad.[13]

In its task of keeping the memory alive of those who had suffered or died at war, the RSL was assisted by the determination of the people and the various governments that the fame of those deeds would not die out. The people insisted on erecting memorials to commemorate the men who had served. Ireland and France had their wayside shrines; Australia was to have its war memorials. Every municipality and town, surely, erected some prominent reminder of the men of the AIF, often including all the names of the men of the district who had served. It is an indication of the pride Australians felt for their troops that these memorials were erected from as early as 1916. Rarely is the soldier-figure depicted in an aggressive attitude, mostly he is standing at rest, honouring his dead comrades. Occasionally these memorials dominated the city or town which erected them; no visitor to Melbourne could ignore the Shrine of Remembrance nor could anyone fail to notice Goulburn's memorial tower. The most prominent of them all was the Australian War Museum, or Memorial, as it later became, begun in London in 1918, temporarily housed in Melbourne and Sydney in the 1920s, and finally located in Canberra in 1941. Officers of the museum began collecting relics, uniforms and memorabilia with almost as much enthusiasm as the ordinary soldier whose diligence at 'souveniring' has passed into legend. The

Anzac Day 1917 – Brisbane. The church predominates

national collection created tremendous interest; a temporary exhibition in Melbourne from 1922–4 attracted 776,810 visitors, in Sydney from 1925–8, 1,324,187 visitors. Associated with the Australian War Memorial were a team of historians, led by C. E. W. Bean, who produced the *Official History of Australia in the War of 1914–18* in twelve volumes. Bean aimed at describing every significant action in which Australians took part and he did so, as often as possible, from the point of view of the ordinary soldier. In volume four, for example, he estimated that about 1,000 persons were mentioned by name. The first volume was published in 1921, the last in 1942.[14]

Despite the memorials and the history, the memory of Australia's contribution to the war was best kept before the people by the annual commemoration of Anzac Day, the anniversary of the landing at Gallipoli on 25 April. The first anniversary in 1916 was celebrated with church services in Australia and a march of Australian troops in London. There was little opportunity for troops to march in Australia until 1920, because of the influenza pandemic in 1919 which prevented public functions. As 25 April 1920 was a Sunday, there was no need to proclaim a public holiday. In Sydney General Birdwood, the former commander of the Australians, took the salute as 5,000 ex-AIF men, in uniform, marched past him in Queens Square. About 20,000 people gathered at the saluting base to watch and afterwards 10,000 attended a memorial service in the Domain. These were rather small numbers of marchers and spectators and were not greatly exceeded in the other cities.[15]

In 1921 the federal government declared 25 April a public holiday but the state governments did not follow that lead. They hesitated not from any lack of respect for the memory of those who had died but because they wanted a solemn observance: 'Whether Australia can keep a public holiday without race meetings and a strenuous public house business is the whole debate in this matter', so the *Sydney Morning Herald* believed. There were church services and small parades of serving men, either navy or army, in each of the capital cities, and many local country and suburban gatherings. One of the most touching of these was the visit to the gates of the Woolloomooloo wharf, whence the first New South Wales contingent had departed. Even without proclamations or regulations as the years passed, people wanted to invest Anzac day with a special, sacred character. In 1922 the *Sydney Morning Herald* reported that

> Although there was no legal obligation in the matter, hotel-keepers generally seem to have observed the recommendation of the United Licensed Victuallers Association that liquor should not be sold during the hours of 10.30 a.m. and 1 p.m. [the hours of the church services] ... One leading hotel, near the waterfront, exhibited on its doors the words, "Closed all day – lest we forget"[16]

The Victorian government determined to legislate to achieve what popular sentiment seemed to want. In 1925 the government introduced a bill to make Anzac Day a public holiday, but a special one on which all shops, hotels, racecourses, theatres and cinemas would be closed. The RSL co-operated with the spirit of the government's intention by organising a march of the returned, which in 1926 attracted 15,000 marchers and 28,000 in 1927. Such success stimulated the other state branches of the RSL so that in 1928 'the march' was a universal way of commemorating the Anzacs. There were 80,000 people at the memorial service at the end of the march in Sydney and 'uncountable thousands' had watched the march. Between 12–15,000 men had marched. In that year, too, the first 'dawn service' took place: a ceremony to commemorate the landing, timed to conclude just as the sun rose, the moment when Australians stormed the hills of Gallipoli.[17]

If the achievements of the Anzac had won such a special place in the hearts of the Australian people, it might be wondered why the commemoration of Anzac day developed so slowly. There were three reasons for this. In the first place people were determined that Anzac day must be sacred and, as they inevitably associated public holidays with secular pleasures, they feared the degradation of the day if a public holiday were proclaimed. For this reason, church services predominated in early celebrations. Secondly, it seems as if people needed to distance themselves from the war before they could bear to think about it too much. There had been so much sorrow, so much anxiety, so much bitterness, that people needed time for the scars to heal. A *Sydney Morning Herald* reporter put this point of view in 1928:

> Sometimes even man ... finds a misery he cannot beat to contemplate. He has come to the end of endurance. He is tired and hopeless. One can understand that thousands of people must have felt like this in the last few years since the war. They did not want to think about it – they did not want to remember. It was too painful ... Now it seems they can bear to look back.

The third reason concerns the reunion aspect of the celebration. Men marched to meet their mates again, to form up in the old battalion, and to spend the time after the march yarning, catching up on gossip. Perhaps in the first few years after the war men had not yet grown apart, so that they did not need to be reunited; as the years went by, they found the need for a special commemoration to bring them together. For all these reasons Anzac day became the 'one day of the year' for many Australians: the day on which all Australians stopped to remember the sacrifice of 'her best sons'.[18]

In various ways, therefore, through institutions and rituals, the returned man was assured of a prominent, permanent place in Australian society. But what of the impact of peace and the effects of the war on those groups of Australians who have made up this study? How did Australian clergymen adjust to the news of peace and how had the war influenced perceptions about the importance of the church? How did Australian children and women fare in the new postwar society? Was it possible to return to prewar conditions or had Australia radically altered?

Clergymen celebrated the armistice as wholeheartedly as any other group of Australians but, true to the understanding of the war they held consistently for four years, when victory came they returned thanks to God, as its source. James Green, a returned chaplain who had seen the fighting at Gallipoli and in France, declared that 'He [God] reinforced the spirit of the warriors, gave discernment to the command, rallied the moral strength of the allies'. The Anglican bishop of Gippsland, George Cranswick, had reminded his people in November 1917 that 'until our people turn to God, we cannot expect him to bestow on us the gift of peace'. He found events justified his prediction. On 4 August 1918 the King and members of the House of Commons, assembled in prayer: 'the effect' the bishop reported, 'was almost instantaneous. During the three months that followed, events of a truly wonderful nature pursued each other'. Victory, then, 'proved' God's providence.[19]

But clergymen had suggested that victory depended on reform and events seemed to deny this because some clergymen, at least, were bemoaning the unreformed condition of Australian society even as late as October 1918. Few faced up to this discrepancy. One who did, S. M. Johnstone, a Sydney Anglican, found in it an additional reason for praising God. 'Shall not', he asked, 'the fact that national victories have been vouchsafed to us before national repentance was marked in us, melt us from our coldness and indifference to the Creator?'.[20]

Unveiling a war memorial in December 1918, at Waverley, New South Wales

Others, ever optimistic, took new heart from the crowds that flocked to churches to celebrate victory. A Melbourne Methodist reported that he had spoken at two services which the people had attended in their thousands; the congregations gave such close attention to his sermons that he remarked 'never have preachers had such audiences in Australia'. Clergymen rejoiced that politicians acknowledged God's role in bringing about the victory: indeed, W. A. Watt, in his first statement about the armistice, invited all Australians to go to church to return thanks to God. The *Church Standard* recorded that the politicians spoke 'without any sense of restraint, with a freedom and naturalness that find expression in the simplest and best words often taken direct from the Bible'. Now that the public openly acknowledged God there was hope 'that a good foundation has been laid for our country's future'. People even sang hymns as they thronged through the streets of Sydney and Melbourne, alternating these with shouts, cheers and the beating of tin-cans.[21]

There is more than an echo in this newfound optimism of the earlier reaction of clergymen to people's response at the outbreak of war. Then, too, crowds had swelled normal church congregations and clergymen had dreamed of a new spirit abroad. That revival had proven as temporary as this one. Soon after the armistice celebrations, the numbers of worshippers dropped back to normal levels. It was only natural that at the end of the war people had wished to do a little more than 'mafficking' in mindless outbursts of joy. They had wished to commemorate the event solemnly and so they had turned momentarily to clergymen. To conclude from this that Australia hovered on the brink of conversion was absurd. It is a measure of how insecure was the grip of the churches on the Australian people that this brief manifestation of a need for religion was taken as the first signs of a revival.

Nor, when they had large audiences, did clergymen do their cause much good by playing on the feuds and divisions that had disrupted Australian life. Instead of emphasising the unity apparent in Australia in the first days of peace, clergymen continued the fights brought into prominence by Archbishop Mannix's intervention in the conscription campaign. Patrick Phelan, bishop of Sale, preached at the main Catholic thanksgiving service in Melbourne, at St Patrick's Cathedral. Such a solemn yet joyous occasion might have inclined the bishop to gloss over the preceding turmoil. Instead, when he spoke of the heroic deeds of the Australian troops, he described them as more praiseworthy because the men had enlisted freely, without need for compulsion: 'their gift of sacrifice and life was a free gift; no cruel law dragged them from their parents and friends'. Nor did Phelan show much sensitivity when he reminded Catholic mothers that their sons, who almost universally received confession and communion before battle, were assured of salvation. The mothers of other Australians, he said, cherished no such consolation. The war had shown 'what little use [on the battlefield was] the Bible-reading clergyman who had no power to forgive sins'. Furthermore, the Catholic mother could follow her son beyond the grave with her prayers; the Protestant mother was taught that such prayers were useless. Nor was Henry Worrall, a Methodist, any more of a peacemaker when, having paid tribute to those who had made the supreme sacrifice, he thanked God that they had not listened to mischievous politicians and cowardly clergymen who had counselled them to stay at home. Is it any wonder that Australians, turning to the churches for solemn commemoration and thanksgiving, should have turned away again when they found disputatious sectarianism, even at the main thanksgiving ceremonies?[22]

The early months of the postwar era witnessed even greater displays of sectarian antagonism than those of the war years. When clergymen as a whole were refused entry to the quarantine stations set up to isolate influenza, Catholics took this as persecution aimed directly at themselves. The activities of the League of Loyalty and other similar groups increased and became institutionalised in newspapers and magazines created to combat Catholicism. In Melbourne, particularly, Catholics retaliated with massive displays of strength. In 1919 Mannix organised an Irish Race Convention to bring the plight of Ireland before Australians; this aroused, of course, the hatred of all those who believed that in championing Ireland, Mannix belittled the Empire. As was customary now in Melbourne, huge crowds endorsed the Archbishop's venture; 10,000 people attended a Pleasant Sunday Afternoon in the Fitzroy Gardens to meet the delegates, and on the same evening 100,000 cheered every speaker at the Richmond Reserve. Speakers moved from one platform to another around the Reserve to allow a portion, at least, of the huge crowd, to hear them.[23]

Illustrated weeklies, such as the *Sydney Mail*, filled many pages with pictures of patriotic young Australians. Most of the children were dressed up like this to raise money. Some might have objected to being so heavily bandaged

The 1920 St Patrick's day procession exceeded all Mannix's previous attempts at showmanship. The crowds were similar, the enthusiasm as intense, but on this occasion the Archbishop's car was escorted by fourteen Victoria Cross winners mounted on grey chargers, while 10,000 ex-servicemen marched behind. Mannix had anticipated Anzac Day celebrations by several years and had embarrassed those who had accused him of disloyalty. There was a clear implication that Mannix was a champion of the patriotic elite. When the Archbishop left on a routine visit to Rome, the League of Loyalty, and other Protestants, campaigned to have the federal government refuse him right of re-entry. The idea apparently appealed to Hughes but it was not implemented and Mannix returned, as he had promised, 'unchanged and unchangeable' to remain a controversial and divisive figure until his death in 1963. Throughout the 1920s he symbolised the sectarian hatred that was the principal effect of the war on the Australian churches.[24]

Growing up in Australia in the 1920s presented children with different problems from those experienced in the war years. Then, the effort had been intense yet simple. There were socks to knit, money to raise, hymns and songs to sing; the war was far away and easily idealised. Peace brought the real nature of the war closer to home. The early pages of George Johnstone's semi-autobiographical novel, *My Brother Jack*, concentrate on the impact of the war on the sensitive young hero, David Meredith. He may have been more conscious of the war because both his parents enlisted, and his mother continued to work as a nurse in a repatriation hospital after demobilisation. Nevertheless there are elements in the way David Meredith experienced the war that might have been shared by many Australian children.[25]

David Meredith's first conscious meeting with his father occurred at a family reunion at Port Melbourne in 1919 when the troopship docked; he was 7 years old. There were flags and triumphal arches and bands in abundance. David was terrified: the 'fear was involved with the interminable blaring of brass bands, and a ceaseless roaring of shouting and cheering, and the unending trampling past of gigantic legs'. The climax of all this fear came when his father arrived in person, a total stranger, of course:

> I was seized suddenly and engulfed in one of the gigantic, coarse-clad figures and embraced in a stifling smell of damp serge and tobacco and beer and held high in the air before a sweating apparition that was a large, ruddy face grinning at me below a back-tilted slouch hat and thin fair hair receding above a broad freckled brow, and then there was a roar of laughter and I was put down, sobbing with fear, and the thick boots marched on and on, as if they were trampling all over me.

We might wonder whether other reunions, outwardly joyous, were as traumatic. Wives finding their husbands strangers, children finding their fathers terrifying.

Helping Australian war victims at the Randwick Military Hospital, Sydney. This became a prominent feature of the Red Cross's post-war activity

David's mother gave refuge to her patients from the convalescent hospital, discharged too soon by an administration desperately short of beds. On Sundays, David and his brother Jack sold postcards in the hospital wards, thronging with visitors, to aid the Red Cross. David hated those Sunday visits, as many other children must have.

> I hated the unending tiring labyrinth of wards, the stretching miles of maimed men in white enamelled cots... the squeaky wheeling of shrouded trolleys, and the shapes and no-shapes that lay hidden beneath the white counterpanes with the red crosses embroidered on them, the lowered false voices of the visitors.

Despite these constant reminders of the horrors, the war itself fascinated David when he discovered his parents' souvenirs, carelessly deposited in the drawer of an old wardrobe. There was a service revolver and a cardboard box of ammunition, campaign ribbons and various regimental badges, a German Iron Cross, and the citation which had gone with his father's Military Medal. There were mysterious French silk postcards, foreign coins and battle descriptions written in the optimistic prose of the *Illustrated War News*. But his love for these memorabilia of war came to a sudden end when he realised the connection between them and the human wrecks his mother brought home. Walking back from school, David passed a photographer's studio, displaying in the window many photographs of young men in uniform.

'They were mostly boyish-looking faces, none of them with the expressions that I had seen at home or in the hospital wards, so that I guessed the portraits had been taken years before, when they had enlisted or just before they had embarked for overseas'. As he was staring at these photographs, an older boy came down the street, kicking a tennis ball. He stopped and stared at them too, for a long time, before he said, '"All of them blokes in there is dead, you know"'.

Perhaps 'David Meredith' was an exaggerated character, an unusually sensitive child suffering a closer involvement with the fate of some returned men than might have been typical for children generally in the 1920s. But no child was allowed to forget. Each April, as Anzac Day drew near, the school papers and magazines would recall the heroism and the achievements of the men of the AIF. There would be a special school ceremony attended by some prominent ex-AIF old boys, and addressed perhaps by a padre who would dwell on the nobility of the sacrifice and its cost. The schools themselves suffered. Many of the teachers who had enlisted left the service on their return to Australia, securing the jobs of the temporaries taken on in the war years, older people whose qualifications were not always high. Some soldiers who did return to teaching were 'so disabled to be almost unfit to carry on' as a New South Wales report noted ominously. If the war 'got on men's nerves' as many ex-diggers testified, might it not also have turned some previously enthusiastic teachers into sour and unpredictable masters?[26]

More than anything else, war experience forged bonds of mateship which separated returned men from their wives and their children. 'Peggy', in the *Soldier*, had dreamed in the first days of peace that all Australian patriots would be united by their common sacrifice. Women had tried desperately to contribute to the war effort in meaningful ways so as not to be denied membership of the patriotic elite. But their hopes were frustrated. Service abroad was the only criterion the RSL demanded for membership; few women qualified. Even at the informal level, many men preferred the company of the mates who had been through it to the love of their wives.

Graham McInnes, a boy in Melbourne in the 1920s, who later recalled his experiences in *The Road to Gundagai*, remembered how much time he spent waiting for his stepfather outside the Naval and Military Club: 'I must have spent longer in it, and even longer waiting outside it than in or out of any institution in my whole boyhood'. Finally, as a teenager, when his stepfather took him inside, did McInnes realise what it was that tempted men to devote so much time to the Club. 'It was not, as Mother sometimes hinted, Demon Rum or even its more probable Australian equivalent, Foster's Lager, Carlton Ale or Melbourne Bitter. It was, rather, the Anzac Dream'. At the bar the boy found that

> Each man had in his hand either a glass or a silver tankard. Their mouths roared open with meaningless ferocity and frightening geniality as they

bellowed at each other across their drinks or broke into cannon roars of gusty laughter ... They were all veterans with the R.S.S.I.L.A. badge in their lapels, but their talk was of current matters ... But beneath it all lay a lazy sense of camaraderie, of some secret shared in common and which excluded me, not only because I was of another generation, but because I had not been 'over there'; because the names of Gallipoli, Gaba Tepe, Mudros, Anzac Cove, the Somme, Passchendaele, the Ancre, Villers-Bretonneux, held for me no common memories softened by time ...[27]

Such memories excluded Australian women as firmly as children because neither group had any real part in this new national institution. At an organisational level the lives of Australian women did revert to normality soon after peace was declared. Most of the money-raising comforts funds closed and the business and entrepreneurial skills, so painstakingly learnt, lapsed, as most women became full-time wives and mothers again. It would not require much imagination to see that the transition might not always have been smooth. The woman whose husband was at war was independent, she managed the house, handled the money, took all the decisions. On her husband's return she had to learn again to be submissive, to leave things in his hands, to be, at best, a partner, rather than a manager. She had to learn to tolerate his new friends and to accept that there was a part of his life which she could not share. In the early days of his demobilisation especially, but often for much longer, she had to be his emotional support as he struggled to cope again with domestic and civilian life. And in many cases she had to learn to live on his pension, if he did not return, or if he came back incapacitated.

Such strains proved too much for many marriages. In 1914 there were 619 divorces throughout Australia, with the highest incidence in New South Wales (297), and Victoria (244). This pattern had been stable for many years and remained so through the war years, despite a slight upward drift towards the end, which saw 721 divorces in 1918. From 1919 onwards, however, there was a significant increase: 879 in 1919, 1,046 in 1920, 1,383 in 1921, 1,248 in 1922, 1,463 in 1923 and 1,536 in 1924. There was no change in the divorce laws to explain this increase, nor was the social stigma attached to divorcees noticeably overcome. It would seem that the strain of the postwar years was a contributing factor. How many marriages followed the pattern of the Merediths in *My Brother Jack* is, of course, unknown, but their experience might serve as some kind of guide in the absence of other types of evidence. David Meredith's father became a worried and frustrated man. He had been gassed in France and he feared that his bronchitis was the portent of a major lung disease. He was frustrated by his failure to make anything of his life – there was no chance of advancement in his job and, of course, he had glimpsed wider horizons abroad. All this made him 'morose, intolerant, bitter and violently bad-tempered'. David recorded that he could 'hardly recall a night when I was not awakened in panic by the stormy violence of my parents' quarrels'. Hardly a happy life for either of these people who had served their country well.[28]

The war, in fact, confirmed male domination of Australian society. Many members of the AIF experienced strong revulsion for the ways of English girls, their work and their social customs. Returning Australians determined that their women would not be similarly 'degraded'. Those women who had found paid employment during the war years succumbed to very strong pressure to surrender their jobs in favour of the returning heroes. There was no great expansion in employment prospects either during or immediately after the war. Denied participation in the Anzac myth, Australian women were required to be submissive and to bear the new generation of Australians for whom the men of Anzac had sacrificed all. Ironically, the war had been fought on behalf of the 'defenceless women and children' of the world; in Australia, at least, they did not derive much obvious benefit from it.

If Australians were not sympathetic towards the Kaiser, they showed little sympathy, either, for the German-Australians in their midst. The report on 'enemy aliens' in the public service was completed in 1919 and recommended, as we have seen, that 'enemy subjects' be permanently excluded from public service employment. The personal resentment towards German-Australians at work and socially may have endured for some years: unfortunately it is very hard to find evidence. The internees and their families suffered most. At first it seemed that the government had decided to treat them leniently. In December 1918 Senator Pearce announced that many of the cases 'wear a different complexion today to what they wore while the war was proceeding'. Mr Watt, acting prime minister, concurred, saying that each case would be given careful review 'to see whether, with due regard to the safety of the Commonwealth, clemency can be shown'. By June 1919 it was clear that clemency was hardly a consideration: the government had determined that all the internees would be deported. The military authorities had begun sending letters to the wives of internees which began, ominously, 'It is possible that your husband will be deported. If so, you and your children will have to accompany him'. The wife could remain if she were a 'British subject before [her] marriage'; the children were free to stay if they had been born in Australia.[29]

Members of the Labor opposition in federal parliament objected to the severity of these decisions and appealed for clemency in particular cases. Mr Carboy, the member for Swan, Western Australia, mentioned the plight of a German who had been in Australia for thirty-six years, had been naturalised for thirty, and was a widower, with one adult daughter. He was to be deported but his daughter, born in Australia of an Australian mother, could not obtain a permit to accompany him. In effect, the government imposed an enforced separation on these two people. Mr Higgs, member for Capricornia, read from an official letter to one of the women awaiting deportation:

you will be allowed to take 84 lbs of baggage with you ... You will be permitted to take £50 sterling, or its equivalent in valuables. With regard to your farm, you may appoint an attorney to look after your interests, but its disposal will be decided by the Government.

When Senator Gardiner from New South Wales brought a similar case to the attention of the Senate, he did not receive a sympathetic hearing: Senator Senior, a Labor man who had followed Hughes over conscription, interjected, 'How can you speak like that, after reading how Germany treated our own people' and Senator Guthrie dismissed the Labor leader as 'a good old Hun advocate'.[30]

In an urgency debate on the fate of the internees, the acting prime minister, W. A. Watt, put the government's case. He stressed that deportation was treated as a question of security: 'This community must protect itself'. He believed that there were 'in Australia today Germans and German-Australians ... who are as truculent as they were in the early stages of the war'. Watt regretted the necessity but argued that 'Even if there is a slight injustice in some part of the procedure adopted, the safety of this community is more important than the display of sentiment towards a particular class of people'. There were large-scale protests about the deportation of some notorious German-Australians, particularly in the case of Father Jerger, a Passionist priest, whom Catholics saw as a victim of the government's sectarian bias. Nevertheless, the deportations proceeded. Famous or obscure, wealthy or poor, enemy subjects were booted out of Australia in the interests of national security.[31]

The immediate postwar years gave no indication that Australian society would revert to its prewar innocence and placidity. It is a commonplace that English novelists, writing of prewar society from a postwar perspective, created a highly romantic picture of life before the war. Society was unified, pleasure available to all, life idyllic; even the weather was perfect, no one could remember a better summer than that of June–July 1914. We do not want to fall into the trap of seeing Australia in a similarly romantic and idealised way. Of course there were problems, tensions and antagonisms evident before 1914. But there was innocence and naïvete, too. A sure faith in the virtues of the British Empire and a confidence that all Australians shared the same vision of a glorious future. The experience of war blew all that away. The people were forced to confront division and class antagonism. Sectarian hatreds threatened to engulf social life. Even the great Australian leveller, the passion for sport, had been shown to be, at least, insecure. Australian casualties had been appallingly high, the flower of a generation had been destroyed. The Australian people had paid a very high price. Never again would they march so lightheartedly to war.

NOTES

Chapter One: THE WAR IN AUSTRALIA
1. Ernest Scott, *Australia During the War*, vol. xi of *The Official History of Australia in the War of 1914–18*, Sydney, 1936, p. 871.
2. *Australian Worker*, 6 and 13 August 1914; cf. Dan Coward, The Impact of War on New South Wales, Ph.D. Thesis, Canberra, 1974, pp. 46–9.
3. *Australian Worker*, 27 August and 15 October 1914.
4. *Church Standard*, 7 May 1915; *Argus*, 10 May 1915; *Argus*, 26 April 1916 (Pearce).
5. Scott, *Australia During the War*, op. cit. p. 871.
6. See L. L. Robson, 'The origin and character of the First A.I.F., 1914–18: some statistical evidence', *Historical Studies*, vol. 15, no. 61, p. 738. Robson shows that 22 per cent of the AIF were labourers, 20 per cent workers in industry, 17 per cent workers in primary industry, 12 per cent workers in commerce, 9 per cent transport workers, 5 per cent clerks, 5 per cent professional and 10 per cent other and unknown.
7. Cf. Dan Coward, 'Crime and Punishment: The Great Strike in New South Wales, August to October 1917', in John Iremonger, John Merritt and Graeme Osborne (eds), *Strikes: Studies in Twentieth Century Australian Social History*, Sydney, 1973, pp. (5)1–80.
8. C. J. Dennis, *Digger Smith*, Angus & Robertson, Sydney, 1920, p. (1)2.

Chapter Two: A HOLY WAR?
1. Commonwealth of Australia, *Census*, vol. 1, pt 1, Melbourne, 1911, p. (2)01; Church of England, *Australian Church Congress, Brisbane, 1913, Official Record*, [Brisbane, 1913?], p. (2)47.
2. Richard Ely, *Unto God and Caesar*, Melbourne, 1976, pp. (1)12–17.
3. R. M. Crawford, *A Bit of a Rebel*, Sydney, 1975, Chapter XIII, 'Professor Wood Must Go', pp. (2)03–31.
4. F. B. Boyce, *Fourscore Years and Seven*, Sydney, 1934, p. (1)51 (Wright); H. M. Moran, *Viewless Winds*, London, 1939, p. (1)59 (Kelly); Gilbert White, *Leadership Unity Hope, Three Addresses*, Sydney, n.d. [1916], p. (1)3.
5. T. B. McCall, *The Life and Letters of John Stephen Hart*, Sydney, 1963, p. (6)0.
6. *Argus*, 10 August 1914; *Daily Telegraph*, 10 August 1914.
7. *West Australian*, 11 August 1914; *Brisbane Courier*, 14 August 1914; *Advertiser* (Adelaide), 12 August 1914.
8. *Advertiser* (Adelaide), 4 August 1914.
9. *Presbyterian Messenger*, 28 August 1914.
10. *Advocate*, 15 August 1914 (Cm); *Freeman's Journal*, 13 August 1914 (Kelly).
11. Cf. *Australasian Catholic Directory for 1914*, Sydney, 1914; H. M. Moran, *Viewless*

Winds, London, 1939, p. (2)2; Commonwealth of Australia, *Census,* vol. 1, pt 1, Melbourne, 1911, p. (2)07 (literacy).
12. *Methodist* (Sydney), 22 August 1914.
13. *Australian Christian World* (Sydney), 12 March 1915 (Ferguson).
14. *Argus,* 20 January 1915.
15. *Church Standard,* 30 April 1915; *Presbyterian Messenger* (Melbourne), 21 May 1915.
16. *Argus,* 8 May 1915.
17. T. B. McCall, *Life and Letters of John Stephen Hart,* Sydney, 1963, p. (6)0 (Clarke); *Argus,* 10 May 1915 (Clarke and Borland's sermons); *Daily Telegraph,* 10 May 1915 (Ferguson and Wright); *Advocate,* 15 May 1915 (Carr).
18. *Methodist,* 22 May 1915; James Norman, *John Oliver North Queensland,* Melbourne, n.d. [1956?], p. (7)8 (Mackay); letter from John L. May to author 28 August 1973.
19. *Australian Christian World,* 15 January 1915 (Ruth); Church of England, Diocese of Brisbane, *Yearbook for the Diocese of Brisbane 1915,* Brisbane, 1915, p. (1)5.
20. *Daily Telegraph,* 2 August 1915; *Advertiser* (Adelaide), 5 August 1915; *Southern Cross* (Melbourne), 16 July 1915.
21. *Church Standard,* 31 March 1916; Church of England, Diocese of Wangaratta, *Diocesan Synod 1916 Address of the President,* Wangaratta, 1916, p. (4); *Spectator* (Melbourne), 5 March 1915; *Annals of the Sacred Heart,* February 1917.
22. Novar Papers, National Library of Australia, MS 697/7447; *Southern Cross,* 16 July 1915 (Lynch).
23. *Advocate,* 26 August 1916; *Presbyterian Banner* (Adelaide), February 1915; *Advocate,* 9 October 1915 (Tregear); *Presbyterian Messenger* (Melbourne), 4 September 1914.
24. T. B. McCall, *The Life and Letters of John Stephen Hart,* Sydney, 1963, p. (4)7.
25. B. L. Webb, *The Religious Significance of the War,* Sydney n.d. [1915?], *passim.*
26. Minutes of a special meeting of the Hay Methodist Circuit, 17 November 1915 and 25 October 1916, Methodist Historical Society, Sydney; *Riverine Grazier,* 3 November 1916.
27. *Australian Christian World,* 1 June 1917.
28. Rohan Rivett, *Australian Citizen,* Melbourne, 1965, p. (7)1.
29. *Advocate,* 6 May 1916 (Carr); *Methodist,* 6 May 1916 (Carruthers).
30. *Australian Worker,* 13 August 1914.
31. See Michael McKernan, 'An Incident of Social Reform, Melbourne, 1906', *Journal of Religious History,* vol. 10, no. 1, June 1978, pp. (7)0–85.
32. *Southern Cross,* 14 January 1916.
33. *Advocate,* 14 October 1916; for the Protestant position see, for example, *Presbyterian Messenger* (Melbourne), 23 November 1917.
34. *Advocate,* 14 October 1916.
35. Scott, *Australia During the War, op. cit.,* p. (3)52.
36. *Presbyterian Messenger* (Melbourne), 20 October 1916.
37. P. Cardinal Gasparri to Count de Salis [British envoy at the Vatican], 22 August 1918, Australian Archives Accession CRS A1606, item SC F42/1, Canberra; Patrick Cunningham, 19 March 1917, Kelly Papers, Sydney Diocesan Archives; 'Irish Catholic', 20 November 1917, *ibid; Daily Telegraph,* 19 March 1917.
38. *Sydney Morning Herald,* 21 November 1917; 11 March 1918 (St John's and Balmain); *Freeman's Journal,* 13 June 1918 (O'Reilly).
39. *Southern Cross* (Melbourne), 3 November 1916.

Chapter Three: SEEDPLOTS OF EMPIRE LOYALTY: THE SCHOOLS AT WAR
1. Victorian Education department, *War Record,* Melbourne, 1919, p. (5).
2. *Report of the Minister of Public Instruction 1914,* Sydney, 1915, p. (2).

3 S. G. Firth, 'Social Values in the New South Wales Primary School 1880–1914, An Analysis of School Texts', *Melbourne Studies in Education 1970,* Melbourne, 1970, has the best discussion of the dominant values in the pre-war school
4 *Fortlan,* October 1914, pp. (5)2–3; *Sydneian,* 1 September 1914, p. (1)7; *ibid,* p. (1)8; *Pegasus,* August 1914, p. (4).
5 *Fortian,* December 1914, p. (8)8; *Record,* September 1914, p. (1).
6 *Bathurstian,* October 1914, p. (8)91; *High School Chronicle,* April 1915, p. (1)7.
7 *Sydneian,* September 1914, p. (1).
8 *High School Chronicle,* November 1914, p. (4).
9 *Pegasus,* May 1915, p. (5); *Ascham Charivari,* November 1914, p. (5).
10 *Sydneian,* September 1914, p. (1)7.
11 *St Joseph's College Annual,* December 1914, pp. (9)–10.
12 Education department (NSW), 'Record of Service in Two Wars' (typescript), Mitchell Library; MS A4117; Victorian Education department, *War Record,* p. (2)14; Dan Coward, The Impact of the War on New South Wales, Ph.D. Thesis, Canberra, 1974, p. (2)1 (salaries).
13 Gilbert M. Wallace, *How we Raised the First Hundred Thousand: An Account of Two Years' Work (1915–1916) for the Education Department's War Relief Fund Victoria,* Melbourne 1916, pp. (1)0, 15; *School Paper for Grades VII & VIII,* 1 September 1914, p. (1)59 (Tate); *School Paper...,* 1 October 1914, p. (1)64 (Gillies); *School Paper...,* 1 July 1915, p. (9)0 (Young Workers), and 1 August 1915, supplement, p. iii (Tate).
14 Victorian Education department. *War Record,* p. (2)12; *High School Chronicle,* April 1915, p. (3); *Babbler,* June 1917, p. (6).
15 *Aurora Australis,* September 1915, p. (3) (PLC); *Ascham Charivari,* September 1914, p. (6).
16 *Babbler,* November 1917, p. (5).
17 *High School Chronicle,* December 1915, p. (1)1; *Babbler,* November 1917, p. (6); *Fortian,* November 1915, p. (6)9.
18 *Magazine of the Girl's Grammar School Rockhampton,* 1916, p. (9).
19 *Newingtonian,* September 1917, p. (6)95; *Sydneian,* September 1917, p. (2)1.
20 *Freeman's Journal,* 18 July 1918.
21 *The King's School Magazine,* September 1918, p, 999; *Newingtonian,* December 1918, p. (8)39; *Caulfield Grammar School Magazine,* June 1919, p. (4)09; *Scotch Collegian,* December 1918, p. (2)75; Greg Dening, *Xavier A Centenary Portrait,* Melbourne 1978, p. (1)13.
22 *Scotsman,* December 1918, p. (6); *Corian,* May 1916, p. (1)0, report of headmaster's speech, December 1915; *Sydneian,* September 1915, p. (1)3, and November 1915, p. (1)7; *Sydneian,* September 1918, p. (6) (Cunningham), and December 1918, p. (5)7 (honour roll).
23 *Scotch Collegian,* December 1915, p. (2)25; J. T. Laird (ed.), *Other Banners: An Anthology of Australian Literature of the First World War,* Canberra, 1971, p. (1)0.
24 *The Kings School Magazine,* September 1916, p. (5)98, and March 1916, p. (5)24.
25 *Report of the Minister for Public Instruction 1915,* Sydney 1916, p. (2) (unqualified teachers); Education department (NSW), 'Record of Service in Two Wars' (enlistment); Victorian Education department, *War Record,* pp. (6), 10.
26 Victorian Education department, *War Record,* p. (4); *Pegasus,* December 1916, p. (3); Education department (NSW), 'Record of War Service in Two Wars' (national anthem).
27 *Pegasus,* December 1915, p. (4)9; *Scotch Collegian,* August 1915, p. (7)6; *Scotch Collegian,* December 1916, p. (1)87; *Newingtonian,* March 1917, p. (6)49.
28 *St Joseph's College Annual,* December 1916, p. (1)7; *Paradian,* December 1917, p. (1)05.

29 *Scotch Collegian,* December 1916, p. (2)21, December 1917, p. (2)05; *Argus,* 23 and 31 August 1917.
30 *Pegasus,* May 1916, p. (3)9; *The Kings School Magazine,* March 1917, p. (6)97; *Pegasus,* May 1915, p. (4).
31 Victorian Education department, *War Record,* p. (3); *Armidalian,* September 1915, p. (2).

Chapter Four: 'TO WAIT AND WEEP': AUSTRALIAN WOMEN AT WAR
1 Beverley Kingston, *My Wife, My Daughter and Poor Mary Ann,* Melbourne, 1975, p. (6)2.
2 *First Annual Report of the Australian Branch of the British Red Cross Society for Year Ending 7 August 1915,* Melbourne, 1915, *passim.*
3 British Red Cross Society, New South Wales Division, *Report to 30 November 1914,* p. (3); *First Annual Report of the Australian Branch of the British Red Cross Society for Year Ending 7 August 1915.*
4 L. Broinowski, *Tasmania's War Record 1914–1918,* Hobart, 1921, p. (1)86; Ernest Scott, *Official History of Australia in the War of 1914–18,* vol. xi, *Australia Puring the War,* Sydney, 1936, p. (7)05; Red Cross Society Australian Branch, untitled pamphlet, [on knitting] Mitchell Library, p. (2); New South Wales Education department, Record of Service in Two Wars, [typescript] Mitchell Library, MS A4117. British Red Cross Society, Victorian Division, *Report … 1915,* pp. (3)6–8 (list of branches).
5 M. A. Harris, *Where to Live, A.B.C. Guide to Sydney and Suburbs,* Sydney, 1917.
6 British Red Cross Society, New South Wales Division, *Report … 1917.*
7 *Red Cross Record,* October 1916, p. (1)3; *Downs Red Cross Herald,* 3 August 1916, p. (3), April 1917, p. (3), October 1917, p. (3), 6 December 1917, p. (4).
8 Scott, *Australia during the War, op. cit.,* pp. (8)82–7.
9 Australian Comforts Fund, Shipping Report 25 January 1917, Mitchell Library, MS 142 item 1 (lost case); Samuel H. Bowden, *The History of the Australian Comforts Fund,* Sydney [1922], p. (2)7 (eggs); *War Chest Review* (NSW), April 1919.
10 *War Chest Review,* November 1918 and April 1919.
11 *War Chest Review,* May 1918, p. (4) (membership lists); balance sheet of garden rete, 16 May 1917, Mitchell Library, MS 142; C. Drake-Brockman (ed.), *Voluntary War Workers' Record,* Melbourne, 1918, p. (3)8 (ACF membership lists, Victoria).
12 *Soldier,* 15 September 1916; 19 January 1917 (poem); 19 October 1917; *Red Cross Record,* October 1918, p. (1)7.
13 Australian Archives Accession, MP 943/5, Box 27, Melbourne; R. A. Kirkcaldie, *In Gray and Scarlet,* Melbourne, [1922], pp. (9)–10, 38; *Report upon the Department of Defence from the First of July 1914 to Thirtieth of June 1917,* Melbourne, 1917, vol. 1, p. (1)97 (numbers of nurses).
14 *Sun* (Sydney), 2 November 1916; *A.W.S.C. Despatch,* 1 May 1917, p. (4) (Victoria Barracks).
15 Letter to minister of Defence, 30 November 1916, reprinted in *A.W.S.C. Despatch,* 1 February 1917, p. (3) (numbers); *ibid,* for correspondence between Defence department and Miss Jacob.
16 *A.W.S.C. Despatch,* 1 March 1917, p. (5), and 1 August 1917, pp. (4)–5 (march).
17 *A.W.S.C. Despatch,* 1 June 1917, p. (2), and 1 October 1917, pp. (4)–5 (strike reports).
18 Scott, *Australia During the War, op. cit.,* p. (8)74 (enlistment rate); *Soldier,* 18 August 1916; letter from mother, 3 September 1916, Evelyn Davies Papers, Australian War Memorial, DRL, 3398, 3rd Series.
19 *Soldier,* 15 June 1916.

20 Letters from mother, 16 January 1916, 3 September 1916, 1 and 17 December 1917, 24 February 1918, 25 December 1917, Evelyn Davies Papers.
21 Cf. C. R. Badger, *The Reverend Charles Strong and the Australian Church*, Melbourne, 1971, pp. (1)45–8; Mary Booth Papers, Mitchell Library, MS 1329/1, 183 (Centre for Soldiers' Wives and Mothers).
22 *Soldier*, 14 July 1916.
23 *Argus*, 20 January 1915 (Wazir); *Sydney Morning Herald*, 15 February 1916.
24 *Sydney Morning Herald*, 12 June 1916 (referendum returns), 7 June 1916 (Ethel Turner), 31 May 1916 (Mrs Lee Cowie) and 9 June 1916 (Defence Union).
25 *Soldier*, 13 October and 11 August 1916.
26 G. H. Knibbs, *Official Year Book of the Commonwealth of Australia, 1901–1919*, Melbourne, 1920, p. (1)57.
27 Australian Archives Accession, MP 367, *A526f2f320*, Melbourne, letters, 15 and 26 February 1917, 27 November 1916 and 8 December 1916 (department's reply); *Soldier*, 12 January 1917 (Cleary's view); 8 December 1916.
28 Kelly Papers, St Mary's Archives, File: Kelly, War Conscript, Chaplains, 1915–27, letter from Hughes, 5 September 1917 and copy of Kelly's reply, 15 September 1917.
29 Letter from mother, 24 March 1918, Evelyn Davies Papers; *Soldier*, 16 August 1918.
30 *Soldier*, 17 August 1917.

Chapter 5: 'MUDDIED OAFS' AND 'FLANNELLED FOOLS': SPORT AND WAR IN AUSTRALIA

An earlier version of this chapter appeared in Richard Cashman and Michael McKernan (eds), *Sport in History*, Brisbane, 1979. I am grateful to the University of Queensland Press for permission to use that material.

1 R. E. N. Twopeny, *Town Life in Australia*, Melbourne 1973 (London, 1883). p. (2)04; Anthony Trollope, *Australia*, (P. D. Edwards and R. B. Joyce, eds), Brisbane, 1967, p. (7)33.
2 Chris Cunneen, 'The Rugby War: the Early History of Rugby League in New South Wales 1907–1915', in Richard Cashman and Michael McKernan (eds), *Sport in History*, Brisbane, 1979, pp. (2)97, 303.
3 *Pastoral Review*, 15 August 1914; *Sport*, Melbourne, 11 September 1914, 21 August 1914 (St Kilda).
4 *Sydney Sportsman*, 16 September 1914 (Darcy), 11 November 1914 (racing).
5 *Pastoral Review*, 15 August 1914 and 16 February 1915. In his spelling of 'mudded', Dr Lang may well have been following traditional Australian usage.
6 Scott, *Australia During the War, op. cit.*, pp. (3)13–19 (enlistment); *Argus*, 6 July 1915 (Rentoul); *Sport*, 9 July 1915.
7 *Wesley College Chronicle*, May 1915; *Sport*, 23 April 1915; *Sporting Judge*, 26 February, 4 March 1916.
8 New South Wales Cricket Association, *Annual Report Balance Sheet Record of Matches Season 1914–15*, Sydney, 1915, p. (8); *Pastoral Review*, 16 August 1917; *Pastoral Review*, 16 June 1916.
9 *Bulletin*, 29 April 1915 (Rugby); *Age*, 15 July 1915 (VFA); Bernard Barrett, *The Inner Suburbs, The Evolution of an Industrial Area*, Melbourne, 1971, shows the class boundaries of Melbourne's inner suburbs at the turn of the century.
10 Ross Topham, 'The Stricken Magpie, The C.F.C. and the "Collingwood Spirit"', *Meanjin*, Winter 1975, p. (1)58; *Age*, 22 July 1915.
11 *Sydney Morning Herald*, 2 August 1915; *Sydney Sportsman*, 4 August 1915.
12 *Bulletin*, 23 September 1915; New South Wales Cricket Association, *Annual Report Balance Sheet Record of Matches Season 1913–1914*, Sydney 1914, pp. (2)4–5, *Season*

1914–1915, Sydney, 1915, pp. (3)8–9; *Sydney Sportsman,* 29 September 1915.
13 *Bulletin,* 30 December 1915, 15 July 1915 (Bendigo), 5 August 1915 (Wodonga).
14 *West Australian,* 9 and 12 August 1915.
15 *Advertiser,* 3 April and 22 May 1916; 21 August 1916 (match report).
16 *Bulletin,* 27 January 1916, 2 March 1916 (balance sheets).
17 *Sporting Judge,* Melbourne, 18 March 1916.
18 *Sporting Judge,* 25 March 1916.
19 Council for Civic and Moral Advancement, *The Case against 'The Stadium' in War Time,* Sydney, 1916, pp. (1)–3.
20 *Sydney Sportsman,* 30 August 1916; letter from L. Darcy to R. L. Baker, 15 March 1917, MP 95/1, box 5, file W.E. 28.4.1917, Australian Archives, Melbourne.
21 *Sydney Sportsman,* 22 November 1916, 4 July 1917 (Coady).
22 These letters, resolutions and replies are to be found in the file 'Sport, Restrictions on' in Prime Minister's department, correspondence file, A2, 1918/1151, Australian Archives, Canberra.
23 Commonwealth of Australia, *Parliamemary Debates,* vol. LXXXII, 11 July 1917, p. (8); *Sydney Morning Herald,* 13 September 1917.
24 *Sydney Sportsman,* 1 December 1917.
25 This correspondence is also contained in the file 'Sport, Restrictions on', Australian Archives, Canberra.
26 *Ibid.*
27 *Sporting Judge,* 23 September 1916 (VCA) and 26 February 1916 (SMFC); *Sydney Morning Herald,* 24 July 1917.
28 Report of Lieutenant J. Lecky, 27 August 1917, Australian War Memorial, DRL 1121.
29 *Sydney Sportsman,* 29 March 1916; *Soldier,* 30 June 1916.

Chapter 6: FROM HERO TO CRIMINAL: THE AIF IN BRITAIN, 1915–19
 1 Norman Hale, letter, 19 September 1916, Australian War Memorial (hereafter AWM), file 12/5/234; G. H.J. Davies, diary entry updated, AWM, DRL 789, 2nd Series; A. A. Cameron, letter, 11 July 1916, AWM, DRL 1st Series.
 2 A. A. Cameron, letter, 11 July 1916, AWM, DRL 1st Series; A. E. C. Bray, diary, p. (1)26, Mitchell Library (hereafter ML), 1273/2; Peter Callinan, diary entry, 12 September 1916, AWM DRL, 1st Series; E.J. Martin, letter, 1 January 1917, ML, MS 2881/4; F.J. Brewer, diary entry, 28 August 1917, ML, MS 1536/2.
 3 C. H. Thorp, *A Handful of Ausseys,* London, 1919, pp. (6)8, 78; T. Darchy, diary entry, 28 August 1917, ML, MS 1178/1; M. M. A. Greig, letter, 28 January 1917, ML, MS 925; W. D. Baldie, letter, 7 January 1918, AWM, DRL 1st Series.
 4 N. G. Ellsworth, letter, 5 December 1915, AWM, DRL 1st Series; F. J. Brewer, diary entry, 1 September 1917, ML, MS 1536/2; A. A. Cameron, letter, 11 July 1916, AWM, DRL 1st Series.
 5 *London Opinion,* 1 April 1916; *Daily Mail,* 24 April 1916.
 6 *Daily Mail,* 26 April 1916; *The Times,* 26 April 1916; N. G. Ellsworth, letter, 26 April 1916, AWM, DRL 1st Series.
 7 *John Bull,* 13 May 1916; *The Times,* 17 April 1916.
 8 *John Bull,* 26 August 1916; *Daily Telegraph,* 25 July 1916; *Daily Express,* 8 August 1916; *Daily Mail,* 5 September 1916 (Northcliffe).
 9 *Military Mail,* 30 June 1916 (Bean); *Morning Post,* 8 July 1916; *Daily Mirror,* 10 August 1916.
10 *Daily Telegraph,* 27 July 1916; *Evening Standard,* 13 June 1916; *Sunday Times,* 2 July 1916 (advertisement).

11 J. G. Ridley, letter, 25 August 1916, AWM, DRL 6428; *Weymouth Telegram,* 3 December 1915 (Dr Perrin); J. G. Ridley, letter, 22 August 1916, AWM, DRL 6428 3rd Series.
12 *John Bull,* 22 July 1916.
13 C. A. L. Treadwell, *Recollections of an Amateur Soldier,* New Plymouth, New Zealand, 1936, p. (1)76; T. E. Bradshaw, letter, 11 January 1918, AWM, DRL 1st Series; W. D. Gallwey, letter, 2 January 1917, AWM, DRL 1st Series.
14 J. J. Marshall, letter, 24 November 1916, ML, MS 1164/3; B. Job, letter, 29 July 1917, ML, MS 2872; J.J. Marshall, letter, 25 November 1916, ML, MS 1164/3 (St Paul's and Big Ben); T. Darchy, letter, 11 March 1919, ML, MS 1178/5; cf. Harold S. and Marjorie Z. Sharp, *Index to Characters in the Performing Arts,* New Jersey, 1969.
15 Thorp, *A Handful of Ausseys,* p. (1)46; J. G. Ridley, letter, 23 August 1916, AWM, DRL 6428; *Matrimonial Times,* October 1916; A. D. Coxhead, letter, 25 May 1918, AWM, DRL6697 3rd Series.
16 L. A. G. Boyce, letter, 16 December 1917, AWM, DRL 1167 1st Series; A. A. Barwick, diary, p. (1)71, ML, MS 1493; J. O. Maddox, letter, 6 October 1918, ML, MS 2877/4; S. T. Brooks, letter, 4 March 1917, AWM, DRL 726 2nd Series; G. Hettick, letter, 6 June 1917, AWM, 12/5/234.
17 B. Job, letter 29 July 1917, ML, MS 2872; W. E. Baker, diary entry, 5 January 1917, DRL 1st Series; W. D. Gallwey, letter, 2 January 1917, AWM, 12/11/4802; N. G. Ellsworth, letter, 24 January 1916, AWM, 12/11/1146.
18 N. G. Ellsworth, letter, 28 March 1916, AWM, 12/11/1146; L. V. Bartlett, diary entry, 14 May 1918, ML, MS 959; Thorp, *A Handful of Ausseys,* p. (8)6; A. A. Barwick, diary entry, 13 May 1918, ML, MS 1493.
19 *British-Australasian,* 9 March 1916; G. E, Edmondson, letter, 22 July 1916, ML, MS 1244/1.
20 C. Francis, magistrate, writing to Home Secretary, 26 June 1916, HO 45, 10523/140266/3, Public Records Office, London.
21 W. D. Gallwey, letters, 21 September 1917, 2 January 1917, AWM, 12/11/4802; *Salisbury Times,* 9 August 1918 (brothel); J. J. Marshall, letter, 24 November 1916, ML, MSS 1164/3.
22 W. D. Gallwey, letters, 14December 1916, 21 September 1917, AWM, 12/11/4802; an Army Council committee examined the problem of venereal diseases and agreed that the provision of prophylactics would be a solution but added: 'under no circumstances should that view be presented to the Colonial Office for transmission to the Dominions', HO 45, 10802/307990/33, Public Records Office, London; Report of a conference held at the Home Office, 3 August 1917, HO 45, 10802/307990/30, Public Records Office, London (figures on venereal diseases).
23 A. A. Cameron, letter, 23 July 1916, AWM, 12/11/627; he also noted that 'you have a good chance of drawing a cash prize' in going with English women, from the context this was a reference to contracting a venereal disease; L. A. G. Boyce, letter, 11 November 1916, AWM, 419/11/22.
24 *Herald* (Melbourne), 7 January 1918; *British-Australasian,* 11 October 1917 and 25 July 1918.
25 W. D. Gallwey, letter, 23 July 1917, AWM, 12/11/4802; AIF marriage returns, MP 367, file A526/2/320, Australian Archives, Melbourne; L. F. S. Elliott, 28 October 1917, AWM, DRL 1st Series.
26 N. G. Ellsworth, letter, 6 March 1916, AWM, 12/11/1146; W. D. Gallwey, letter, 23 January 1919, AWM, 12/11/4802; N. G. Ellsworth, letter, 6 March 1916, AWM, 12/11/1146; Thorp, *A Handful of Ausseys,* p. (1)56; L. F. S. Elliot, letter, 28 October 1917, AWM, DRL 1st Series; W. D. Gallwey, letter, 23 July 1917, AWM, 12/11/4802; AIF marriage returns, MP 367, file A526/2/320, Australian Archives, Melbourne.

27 *Western Daily Press,* Bristol, 21 July 1916 ('poor type'); *British-Australasian,* 13 November 1919; *Argus,* 2 October 1918; *Age,* 2 October 1918; *Argus,* 8 January 1919.
28 *Weymouth Telegram,* 25 January 1918.
29 *Weymouth Telegram,* 21 February 1919 (later developments), 22 February 1918 (AIF reaction); *Western Daily Press,* Bristol, 11 April 1919 (House of Lords).
30 Gunner S. W. Hodge, *Evening Standard,* 2 August 1916; A. D. Coxhead, letter, 27 July 1918, AWM, 3 DRL 6697; F. J. Brewer, diary entry, 27 August 1917, ML, MS 1536/2.
31 W. D. Gallwey, 21 September 1917, AWM, 2 DRL 785; in private life Gallwey had been a bank clerk.
32 A. A. Barwick, diary entry, 1 May 1918, ML, MSS 1493; *British-Australasian,* 10 January 1918; *British-Australasian,* 17 January 1918; *Daily Mail,* 14 July 1916.
33 A. A. Barwick, diary entry, 18 May 1918, ML, MSS 1493.
34 G. H. Richards, *Spectator,* 4 August 1917.
35 G. H. Richards, *Spectator,* 4 August 1917; L. F. S. Elliott, letter, 11 July 1918, AWM, 12/11/1191; Norman Hale, letter, 19 September 1916, AWM, 12/5/234; Sister A. Donnell, letter, 11 January 1918, ML, MS 1022/2.
36 J. G. Ridley, letter, 24 August 1916, A WM, 3 DRL 6428; Thorp, *A Handful of Ausseys,* p. (1)22; N. G. Ellsworth, letter, 28 March 1916, AWM, 12/11/1146.
37 J. S. Bambrick, letter, 7 January 1917, AWM, 2 DRL 157; B. Job, 3 September 1917, ML, MS 2872; *Salisbury Times,* 1 September 1916; Thorp, *A Handful of Ausseys,* p. (1)47; A. A. Barwick, diary entry, 17 June 1918, ML, MS 1493.
38 *Weymouth Telegram,* 2 March 1917; W. D. Gallwey, 21 September 1917, AWM, 12/11/4802; N. G. Ellsworth, 24 February 1917, AWM, 12/11/1146; Thorp, *A Handful of Ausseys,* p. (1)65; *British-Australasian,* 6 June 1918.
39 *Weymouth Telegram,* 24 December 1915.
40 *Weymouth Telegram,* 25 February 1916, 24 March 1916.
41 *Weymouth Telegram,* 24 August 1917, 28 December 1917, 18 July 1919 (Jenkins).
42 *Salisbury Times,* 27 July 1917, 25 May 1917, 24 August 1917 (ungrateful act); *Western Daily Press* (Bristol), 15 April 1919; *Salisbury Times,* 23 August 1918 (rape).
43 *Salisbury Times,* 21 March 1919, 11 April 1919, 18 April 1919; *Morning Post,* 19 June 1919 (Epsom riot).
44 *Salisbury Times,* 12 December 1919.
45 Minutes of the War Cabinet, 14 November 1918, Cab 23/8, 502(1), Public Records Office, London.
46 J. O. Maddox, diary, 14 May and 11 June 1919, ML, MSS 2877/5; A. E. C. Bray, diary, 14 February 1919, ML, MS 1273/2; T. Darchy, diary, 9 May 1919, ML, MS 1178/3.

Chapter 7: MANUFACTURING THE WAR: 'ENEMY SUBJECTS' IN AUSTRALIA

1 G. H. Knibbs, *Census of the Commonwealth of Australia* taken for the Night between 2nd and 3rd April 1911, Melbourne, 1912, pp. (1)45, 127.
2 *Barossa News,* 7 August 1914; *Kapunda Herald,* 7 August 1914; *Advertiser,* 4 August 1914; *Daily Advertiser,* 7 August 1914; *Advertiser,* 5 August (Bagner) and 7 August 1914 (Blacket); *Kapunda Herald,* 7 August 1914.
3 *Advertiser,* 6 August 1914; *Kapunda Herald,* 14 August 1914 (Duhst); *Advertiser,* 7 August 1914.
4 *Advertiser,* 24 October 1914; *Barossa News,* 11 September 1914; *Mount Barker Courier,* 18 September 1914.
5 *Barossa News,* 23 October 1914 (Kliche) and 13 November 1914 (Schulz); *Mount Barker Courier,* 16 October 1914.

NOTES 233

6 Correspondence relating to trading with the enemy is found in the Attorney-General's department's correspondence files, War Series, CRS A456, W6f11/37 (Palings and Watson) and W8/6/[3] (Commercial Bank), Australian Archives, Canberra.
7 *Advertiser*, 15 January 1915, and Attorney-General's department, correspondence files, War Series, CRS A456 W8/14/-, 'Pastor Nickel' (Glynn's letters 21 and 25 January 1915), Australian Archives, Canberra.
8 *Kapunda Herald*, 27 November 1914; Report of Aliens Committee CRS A456, W8/1/-, Australian Archives, Canberra.
9 Australian Archives Accession, MP 16, 14/3/636, Melbourne (Bishopscourt), and CRS, B543, 175/1/2186, Canberra (Dr Kilmar).
10 Letter from General Foster to Senator Pearce, 27 March 1917, Defence department, CRS, B543, W155f1/82, Australian Archives, Melbourne; *Mount Barker Courier*, 21 August 1914; *Mount Barker Courier*, 27 November 1914; General Foster removed the guard in August 1916; see file above.
11 For these and many other cases, see Australian Archives Accession, MP 367/1, file 512/3/1319, Melbourne.
12 These complaints are found in Australian Archives Accession, CRS A2, item 17/4053, Canberra.
13 See Australian Archives Accession, A456, W8/9/[2], Canberra; *Advertiser*, 15 March 1916 and 24 February 1915.
14 *Advertiser*, 6 September 1915, 4 September 1915, 10 January 1917; *Barossa News*, 3 December 1915; *Advertiser*, 2 January 1916.
15 *Barossa News*, 16 April 1915; *Advertiser*, 23 December 1915.
16 *Advertiser*, 26 and 18 June 1915.
17 *Australian Worker*, 27 May 1915.
18 *Advertiser*, 28 and 30 November 1914, 19 December 1914, 25 January 1916 (brewery).
19 Australian Archives Accession A456, W8f15/[3], Canberra (Ludersen); *Advertiser*, 28 July 1915 (Wettel), *Advertiser*, 17 March 1915 (voluntary internment).
20 *Advertiser*, 13 November 1914; 17 September 1915 (Holman); 23 March 1916 (Holman); 25 May 1916 (Premiers' Conference).
21 Letters from mother, 17 December 1917 and 24 February 1918, Evelyn Davies Papers, AWM, 3 D RL 3398; the cases are documented in the papers of the Royal Commission, Australian Archives Accession, CP 661/11, item Bundle 1, Canberra.
22 *Daily Herald* (Adelaide), 7 September 1914 (votes); *Advertiser*, 26 August 1916; 25 September 1916 (petition); Joan Rydon, *A Biographical Register of the Commonwealth Parliament 1901–1972*, Canberra, 1975, p. (5)7.
23 *Mount Barker Courier*, 5 March 1915, 9 April 1915.
24 *Advertiser*, 2 November 1917 (rejection was carried nineteen to thirteen); *Advertiser*, 12 November 1917 (federal disenfranchisement).
25 *British-Australasian*, 7 March 1918.
26 Australian Archives Accession, MP 95/1, Box, Wfe 22.12.17, Melbourne; *Advertiser*, 25 March 1916 (telephones); Australian Archives Accession, MP 95/1, Box 9, Wfe 19.5.17 (Kahn).
27 *Mirror*, 29 August 1915, 3 October 1915.
28 *Mirror*, 24 February 1917.
29 *Register*, 7 September 1914, 9 September 1914; *Advertiser*, 17 March 1916 (Pischul).
30 *Kapunda Herald*, 13 August 1915; the letters from German-Australians expressing disloyalty are found in the weekly intelligence reports, Australian Archives Accession, MP 95/1, various boxes, Melbourne.
31 *Ibid*, MP 95/1, various boxes, Melbourne.
32 *Kapunda Herald*, 4 January 1918.

33 Report of Aliens Committee, 10 December 1918, Australian Archives Accession, A456 W8/1/–, Canberra (statistics).
34 Brittain's reports, Australian Archives Accession, CP 78/24, item 89/228.
35 Personal record of Sergeant P. J. Braine, guard at Holdsworthy, Australian War Memorial, File 181. 11 12/21; Australian Archives Accession, CRS A2, item 1917/4290.
36 *Ibid,* item 1917/4051 (Tannenberg).

Chapter 8: THE OTHER AUSTRALIA: WAR IN THE COUNTRY
1 *Mount Morgan Chronicle,* 28 August 1914; *Ballarat Courier,* 8 August 1914.
2 *Bendigo Advertiser,* 10 August 1914; *Goulburn Evening Penny Post,* 8 August 1914; *Mount Barker Courier,* 7 August 1914; *Naracoorte Herald,* 11 August 1914.
3 *Yass Courier,* 24 August 1914; *Ballarat Courier,* 8 August 1914; *Bendigo Advertiser,* 10 August 1914.
4 *Yass Courier,* 13 May 1915; *Kapunda Herald,* 2 October 1914; *Barossa News,* 16 June 1916; *Kapunda Herald,* 14 August 1914; Report of recruiting trip by Lieutenant Elfield to New South Wales Sportsmen's Recruiting Committee, 3 June 1917, Australian War Memorial file DRL 1121.
5 *Bendigo Advertiser,* 7 April 1916; L. L. Robson, 'The Origin and Character of the First A.I.F., 1914–1918; Some Statistical Evidence', *Historical Studies,* vol. 15, no. 61, October 1973, p. (7)45.
6 *Mount Barker Courier,* 28 August 1914; *Daily Advertiser,* Wagga, 8 May 1915; *Kapunda Herald,* 11 September 1914; *Tamworth Observer,* 19 August 1914.
7 *Yass Courier,* 20 August 1914.
8 *Kapunda Herald,* 13 August 1915.
9 *Mount Barker Courier,* 14 January 1916, 27 August 1915 (Robbie) and 19 November 1915 (Robbie's enlistment).
10 *Mount Barker Courier,* 28 May 1915; *Yass Courier,* 16 September 1915.
11 *Alert,* Maryborough, 26 January 1917; *Bendigo Advertiser,* 11 April 1916.
12 *Bendigo Advertiser,* 15 April 1916 (figures); New South Wales, Parliamentary Papers, vol. II, Sydney, 1916, p. (9)97.
13 *Yass Courier,* 20 August 1914 (well wishers); *Albury Banner,* 14 August 1914; 17 August 1914 (Wagga); *Barrier Miner,* Broken Hill, 13 August 1914; *Ballarat Courier,* 2 May 1916; *Kapunda Herald, passim; Mount Morgan Chronicle,* 7 September 1917; *Barossa News,* 25 August 1916 and 19 April 1918.
14 Report by Lieutenant W. G. Williams to New South Wales Sportsmen's Recruiting Committee, [n.d.], report by Fred J. Bohm, 17 October 1917; and report by Lieutenant Elfield, all in Australian War Memorial file DRL 1121.
15 *Bendigo Advertiser,* 15 April 1916; *Mount Barker Courier,* 13 March 1916; *Tamworth Observer,* 28 September 1915 (Gunnedah).
16 *Goulburn Evening Penny Post,* 12 September 1914; *Albury Banner,* 21 August 1914; *Alert,* 11 September 1914.
17 *Mount Barker Courier,* 21 August 1914; *Kapunda Herald,* 11 September 1914 (farewell), 2 October 1914 (patriotic tennis dance) and 9 October 1914 (Freeling); *Yass Courier,* 17 May 1915; *Daily Advertiser* (Wagga), 17 May 1915.
18 *Mount Morgan Chronicle,* 7 August 1914; *Northern Star,* 6 August 1914.
19 *Barrier Miner,* 9 August 1915.
20 *Yass Courier,* 13 and 20 August 1914.
21 *Mount Barker Courier,* 23 June 1916; K. Fewster, Goulburn, New South Wales, 1914–1918: The Impact of the Great War on the Town and Its People, BA (Hons) Thesis, Australian National University, 1975, p. (9)0.
22 *Daily Advertiser,* 24 October 1916.

23 *Mount Morgan Chronicle;* 27 October 1916; *Alert,* 16 November 1917; *Barrier Miner,* 19 December 1917.
24 *Tamworth Observer,* 18 October 1916; *Ballarat Courier,* 19 December 1917.
25 *Kapunda Herald,* 13 October 1916; *Tamworth Observer,* 4 December 1917 (ex-teacher).
26 *Barrier Miner,* 7 December 1917.
27 *Mount Barker Courier,* 27 October 1916.
28 *Naracoorte Herald,* 17 October 1916; *Mount Barker Courier,* 12 and 27 October 1916.
29 *Ballarat Courier,* 21 October 1916 (Phillips); *Bendigo Advertiser,* 18 October 1916 (Dunstan); *Mudgee Guardian,* 30 October 1916 (Ellis).
30 *Yass Courier,* 20 August 1917.
31 Report of Lieutenant H. G. Williams to the New South Wales Sportsmen's Recruiting Committee, 30 August 1917, Australian War Memorial file DRL 1121 (Lithgow); *Yass Courier,* 20 August 1917; *Tamworth Observer,* 16 and 18 August 1917; Dan Coward, The Impact of War on New South Wales, Some Aspects of Social and Political History 1914–1917, Ph.D. Thesis, Australian National University, 1974, p. (4)01.

Chapter Nine: THE GREY YEARS
1 Scott, *Australia During the War, op. cit.,* p. (4)45.
2 *Sydney Morning Herald,* 9 November 1918.
3 *ibid,* 9 November 1918, 12 November 1918.
4 *ibid,* 12 November 1918.
5 *ibid,* 13 November 1918.
6 *Yass Courier,* 14 November 1918; *Albury Banner,* 15 November 1918.
7 *Ballarat Courier,* 12 November 1918; *Tamworth Observer,* 13 November 1918.
8 *Sydney Morning Herald,* 13 November 1918; *Soldier,* 15 November 1918, 11 October 1918.
9 Humphrey McQueen, The Spanish Influenza Epidemic in Australia, 1918–1919 (typescript), pp. (1), 8, 9.
10 Scott, *Australia During the War, op. cit.,* p. (8)27; 'Leslie Parker' (Angela Thirkell), *Trooper to the Southern Cross,* Melbourne, 1966 (London, 1934).
11 Heather Radi, '1920–29', in F. K. Crowley (ed.), *A New History of Australia,* Melbourne, 1974, p. (3)61.
12 Scott, *Australia During the War, op. cit.,* p. (8)46.
13 G. L. Kristianson, *The Politics of Patriotism,* Canberra, 1966, p. (2)34; Scott, *Australia During the War,* p. (8)53.
14 Australian War Memorial Museum, *Guidebook,* Sydney, 1928, p. (3).
15 *Sydney Morning Herald,* 26 April 1920.
16 *ibid,* 26 April 1921 and 1922.
17 Mary Wilson, 'The Making of Melbourne's Anzac Day', *Australian Journal of Politics and History,* vol. 20, no. 2, pp. (1)97–209; *Sydney Morning Herald,* 26 April 1928.
18 *Sydney Morning Herald,* 26 April 1928.
19 James Green, *The Angel of Mons,* Sydney, n.d., p. (2)4; G. H. Cranswick, *Presidential Address ... to the First Session of the Fifth Synod,* Sale, 1917, p. (8); G. H. Cranswick, *Presidential Address ... to the Third Session of the Fifth Synod,* Sale, 1919, p. (1)1.
20 Church of England, Diocese of Sydney, *Minutes of Synod,* Sydney, 1918, p. (2)2.
21 *Spectator,* 20 November 1918; *Church Standard,* 29 November 1918.
22 *Advocate,* 23 November 1918; *Argus,* 13 November 1918.
23 *Advocate,* 8 November 1919.
24 N. Brennan, *Dr Mannix,* Adelaide, 1964, p. (1)76; *Advocate,* 20 May 1920.

25 George Johnston, *My Brother Jack*, London, 1967, p. (1)0.
26 *Report of the Minister of Public Instruction for the Year 1919,* Sydney, 1920, p. (3)3.
27 Graham McInnes, *The Road to Gundagai*, Melbourne, 1970, pp. (2)45, 247, 248–9.
28 Commonwealth of Australia, *Yearbook of the Commonwealth of Australia for 1924*, Melbourne, n.d., p. (4)99; Johnston, *My Brother Jack*, p. (4)0.
29 Commonwealth of Australia, *Parliamentary Debates,* vol. 88, p. (9),793 (Pearce), p. (1)0,005 (Watt), p. (1)0,249 (circular).
30 *ibid*, p. (1)0,252 (Corboy); vol. 89, p. (1)1,610 (Higgs); vol. 88, p. (1)0,106 (interjections).
31 *ibid*, vol. 89, p. (1)1,620.

INDEX

Adamson, L. A. 99–101
Albiston, Rev. W. 32
Albury (NSW) 181, 189, 190, 205
All Saints College, Bathurst 47
Angaston (SA) 182, 189
Anti-German League 169, 170
Anzac Day 213–15, 219, 221
   in London 120–2
Armidale (NSW) 20, 184, 188
Armidale School 64
armistice, reaction to news of 2017
Ascham School 48, 53
Asche, O. 128
Ashmead-Bartlett, E. 24
Australasian League of Honour 53
Australia, fears for safety of 1, 7, 150, 196–7
Australian Comforts Fund 73–7
   class nature of 76
   fundraising methods 75–6
   organisation 73,
   sock fund 73–4
   statistics 75–6
Australian Imperial Forces 6, 7, 8, 9, 10, 11, 22, 24, 25, 27, 38, 56, 57, 60, 63, 64, 65, 70, 73, 78–9, 86, 89, 90, 91, 92, 98, 99, 103, 111, 114, 116, 126, 133, 134, 136, 137, 139, 141, 147, 150, 154, 162, 164, 165, 166, 167, 178, 182, 183, 187, 190, 192, 197, 198, 200, 209, 210, 212, 213, 220, 223
   and bigamy 138
   and British nurses 131
   and class distinctions 140–3
   and criminal activity 145–7
   and employment 210–11
   and marriage in Britain 90, 134–7
   and prostitutes 132–3
   and relatives in Britain 116, 129
   and riots 86, 146–7
   and slouch hats 123, 124, 143–4, 219
   and tea parties 142
   and venereal diseases 92, 133–4
   and women 131–9
   as tourists 127–8
   attitudes to working women 129–30
   Australian nurses in 79–80
   Australian opinions of 6, 22, 24, 86
   British opinions of 120–21, 122–5, 131, 144–5, 147–8
   farewells to departing troops 183–4
   provision of comforts for 73–7
   reception of, in postwar Australia 149, 209–10
   repatriation of 209
   rural composition of 182
Australian Jockey Club 68, 97
Australian Labor Party 2, 7, 20, 84, 223
Australian War Memorial 117, 212–13
Australian Women's Service Corps 80–2, 89
   class nature of 81

Bagner, E. W. G. 152
Baker, R. L. 110
Baldie, W. D. 120
Ballarat (Vic) 180, 205
Barnett, A. N. 164–6
Barrett, Dr J. W. 67
Barwick, A. A. 129, 131, 142, 144
Bean, C. E. W. 9, 22, 122, 182, 213
Bega (NSW) 187, 189
Bendigo (Vic.) 181
Bigamy 138

237

Biggs, L. V.   14
Binginwarri (Vic)   196
Birdwood, Sir W.   213
Black, G.   109
Blacket, J.   152
Bohm, F. J.   189
Border Town (SA)   197–8
Borland, Rev. W.   25
Boxing   94, 97, 104, 108–9, 111
   and recruiting   104
Boyce, L. A. G.   129
Bradshaw, T. E.   126
Brandt, Rev. D.   104
Braund, Lieut-Col   184
Bray, A. E. C.   118, 149
Brennan, F. (MHR)   177
Brewer, F. J.   120
Britain, Australian complaints
   about   119–20, 142–4
   Australian opinions of   11, 22, 118, 139–43, 144
   first reactions to   118–20
   see also 'home'
British Empire   1,
   and school texts   43–4, 118, 120, 139–40
   Australian opinions of   1, 13, 116, 126
   children's opinions of   47
   clergymen's opinions of   18, 20, 22
Brittain, J. I.   174–5
Broken Hill (NSW)   4, 5, 189, 192, 193, 195, 197
Brookes, H.   32
Brothels   133, 134
Brown, F. E.   59
Burns, J. D.   59–60

Callinan, P.   118
Cambridge (UK)   120
Cameron, A. A.   118, 120
Cameron, Rev. D.   38
Campbell, J. D.   95
Carlton Football Club   107
Carr, Archbishop Thomas   19, 25, 32
Carruthers, Rev. J. C.   32
Carruthers, Sir J.   113
casualties and schools   59
   impact of   82–3
casualty lists   25
casualty telegrams   25–6

Catholic church
   Irish heritage of   19, 44
   loyalty of doubted   32, 33, 38
   on Ireland   32
   on war   19, 20
   opinions about   32
   social composition   19–20
Caulfield Grammar School   57
Centre for Soldiers' Wives and Mothers   85
Cerretti, Archbishop Bonaventure   38, 50
Christian Brothers' College, Lewisham   57
Christian Brothers' College, Victoria Parade   63
Christian Brothers' College, Waverley   56
children, adjustment to peace   219–21
   and fund-raising   52–4
   see also schools
'Chu Chin Chow'   128
churches
   and marriage-by-proxy   91
   influence of   41
   position in Australia   14
   reaction to armistice   215–16
   statistics   14
   views on war   16–18
Clarke, Archbishop Lowther   16, 25
class differences in Australia   3–4, 7–8, 9, 11–13, 19–20, 31, 33, 35, 37, 38, 40–1, 44, 49, 56, 63, 70, 72, 76, 81, 88, 89, 93, 94–6, 97, 98, 101, 103–4, 107, 108, 110, 112–13, 141–3, 194, 199, 200
class distinctions in Britain   140–3
Clausen, H. H.   165
Clayton, J. H.   102
Cleary, P. S.   91
clergymen, enlistment of   27–8
   on disloyalty   33
   on sacrifice   23, 25
   on war   17–19, 22–3, 26, 29, 41
   opinions about   16
   role in wartime   16, 42
Clune, Archbishop Patrick   37
Coady, Rev.   110
Coen, Capt.   185
Collingwood Football Club   103, 104
comforts   3, 49, 53, 65, 66–7, 69
   children's contributions to   52–3,

children distracted by 54
see also Australian Comforts Fund
conscription 7–8, 104–5, 195
    and schools 62, 196
    and women 88–9
    Catholic views on 35, 37–8
    effect of campaigns in rural Australia 196–7
    explanations for defeat of referenda 197
    and German-Australians 173–4
    in rural Australia 195–7
    Protestant views on 37, 38
    Red Cross support for conscription referendum (1916) 7, 38; (1917) 8, 84
Cook, Sir J. (MHR) 2, 15
Cooma (NSW) 187, 189
Cooper, Rev. W. H. 23
Cootamundra (NSW) 191
Council for Civic and Moral Advancement 108–9, 110
country, *see* rural Australia
Cowie, Mrs Harrison Lee 87
cricket 101–2, 105
Cullen, Lady 76
Cunningham, R. E. G. 59

Dains, Rev. J. W. 20
Dankel, G. (MHR) 166
Darchy, T. 119
Darcy, Les 97, 104, 110, 112, 115
Darling Downs 70–1, 151
Davies, G. H. J. 118
Davies, Mrs 82–3, 84–5, 93, 164
Dennis, C. J. 12
divorce, statistics of 222
Donaldson, Archbishop St Clair 27
Duhig, Archbishop Sir James 32
Duhst. O. H. 152–3, 166–7
Dunstan, I. J. 198

East Perth Football Club 106
Edinburgh (UK) 129
Edinglassie Primary School (NSW) 69
elections
    federal (1914) 2, 38, 166
    federal (1917) 111, 166, 167
    Red Cross involvement in 72
Elfield, Lieut. 190
Elkan, E. 170

Ellis, A. 198
Ellsworth, N. G. 131, 145
Empire Day 44
enemy subjects 174
    internment of 155
    1916 definition of 156
    registration of 155–6
    see also German-Australians
enlistment 7, 8, 28, 33, 34, 53–4, 56–7, 58, 59, 60, 61, 62, 82, 94, 98, 101, 103, 106, 107, 115, 160, 166, 178, 182, 185, 187, 188, 190, 191, 207
    and 'economic conscripts' 193–4
    and Les Darcy 110
    and schoolboys 58
    and sportsmen 98, 101, 103, 106, 113–16
    Catholic 32, 33
    comparison of rates 187–8
    evidence of local loyalty 187
    of teachers 60
    opposition to 160
    pressure for in rural Australia 185–7
    statistics 3, 6, 8
enlistment rates, of German-Australians 154
    in Catholic schools 56–7
    in rural Australia 189
    schools' contribution 56–8
    and Sydney Rugby Union 103
espionage in Australia 157, 170
Eudunda (SA) 157, 184
exemption courts 197–8
Exeter (UK) 118

Ferguson, Rev. J. 16, 22, 25
'Fife and Drum' (Dr W. H. Lang) 97, 98
Fisher, A. 2, 7, 15
Fitchett, Rev. W. H. 41
Fitzroy Football Club 101, 108
'For England' 59
Forrest, Sir J. 29, 57
Fort Street Boys' High School 46
Fort Street Girls' High School 54
Freeling (SA) 192

Gallipoli 5, 6, 23, 24, 25, 26, 27, 31, 44, 59, 60, 62, 64, 98, 99, 120, 122, 138, 146, 189, 213, 214, 215, 222
Gallwey, W. D. 126, 129, 133, 135, 141,

Geelong College   46, 48, 62, 63
Geelong Grammar School   58
German-Australians
   administrative acts against   167–8
   alienation of   170–3
   and Australian nationality   155–6
   and conscription   173–4
   and enlistment   154
   and parliamentary office   166–7
   and public service   85, 162–6
   defined   150
   denial of work by unionists   161–2
   disenfranchisement of   167, 169
   divided loyalties   152–4, 170, 172
   early reaction to the war   152–4
   in postwar Australia   223, 224
   loyalty of doubted   38, 154, 158–9
   organised opposition to   169
   poverty of   162
   statistics   150–1
   violence against   154, 160–1
Germany, opinions about   1, 20, 62, 154, 187
Gibbs, P.   122
Gibson, Rev. J.   31
Gillies, W.   51
Glasgow (UK)   129
Glynn, P. M. (MHR)   156
Goulburn (NSW)   179, 187, 191, 194, 199, 212
Green, Rev. J.   215
Greenwall, H. J.   122
Greig, M.   119
Gunnedah District Association   190

Haig, Sir D.   201
Hale, N.   118
Hart, Rev. J.   30
Harvey, E. J.   185
Hay, Lady   76
Hay (NSW)   159, 193
Healesville (Vic)   82, 83, 84, 93, 164
Henningham, H.   184
Heydon, L.   40
Hoisler, Rev. R. G.   29
Holland, F.   97
Holman, W. A. (MLA)   27, 40, 86, 104, 164,
Holthouse, H. A.   152
Holy Cross College, Ryde   57
Homburg, J.   179

Homburg, H.   166
'Home'   116, 118, 126, 149
honour boards and schools   56, 58, 62
Hordern, Mrs Cecil   76
horse-racing   94, 95, 97–8, 101, 102, 111, 112–3
Howard, Rev. H.   18
Hughes, W. M. (MHR)   2, 7, 8, 29, 37, 111, 197, 209
   and conscription   35, 80, 87, 89, 195, 196
   and German-Australian franchise   167
   and marriage-by-proxy   90–2
   and rural economy   194
   and sport   111
   and supply of rural labour   198
   opinions about   84
   opposition to Mannix   37–8, 219
   reception in Britain   35
Huntly, Shire of   187

inflation   4, 12, 33
influenza pandemic   209, 213, 217
Inglewood (Vic)   179
internment   155, 158, 161, 172, 174–7
   applications for by German-Australians   162
   conditions in camps   174–5
   demands for   159, 177,
   numbers   156, 174
   riots in camps   175
Ireland   129, 166
Irish Race Convention, Melbourne   217
Irish uprising   32

Jacob, Eleanor   80, 72
Jahn, F. E.   155
Jameson, Miss W. G.   54, 55
Jenkins, Rev.   147
Jerger, Rev.   224
Job, B.   144
Johnstone, Rev. S. M.   215
Johnstone, George   219

Kaiser, Australians hatred of   202, 203–4, 205, 223
Kalgoorlie (WA)   162, 180, 193
Kapunda (SA)   151, 152, 156, 172, 174, 182, 185, 189, 192, 196

Kelly, Mrs George   76
Kelly, Archbishop Michael   16, 19, 32, 35, 37, 91, 92,
   opposition to   40
Kirkcaldie, Nurse   79
Kitchener, Lord, impact of death of   84
Kliche, C. B.   155
Korong Vale (SA)   190

Lady Mayoress's Patriotic League   76
Laird, J. T.   60
Leek, W. H.   165
League of Loyalty   217, 219
Leeper, A.   32
Le Maitre, Rev. E.   27
Lindsay, N.   154
Liquor Trades Defence Union   87
Lismore (NSW)   188, 192
Lithgow (NSW)   199
Lloyd George, D.   148–9
Long, W.   149
London   22, 37, 117, 120, 121–125, 129–131, 209, 212
   and loneliness   128–9
   and prostitution   132–3,
   Australian complaints about   127
   Australian love for   126, 128
Loyalist League   32
loyalty, to Australia   6, 49, 67
   for Empire   2, 6, 44, 67, 95–6
Ludersen, Charles   162
Lutheran church, attacks on   160–1
Lynch, Rev. F.   29

McGoorty, E.   104
McInnes, G.   221
Macintyre, Rev. R. G.   110
McKenzie, G. M.   159
Maddox, J. O.   149
Mannix, Archbishop Daniel   39, 113, 217–19
   and conscription   37, 38
   class views of   40–1
   opposition to   40
   support for   40
   views on war   42
Marist Brothers' College, Darlinghurst   56
marriage-by-proxy   90–1
marriage rates, and war   90
Martin, E. J.   119

Maryborough (Qld)   75, 187, 191, 195
Mason, O.   15
Merrington, Rev. E. N.   31
Messenger, H. H.   95
Miller, Hon. E.   67
Mirror of Australia   168, 169–70
Monash, Gen. Sir J.   209
Moran, Cardinal Patrick   15
Mount Barker   151, 190, 198
Mount Morgan   179, 189
Mueke, H. C. E.   152
Munro-Ferguson, Lady Helen   67, 69
Munro-Ferguson, Sir R.   16
Murray, Mrs Jean   142
Murray Bridge   154, 179, 183, 185, 187, 191,
   defence of   157
Mutch, Mrs   187
My Brother Jack   219

Naracoorte (SA)   179
Newington College, Sydney   55, 57, 62
Nichterlein, Rev. O.   168
Nickel, Rev. Th.   156
Nimmitabel (NSW)   189
Noble, M. A.   105
Northcliffe, Lord   122
North Sydney Girls' High School   47–8, 53, 54, 62
Nuriootpa (SA)   189
nurses in AIF   79–80

Oakey (Qld)   72
Oakwood (NSW)   200
O'Reilly, Rev. M.   41

pacifism   10, 30–31, 84
   and women   65
'patriotic classes' in post-war Australia   207
Patriotic Football Association   107
patriotic funds   97, 200
   and social life   192
   children's contributions   47–8, 50–1
   donations   4
   donations from rural Australia   191
   unemployed workers   4
   Victorian schoolchildren and   51
patriotism
   and ritual   60–2
   children's views of   47

displays of   20, 179
Empire   181
Peake, A. H. (MLA)   167
Pearce, Senator G. F.   6, 162, 174, 223
Perth Football Club   106
Phelan, Bishop Patrick   217
Phillips, S. H.   168, 198
Piesse, Major   157
Plate, O.   169
Port Adelaide Limited Patriotic Football Club   107
Pozières, battle of prayer, special calls for   122, 123
Presbyterian Ladies' College, Sydney   53
prostitution   132–3
prophylactics   134
prisoners, celebration of armistice   205

Queanbeyan (NSW)   189
Queensland Turf Club   113

recruiting   7, 198
   and sport   98–101
   and sportsmen   115
   clergymen's role   26–7
   in rural Australia   183, 185, 187, 188–90
   methods used   189–90
   Victorian campaign   99
Rentoul, Rev. J. L.   99
recruits, descriptions of
Red Cross   8, 10, 67–73, 75, 76, 78, 79, 88, 167, 192, 194, 200, 212, 220
   activities   68–9, 72
   British connection   67
   children's contributions to   48–9
   class nature of   67, 69, 70, 74
   in rural Australia   194
   men's branch   194
   money   68
   organisational structure   67
   political involvement   72
   statistics   68
Reid, Sir G.   51
Renmark (SA)   187
repatriation department   211–12
Returned Sailors and Soldiers Imperial League of Australia
The Road to Gundagai   221
Robbie, G. C.   185–7

Rockhampton Girls' Grammar School   54, 62
Rockstroh, Matilda   165
Royal Commission on German-Australians in the Commonwealth Public Service   164–6, 169
rural Australia
   and the Red Cross   194
   and conscription debates   195–7
   compared with urban Australia   181
   conflict with cities   190
   donations to patriotic funds   180, 191–2
   early reactions to war   178, 191–2
   effect of conscription campaigns   196–7
   effect of war on   178, 198, 200
   importance of newspapers to   179
   patriotic displays   179–80
   reaction to 'great strike'   199
   reaction to news of Armistice   205
   recruiting in   181–3, 187
   rivalries between towns   182, 187
   social activity   192
   unemployment in   192
   war and trade   181
Ruth, Rev. T. E.   27, 32
Ryan, D. H.   159

St Aloysius' College, Sydney   57
St Ignatius' College, Sydney   57
St Joseph's College, Sydney   49, 57, 63
St Kilda Football Club   97, 108
Salisbury (UK)   118, 119, 120, 133, 144, 145, 146, 147, 148
'Scabs Collecting Ground'   200
schoolteachers, views on sacrifice   59
schools   13
   Catholic Australian emphasis of   49
   social teaching of   44
   description of education system   42–5
   effect of war on   221
   private school teaching of   44–5
   reaction to war   45–7
   State social teaching of   43–4
   statistics   43
   school spirit   63
Schulz, A.   155
Schweiger, Rev. E.   29
Scone (NSW)   200

Scotch College, Melbourne   57, 59, 62, 63
Scott, T.   154
sectarianism   15, 41, 217–19
   and schools   62–3
sex roles   66
   and conscription campaigns   89
   and schools   52, 54
   and social reform campaign   86–7
   effect of war on   223
social reform   21, 34–5, 42, 85–8
   Catholic views on   35
soldier settlement   211
South Australian Cricket Association   107
South Australian Football League   107
South Melbourne Football Club   101, 108, 114
Spence, Mrs Valentine A.   114
sport
   calls for abandonment of   107, 111
   and crowds   97–8
   and schools   63
   and recruiting   101
   middle-class reaction to   21, 41, 95
   place in Australian life   94
   restrictions on   111
   voluntary abandonment of   105–6
   working class reaction to   95
Sportsmen's Recruiting Committee   114
Stone-Wigg, Bishop M.   23
Stawell (Vic)   185
strikes
   'great strike'   8, 115
      Australian Women's Service Corps and 'great strike'   81
      'great strike' in rural Australia   199–200
      'great strike' and schoolboys   55
      Red Cross views on 'great strike'   72
Strong, Rev. Dr C.
Stuart, Sir T.   109
Sydney Boys' High School   46, 47
Sydney Girls' High School   47, 52, 53, 62
Sydney Grammar School   46, 49
Sydney Rugby League   97, 104, 108
Sydney Rugby Union   101, 103

Talbot, Rev. A. E.   17
Tamworth (NSW)   188, 196, 199, 205
Tannenberg, M.   177
Tanunda (SA)   151, 154, 155, 160, 189
Tate, F.   52
Temora (NSW)   182
temperance   18, 53, 87, 88, 112
The King's School, Sydney   55, 56, 57, 60
Thomson, Hon. D.   76
Thorp, C. H.   119, 144, 145
Treadwell, C. A. L.   126
Tregear, Rev. G.   29
Trollope, A.   95
Truro (SA)   189
Tudor, F. (MHR)   37
Turner, Ethel   87
Twain, Mark   95
Twopeny, R. E. N.   95

unemployment   4, 33, 161–2
   in rural Australia   192
Universal Service League   35
University of Adelaide   15
University of Melbourne   11, 15, 59
University of Sydney   15, 40

venereal diseases, and AIF   38, 92, 133–4
Victoria Racing Club   97–8
Victorian Amateur Turf Club   102
Victorian Cricket Association   113–4
Victorian Football Association   101
   and recruiting   103
Victorian Football League   101, 103
   and abandonment of games   104, 107–8
   early reaction to war   97
Victorian State Schools' Patriotic League   51

Waddy, Rev. P. S.   60, 63
Wagga Wagga (NSW)   151, 152, 184, 188, 189, 192, 195
Walker, Rev. J.   18
Walklate, Rev. C. J.   196
war
   children's views of   49
   economic consequences of   4, 193–4
   effect on Australia   9, 13, 200
   effect on schools   63
   effect on women   77
   middle class reaction to   94

teachers' views of   60
working class reaction to   4, 33, 70, 94
war brides   134–9
war hysteria   16, 29, 42, 84, 158,
war memorials   178, 187, 212–13
War Precautions Act   155, 197
War Relief Gardeners' League
Watson, J.   155
Watt, W. A. (MHR)   216, 223, 224
   on Armistice   203–4
Webb, Rev. B. L.   30, 31
Wellington (NSW)   189
Wesley College, Melbourne   46, 99–100
Western Australian Football League   106
Wettel, G. V.   162
Weymouth (UK)   133, 145–7
white feathers   29, 185
Wilcannia (NSW)   193
Williams, W. G.   189, 190
women
   and comforts   93
   and conscription campaigns   87–9
   and marriage   90–2
   and social reform campaigns   86
   and work   65–6, 77
   and work in Britain   129–30
   effect of war on   65–6,
   effect of war on social life   92–3
   identification with AIF   73, 82
   in postwar Australia   222–3
   in rural Australia   194
   offers of service   78–81
Women's Patriotic Club   93
Wood, G. A.   15
Woodcock, C. F.   157
Worrall, Rev. H.   28, 34, 217
Wren, J.   112–13
Wright, Archbishop John   15, 17, 25, 109,
Wyalong (NSW)   182

Xavier College, Melbourne   57, 63

Yass (NSW)   75, 180, 181, 182, 185, 187, 192, 194, 199, 205
Young Workers' Patriotic Guild   51